IMPACT

IMPACT

Essays on Ignorance and the Decline of American Civilization

by

EZRA POUND

Edited with an introduction by NOEL STOCK

CHICAGO

HENRY REGNERY COMPANY

1960

Some of the essays in Part I of this volume appeared originally, in part or in whole, in the following publications: *Criterion, Exile, Delphian Quarterly, North American Review,* and *Aryan Path.*

Bellum cano perenne, between usura and the man who wants to do a good job.

OF MISPRISION OF TREASON

MISPRISIO cometh of the French word Mespris, which properly signifieth neglect or contempt; for (*mes*) in composition in the French signifieth *mal*, as *mis* doth in the English tongue: as mischance, for an ill chance, and so *mesprise* is ill apprehended or known. In legall understanding it signifieth, when one knoweth any treason or felony, and concealeth it, this is misprision, so called, because the knowledge of it is an ill knowledge to him, in respect of the severe punishment for not revealing of it. For in case of misprision of High Treason he is to be imprisoned during his life, to forfeit all his goods, debts, and duties forever, and the profits of his lands during his life: and in case of felony, to be fined and imprisoned. And in this sense doth the said statute of 1 & 2 Ph. & Mar. speak when it saith: *Be it declared, and enacted, by the Authority aforesaid, that concealment or keeping secret of any High Treason be deemed and taken only misprision of treason, and the offenders therein to forfeit and suffer, as in cases of misprision of treason hath heretofore been used.* But by Common Law concealment of High Treason was treason as it appeareth in the case of the Lord *Scrope* An. 3 H. 5. and by *Bracton lib. 3. fo. 118.b. & 119.a.*

It is misprision of High Treason, for forging of money, which neither is the money of this Realm of England nor currant within the same.

Misprision of High Treason in concealing of a Bull, c. See the Statute (*El. ca.2*).

It is said in 2.R.3 that every treason or felony includeth in it a misprision of treason or felony. Therefore if any man knoweth of any High Treason, he ought with as much speed as conveniently he may to reveal the same to the King, or some of his Privy Council, or any other magistrate. And misprision in a large sense is taken for many great offences which are neither treason nor felony, whereof we shall speak more hereafter, being in this place restrained to misprision of treason.

See *John Coniers* Case *Dier 296*. That the receiving of one that hath counterfeited the Kings Coin, and comforting of him knowing him to have counterfeited the Kings Coin, is but misprision.

See more of misprision of treason in the Chapter of High Treason, and of Principall and Accessory.

COKE's "INSTITUTES," The Third Part

Contents

INTRODUCTION

Twenty-five years ago, in 1935, Ezra Pound saw that the "education system" of most of the world, and of the United States in particular, was moving towards "the manufacture of robots and tame rabbits." Unfortunately, this horror is no longer in the future. The world of "robots and tame rabbits" is with us here and now; the student of 1960 is trained to look at everything with a sort of idiot simplicity; nothing has a cause, trends simply occur. But, above all, the student must never ask who is in whose pocket. Such a question when asked at all today is asked only at a superficial political level, nor is there any consideration of the fact that there are other means of bribery than straight cash payment, and more than one form of suffocation.

During its best years, from 1917 into the early twenties, the *Little Review* was a rare magazine, a place where you did not have to write an essay if a sentence would do. It was a place, the only place, where Pound, Eliot, Joyce, and Wyndham Lewis could appear all four together, without unnecessary delay. Pound, looking back in 1935, wrote: "Twenty years ago the little magazines served to break a monopoly, to release communication, mainly about letters, from an oppressive control, and they now wither on the stalk because they refuse to go on from where the late Henry James was interrupted." James had got to "money," money as an important element in society, worthy of serious consideration, but had got to it only at the end of his life. During the twenties and thirties the little magazines, purporting to deal with civilization, the arts and amenities thereof, withered because they would not face one of the major realities, in, under, and around the civilization they were supposed to be concerned with; so that a withering was to be expected.

Pound's mind, however else one might describe his mental activity after 1920, certainly did not wither. His mental liveliness in domains impinging on the bread, butter, and freedom of the individual, for instance, is manifest in the essays and extracts collected in the present volume. He entered domains which most of the literati refused to enter; or which, if they did enter, they emerged from with clichés on their lips, victims of "the brainwash."

Pound's emphasis on the importance of money in history amounts to revival of a lost tradition; it is not, as has often been stated or implied, a concentration upon this point to the exclusion of other elements, but is simply insistence on money as a central factor in any civilization where it is a means of exchange and measure of price to facilitate the movement of goods and use of services through the community. He has revived, or helped to revive, interest in various important history books, including neglected works by three American historians —Thomas Hart Benton, Alexander Del Mar, and Brooks Adams—and the ancient Chinese monetary text of Kuan Chung.*

* Senator Thomas Hart Benton, *Thirty Years' View: or A History of the Working of the American Government 1820 to 1850*. (2 vols.; New York, D. Appleton & Co., 1856). A reprint of seventy important pages from Vol. I is available in the Square Dollar Series, Washington, D.C.
There are forty vols. or more by Del Mar in the British Museum, the most recent dated 1903. The only reprints available are *A History of Monetary Crimes, Roman & Moslem Moneys*, and *A History of Netherlands Monetary Systems* (Square Dollar Series).
Kuan Chung, *The Kuan Tzu, Economic Dialogues in Ancient China*, edited and published by Lewis A. Maverick (Carbondale, Illinois, 1954).
For two important vols. by Brooks Adams, see p. 195.

Forty years ago when Pound began writing an epic poem, a poem containing history, he discovered that history without monetary economics is a dead study. Hence his tireless concern since then with the history of money and its ramifications. In the essays printed here, the poet is seen moving through history and his own time setting his facts and ideas in order. He observes, he compares; he believes that real knowledge comes from observation of phenomena, whether poems, banking systems, or the gloss on leaves. Observation is followed by comparison, and, finally, by the critical process, the weeding. It is time, I believe, for a lively English version of the great book in this field, Dante's *De Vulgari Eloquio*. So far as I know there has been no serious discussion regarding the influence of the *De Vulgari Eloquio* on Pound's prose—as regards style, that is—quite apart from the fact that it was in this book that Pound received severe instruction in the use of language and discovered the term *directio voluntatis*, link between Confucius and the best of medieval Europe.

Pound's method effected a reform in literature, it helped to clean up the poetry of his time, but it did not bring him popularity, especially among writers who had no care for perfection. He began to apply the same method of observation, comparison, and weeding to the world of "human events," and if the literary world with its jealousies and investments in books and worn-out literary fashions was hardly pleased with his cleansing process, the world where "business is business" had no use at all for a man who wanted clear statement.

As the building of categories became more exact, the need arose for Pound to define his "laws" and terminology, not only in the field of literature, but in economics, law, history, as well. Any reader who doubts the need for Pound's attempts to erect a clear terminology in monetary economics, or the need for his terminology in 1960, may refer to various unwieldy and blurry, at times inaccurate, meanings attached to the word "money" in current official and academic publications.

By 1920 Pound was studying economics and "current affairs" as an integral part of his work as an epic poet, seeking "threads" running through, and laws binding, the history of the race. The change from aesthetic young man, a brilliant poet passionately interested in the Arts, to a wiser man groping his way to the organic unity binding the Arts to society generally, occurred during the First World War, by way of A. R. Orage, editor of the *New Age*. Pickthall, a *New Age* writer, had been adviser to the Young Turks; C. H. Douglas had observed certain things financial in India and England; and the *New Age* traced the recession of power, away from the people into inner rooms inhabited by inner cliques. It was in the *New Age* office, not in the literary circles of the day, that Pound heard first-hand accounts of important facts that should have been, but were not, in general circulation via the education system and book trade.

For a year or two, say 1917 to 1919, Pound listened, observed, and asked questions of people in a position to know the answers. We might say that at this time his interest in first-hand data on economics and contemporary history ran parallel to his cultural and literary interests. In 1919 or thereabouts he introduced Douglas to Wickham Steed of the London *Times*. By 1920 he was seeing a definite relationship between literature and economics, and in April of that year he published a review of Douglas's *Economic Democracy* in a literary magazine, the *Little Review*. In the *New Age* for March 30, 1922, Pound was able to write an essay on "Credit and the Fine Arts." All his interests now were as one; economics and first-hand data on "current affairs" were seen as parts of a whole. The various "subjects" of the curriculum were but various aspects or angles of the *one* subject, and money was a major reality, whether he was dealing with "Kublai Khan and his Currency," the Medici, or the decline in a certain kind of verbal expression in English from Chaucer to Cromwell.

Against the nineteenth-century "germanic" system of philology, the "compartment" system of learning, particularly as it existed in the United States in 1905, Pound fought for correlation and condensation. Under the "germanic" system a scholar spends his life down an academic hole investigating, say, the back legs of the Argentine ant, without ever considering or being asked to consider the relationship between his own particular study and the rest of human knowledge. Pound believes that this system has trapped many, perhaps even most, of the best minds of the world in useless study, from which, after a certain stage, there is almost no hope of escape. The system has produced scholars without sense of proportion, or people who, if not incapable of exercising such sense, refuse to do so for professional reasons, for fear of what their colleagues will say, etc.

The system has led to some splendid perversions. In the study of literature, for example, we have the descending hunt for minor and ever more minor textual variations, until finally the study of literature is so meaningless that critics can achieve fame by treating of nothing save their own special brand of bellyache in the presence of this or that poem or novel. Students with no knowledge of literature are encouraged to have "preferences," to say what they "like" or "don't like," a complete break with the tradition of respect for significant fact running through Aristotle, Linnaeus and Agassiz. We get such phenomena as disembodied teaching—the teacher so intent on the techniques of teaching that he or she is no longer concerned, except in a minor and casual sense, with the importance or otherwise of the thing being taught. A Professor of

English from Chicago can write an article called "Enrichment of the English Curriculum," mentioning only four texts, not one of them important in the history of English literature. At its most harmless this sort of thing is simply meaningless; but such decay can, if allowed to spread, poison the whole mental life of the race.

In literature, Pound sought and found a critical method to weigh Theocritus and Yeats with one balance. This method he extended to other fields of human knowledge as he gathered material for his Cantos. In constructing the Cantos he made an instrument for determining the specific gravity of any fragment or part of any culture discovered on his journey through history. Whether the instrument is successful or not is not a matter for discussion in this introduction, but I would point out that the Cantos are successful in at least one respect —as a multiple signpost to "areas" of history needing further investigation. A number of matters exposed to view for the first time in the Cantos, or revived there, have since been the subject of fuller treatment by serious authors, whether as a result direct or indirect of the Cantos I cannot say; but in at least three cases that come to mind, *The Medici Bank* by Raymond de Roover, *John Adams and the American Revolution* by Catherine Drinker Bowen, and *Pléthon et le Platonisme de Mistra* by F. Masai, the authors have provided what amount almost to commentaries on particular aspects of the Cantos.

The poet's fight to obtain significant data and to correlate it has, of necessity, been a one-man affair; and this has had its dangers, for one man cannot discover everything of importance, he cannot move through an ideal reading list already arranged in ideal order. Pound missed Francis Neilson, for instance, author of *The Makers of War* and *The Churchill Legend*, who could have saved him a good deal of time and trouble. He did not get to Brooks Adams until the late thirties, although once he had read *Law of Civilization and Decay* he saw immediately that Brooks was more important than the popular Henry. And he now wishes that he had read Agassiz before reading Confucius. However, despite the dangers, the method has been "kept afloat" by Pound's sense of responsibility. He believes intellectual health comes from men taking responsibility each within his own "field"—which does not mean cutting oneself off from the rest of the world, but implies definitely an interest in surrounding "fields," an understanding of the relationship between one's own field and the others, and above all no "passing the buck." Anyone not endowed with an academic turn of mind who has had to plough through academic journals, reviews, proceedings of learned societies, etc., in search of significant fact, will probably suppose as I do, that there is plenty of room in these circles for more clarity and straightness of expression, but especially for a surer and more meaningful method of selecting and assembling data: that is, for more responsibility.

At any rate, Pound set himself a heavy task very early in his career, he took upon himself certain responsibilities, warranted or not as you choose to regard it, but with positive results:

He tested accepted values and attempted to preserve the best. For example, he fought to preserve the individual against outside encroachment, a fight which is clear in the present volume.

He kept his curiosity alive, and sought to keep curiosity alive in others, in order to prevent people becoming bogged down in cliché and superstition.

He sought to maintain a constant flow of significant factual data, in order to prevent "brainwashing."

The total weight of his work has been against the idea of

education as a means of making and training robots to obey the messages fed to them by the robot-masters. He has tried to make people think, as E. E. Cummings noted; he has tried to make them sensitive to the outside world, so that they may live, and help others to live, as human beings.

Whereas in his literary writings Pound is very often near the top of his performance, at any time from the *Spirit of Romance* onwards, in the sort of work collected in this volume he spent many years feeling his way through an unmapped land, gathering facts long out of print or available only in rare pamphlets or the archives of learned societies etc. For this reason I have discarded a large quantity of material and, generally speaking, have attempted to present his mature view as it was, say, in 1940.

NOEL STOCK

I

Essays on Ignorance and the Decline of American Civilization

NATIONAL CULTURE
A *Manifesto* ✌§ 1938

A NATIONAL or racial culture exists when the works (art, letters) of that nation do not and do not need to ask favours
because they have been produced by a member of that particular nation or race. A national American culture existed
from 1770 till at least 1861. Jefferson could not imagine an
American going voluntarily to inhabit Europe. After the
debacle of American culture individuals had to emigrate in
order to conserve such fragments of American culture as had
survived. It was perhaps no less American but it was in a distinct sense less *nationally* American as the usurocracy came
into steadily more filthy and damnable control of the Union.

The distinction between nationalism and non-absorbency
needs stressing. Our revolutionary culture was critical and not
monolingual. A national culture can exist so long as it *chooses*
between other cultures. It obviously descends to the swamps
when it degenerates into a snobism, when it accepts from
abroad instead of selecting. There is no inferiority sense in the
Jefferson-Adams letters. Till at least 1850 the U.S. was respected. The American as such was not at a disadvantage.
Europe looked *to* America; not as to a rich cheese but as to
a model and example.

An American culture has existed and exists in any American
work that imposes itself on foreign judgment, and the quality
of its existence is measured by the quality of that judgment.

3

A distinction exists between a national (or racial) culture and a metropolitan market. The criteria of quick sales, speedy profit etc., belong to Broadway hair oil. The fact that there is more lucre in shoddy and Ersatz is often a mere sign of provincialism. All of which remarks are probably platitude, but are necessary for clearing the ground.

There exist means to reconstruct or coordinate such American culture as is available.

It is possible to learn and apply high and international criteria. It should be possible to establish a communications service between individual components of such culture-containers and engines as humanly exist. One can not create by fiat a phalanx of great writers, or men of genius. One could however establish a certain degree of mental integrity, and an utter and blistering intolerance of certain present habits of sloppiness and bad faith.

Certain inaccuracies (now serving ill will) could be eliminated.

Efforts could be made to establish committees of correspondence between men, in America, who produce or prefer good writing to bad.

There is at the moment no periodical giving even rudimentary information on American thought, let alone correlating that thought with live thought in other countries. To shun such correlation is cowardice. It is also the habit of the American mercantilist age, as indeed of the mercantilist age anywhere.

I do not see a regeneration of American culture while Marx and Lenin are reprinted at 10 cents and 25 cents in editions of 100,000 and Adams' and Jefferson's thought is kept out of the plain man's reach, and out of my reach considering that for three years I have in vain tried to buy John Adams' letters.

Men who impede the examination of the monetary and

financial causes of historic events are a seething corruption. Whether one start that examination before the collapse of our civilization in the war of the 1860's or before the last war that study is to be made. We physicians of the mind can not rest until we have discovered a serum which will make impossible the existence on the American scene of the persons who have impeded this study, wilfully or in abuleia. In most cases the obstruction is a compost of sloth, fear and greed.

The befouling of terminology should be put an end to. It is a time for clear definition of terms. Immediately, of economic terms, but ultimately of all terms. It is not a revolution of the word but a castigation of the word. And that castigation must precede any reform.

An administration that can not or dare not define money, credit, debt, property, capital, is unlikely to provide a durable solution of national chaos or evolve a durable system of national order.

In aiming this manifesto at a few dozen just men I am trying to find out whether they want anything better than the present circumjacent fugg and moral morass.

Do six dozen or six hundred Americans value "a national culture" sufficiently to conserve it

A. By correlated reprint of proofs of its earlier existence?

B. By periodical bulletin of its present products?

C. By keeping sharp the criteria which would prevent a relapse into the narcissism of the U.S. of the late 19th century?

What other measures are they concretely prepared to take for its maintenance? Jefferson and Adams were in position to decide whether the English or French view or idea in a given case were preferable. The snob or member of Harvey's generation or the later derivers are merely there to assure the boob that London says this or the other. The hair oil boys, out for quick profit and exploitation of a fad or fashion.

5

The degradation of American publishing was nowhere more manifest in that from 1917 to 1919 the actual centre of activity in printing work in English was transferred from London to New York. Later it hovered over Paris. Then for the rest of a decade New York did nothing and the centre of publishing live work flopped back to London. This shows contempt for and oblivion of whatever national culture exists. Culture is individual and not national so long as the individual having unusual capacity is forced OUT of his native milieu by material (i.e. economic) conditions and the imbecility or incapacity of the milieu to sustain and coordinate effort.

Concretely, *if* American individuals have to communicate via Europe the national culture will not function to its own best advantage. Provincialism shows equally in four ways.

One, the absurd aping of foreign modes.
Two, the absurd timidity and fear of accepting foreign work in an unknown mode.
Three, neglect of high-grade work done at home.
Four, back-scratching and boosting of tosh *because* it is produced at home.

A national culture has a minimum of components. If the production be simply unconscious we are in a state of folk culture only. Any more developed phase must of necessity include criteria which are, as criteria, capable of comparison with the best alien criteria.

In one sense it can almost be said: there are no alien criteria.

The hair oil boys of course could not sustain foreign criteria for a week. The "bright and slick" goes *once* with the European. The seventh issue of any of the hair oil organs is identical with the first. The issues of a serious periodical are all different, one from the others. *Cantleman's Spring Mate* is not confoundable with a chapter from *Ulysses*.

It is or should be obvious that H. James asked no favours of French and English contemporaries. He was sold in French in the 1880's, and his later small sales were due not to inferiority but to his superiority to the foreign reader's capacity.

I suppose in the long run Jimmy Whistler was not so good a painter as Manet but he had a damn good run for his money. I don't recall any British painter of his time cropping up in a poem by Mallarmé.

In our own day and vocation it can't be said that either Mr. Eliot nor the undersigned have exactly looked UP to British contemporaries. It can't be said that an alteration on Mr. Eliot's passport has altered the essential Americanness of his work. H. James' death-bed change of citizenship was the one last and possible defiance that he could hurl at the scum in the White House.

Eliot's real criticism of England was written some years before he committed the technical change.

> crawls between dry ribs
> To keep our metaphysics warm.

Out of Gautier and the Bay State Hymn Book, but no soft Victorian slither converging.

Williams is American by program, and in so far as his nationality is factitious it has an immediate local appeal. His verity, despite a provincial top-dressing, has driven into, even into some silly young Britons. You have here some of the best work done on the ground, but you have also the proof that race is stronger than program.

The American culture is Franco-English, it is at the start the culture in the bone of the one English segment that ever in all history threw off the tyranny of the conquerors of the

Island. And it is then lightened, brought into clearer demarcation by a French ideation plus, for all I know, climate.

Henry James is as New England as Henry Adams because of the same racial origins and mixed by education with the same other chemical. The national culture was there in Jefferson-Adams. Van Buren was too busy on necessary public jobs to *learn* much of it. If you can conceive an idle Van Buren I suspect he might have imbibed quite a good deal of it.

Whitman was neglected by prigs, and then the snobs overlooked the part of him which was quite simply exotic.

Williams is international. Cummings on the other hand who has been driven abroad for his two major subjects (*Enormous Room* and the Russia of *Eimi*) is indelibly New England. And, though it be almost axymoron to say so, "Whitman's one living descendant."

There is I think little doubt that I should have more quickly attained a unity of expression had I been also New England without disorderly trek of four or five generations across the whole teeming continent.

Zukofsky is in the American vein in his essays on Henry Adams, and *Meet Baruch Spinoza*.

As to Ersatz & Margarine

The pseudoculture insists on staying 20 years or so behind Europe. I have always advised against this. The press is always all for it. Nothing will induce the American press to print contemporary news of Europe.

In closing and before I divagate, I should advise

ONE: a decision as to the bases of our national culture.

TWO: a serious constructive program, complete with possible methods of organization before I hear any more about destructive programs.

8

I mean to say there is one point in the constitution which has not been tried and which the infamies infesting the White House for the past decades do not and dare not try: namely the right of congress to determine the value of money.

We had a basis for civic order in the time of Jackson and Van Buren. A new order must at least incorporate that base. Once that is done we can consider modernization of other components and decide whether and/or how far a more modern articulation is possible or desirable. By possible, I mean initiable in time and in our time, without loose analogies to European needs and possibilities. An ORDER yes, but per force an American order. A *directio voluntatis* certainly, but in writing the details of a program this directio must take count both of its own driving force and material obstacles.

The excuse for materialism exists only when the sane man is faced by doctrinaires who do not see the reality of these obstacles. As the worship of inertia it is not even a philosophy, it is merely sub-human. Though it is a quite natural excess of a short-distance thinker suffering from irritation. Even poor Charlie Marx couldn't carry it into his theory of values, and as a working system Russia knows it's a washout.

The total democracy bilge, by which I mean the clichés, the assumptions, the current cant about "the people" arose from sheer misunderstanding or perversion. Perversion of ideas by means and by misuse of words.

The disequality of human beings can be observed, if you take long enough, from the reports in the English Journal (organ of teaching in secondary schools). There is no more equality between men than between animals. Jefferson never thought that there was. I say "Jefferson" because J. Adams might be abused as a monarchist, which he wasn't. I say Jefferson because I want the extreme case, the inventor or impresario of our democracy.

9

Equality before the law courts, equality in the sense of there being no insurmountable obstacles imposed by arbitrary classification and arbitrary limits of categories. Liberty: to do that which harms not another.

To ORGANISE in our barbarism, in our utter and rabbity inconsequence, an hierarchy and order is not an affair of decades. We can not, or at any rate we have not organized one clean book club, we have not organized even committees of communication, we have not one publication that serves as postal system for ideas between the few hundred top-notch (however low the top be) intelligentsia. And until a selection of the intelligentsia can organize something, until they can set up at least a model they can not expect the 120 or whatever million to copy it.

We have, god pity us, an "Institute." Is it organized? Has it a status official or other? Can even a member of it ascertain what it has done? Has it even a bulletin? Has it records?

Flaubert cannot meet Turgenev at the Goncourts in every decade, and 30 or 200 men of talent can not be created on demand, but at least standards of intellectual probity COULD be observed. At least protests could be registered against the more flagrant rackets, against the worst malpractices of the press and the book trade, and more violent inaccuracies of so-called books of reference.

Thirty or 200 persons "elected" because of superior services to American letters could were they not a farce demand and obtain the publication of essential parts of our heritage.

Were there any general spirit among them their recommendation of such publication would also place the publication on a perfectly practical level. The umpteen hundred dead libraries in the umpteen etc pseudo-universities and travesties, plus the public (so) libraries (called) would absorb (that is the just word) enough copies to cover the printing expenses.

Until you root out the mercantilist morale by acid you will have no decent America. Ivar Kreuger was boomed in the Sat. Ev. Post as more than a financial titan. And that state of belly tickling sycophancy still festers.

FOR A NATIONAL CULTURE the first step is stocktaking: what is there of it *solid*. The second step is to make this available and to facilitate access to it.

DESTRUCTION BY TAXATION

London, January 7, 1936

Dear E.P.,

Pending engaging a whole-time secretary to correspond with you, I suggest that you concentrate on the subject of taxation as a form of modern highway robbery combined with iniquitous interference with the freedom of the individual.

Yours ever,

C. H. Douglas

THE British tax system is black infamy and the sooner at least a nucleus of literate Englishmen know why it is black infamy the sooner England will take the road towards national health.

Nowhere is the decadence of parliamentary systems more blatant. The House of Commons was founded mainly to *stop* governmental extortion. It was set up as barrier to unbridled and inane greed of Royalty. When Royalty was reduced to a bit of theatrical stage play, the Commons were led down the garden path and have long since forgotten what their predecessors were made for.

The British taxpayer need not pay two pounds for every sovereign spent by his government.

There are probably not six men in the Commons and Lords who have the intellect required to distinguish a tithe from a tax, or a just payment from an extortion.

A tithe is a payment made in something the payer has. A tax is normally paid in money.

A tithe is strictly proportional to production. Justice from time immemorial has limited tithe to a tenth or a ninth. More was considered evil and less inadequate for the good conduct of the state.

Extortion is forced payment of an exaggerated sum. One of the prime means of extortion is that of insisting on payment in something which the payer has not, and which he can only obtain at a price unjustly high.

In present circumstances your taxes are to be paid in money. And the taxpayer is too illiterate in matters of money to ask what money is; who issues it; under what circumstances is it obtainable? (1938)

The Dismantled Manor House

So far as I know no 100% honest monetary policy has been officially proposed in the British Parliament since the Bank of England was founded. Nor has any of the larger religious bodies in England come out for common monetary honesty.

The farm hand does not eat more because the paintings by Raeburn or Constable are taken out of the Manor House and put in the dealer's cellar under a black and iniquitous inheritance tax.

The obscuring of the sense of the *nature* of money has destroyed all these fine things uselessly. The dismantled Manor House, that could be and ought to show a model of how to live, is made a skeleton for no purpose.

If any hedger, or ditcher got a half-ounce more beefsteak because the Manor House library was sold off and its pictures put up to auction, there might be some justification in taxes. But there is no justification in taxes as now suffered in Britain. (1939)

Feasible Justice

A sane and decent tax system should, and if you grant the possibility of the electors having even a small particle of good sense, could have the following characteristics.

1. Aiming at feasible justice it could, as Mencius said it should, consist in a share of the available products. Mencius used very considerable lucidity in demanding a share, not a fixed charge, which latter might not be available in a poor farm year, or produce in a rich year a reserve against famine or future contingency.

2. The system should aim at minimum cost of collection. Mr. Jefferson had some pithy remarks on the price of tobacco in France, in relation to what the producer got, what the government got as profit, and the cost of gouging out of consumers.

3. The convenience of the collection should be considered, though this might be considered as component in the cost of same.

4. It should encourage production, not sabotage it. I have a letter of decades back suggesting that I specialize in examining taxation as highway robbery. The *Secolo* of Genoa recently managed to print a line referring to the current tax system as "un furto organizzato che punisce ogni atto produttivo." The mills grind slowly. It takes time to get simple ideas past a copy desk.

5. It should not create crime, i.e. it should not penalize simple and often useful activities, by making them crimes by statute. The bootlegger in the A.H. of the army understood perfectly well that his profession could only function when there was a tax on, or prohibition of booze. (1959).

14

AN INTRODUCTION TO THE ECONOMIC NATURE OF THE UNITED STATES 🦢 1944

The Title

THIS is not a Short History of the Economy of the United States. For forty years I have schooled myself, not to write the economic history of the U.S. or any other country, but to write an epic poem which begins "In the Dark Forest," crosses the Purgatory of human error, and ends in the light, "fra i maestri di color che sanno." For this reason I have had to understand the nature of error. But I don't think it necessary to refer to each particular case of error.

I do not believe that the method of historiography has progressed much since the days when Confucius selected the documents of the old kingdoms, and condensed his conclusions in the *Great Digest*. Aristotle towards the end of his life arrived at a similar method, in his collection of Greek State Constitutions. Voltaire used the "human" method which hinges on chance and the personal element. A prince eats a pudding and dies of acute indigestion at a critical moment. Caesar Borgia said: "I had anticipated everything except being bed-ridden the day my father died." Michelet analyzes the motives of different social groups and tells us that the manual labourer

Translated from Italian by Carmine Amore.

wants to own a shop because he thinks shop-keepers don't work. Another method consists in analyzing certain mechanisms invented to humbug the public. Perhaps it is the renewal of an Aristotelian tendency but, in any event, it is suitable for the present narrative, and I am following it in this essay or definition, of the struggle between the people and the usurers, or financiers, in the colonies, and then in the United States of North America.

Towards the end of the Eighteenth Century the settlers, driven by the desire for freedom of conscience, hardened by privations, favoured and betrayed, reached a certain degree of prosperity, thanks to their own hard work and a sane system of using paper money as a means of exchange that freed them, temporarily, from the pincers of the Bank of England.

The settlers, or colonizers, in Pennsylvania and in other colonies, irritated by the disappearance of metal money, understood that any other document could be used for book-keeping and as a certificate of what the bearer was entitled to receive in the market. The agriculturists who arrived in the new country, while they cleared the forests and prepared their camps, lacked the power to buy what was necessary to build houses, to buy ploughs, and to make a living. So the governments of several colonies began to lend paper-money for these purposes. Pennsylvania chose the best method adapted to the conditions—repayment in ten or twelve years, and lending amounts up to one half the value of the farm. Those who lent the money, living near to those who had received the loan, could judge the character of the borrowers. This arcadian simplicity displeased the London monopolists and the suppression of this competition, together with other irritants, provoked the 1776 "Revolution."

The clearness of comprehension on the part of the revolutionary leaders is registered in diaries and "memoirs" of the times, and particularly in the notes of John Adams who, among other things, had been sent to Europe to organise the credit for the new State, and who secured the first loan from Holland.

It is to be understood that the experience of John Adams was neither theoretical nor abstract. Firmly convinced of the capacity of the Americans to produce farm products and merchandise, he met, and overcame, all the insidiousness of Europe. He convinced the Hollanders of the solidarity of the American guarantees by comparing the insignificant debt of the United States with the great debt of England.

I repeat: his notes are neither abstract nor theoretical. It was a question of paying the war expenditures with tobacco. The intimate letters and conversations, verified by the friends of Adams, contain concrete concepts as, for example: "It is necessary to keep up the idea that this paper is good for something," meaning that the note can be exchanged for actual goods.

It was understood that the Navy depended on iron, timber, tar, and not on the manoeuvres of a false finance.

Some time later the bankers published projects for the extension of credit, "funding," or the institution of a public debt. Adams faced the terrors of inflation by saying that a diminishing buying power of the paper money functioned as an unevenly distributed tax, a tax that hit those with a fixed salary, or living on an income; that the businessmen would have the best of it; and that, in any event, an inflation of this kind would not have created a public debt *with interest*.

It was understood that credit is Paul's supposition that Peter will pay. It was understood that the base of the real credit of the thirteen colonies was their capacity to work, taken together with the truly great possibility of future production limited then, not by nature, fields, vegetation, but only by the number of inhabitants.

Washington was able to win the war because he resisted to the bitter end. Washington won, but not without indebtedness to the tenacity and good sense of Adams the negotiator.

History, as seen by a monetary economist, is a continuous struggle between producers and those who try to make a living by inserting a false system of book-keeping between the producers and their just recompense.

The Bank of England was based on the discovery that instead of lending money, the Bank's paper could be put out on loan. The Philadelphia financiers, not entirely severed from their friends in foreign countries, saw the possibility of speculation and the monopolizers of money tried their usual tricks on a thick-headed public.

Financiers and congressmen bought up the promises-to-pay of the single states, valued at 20% of their face-value, and then the nation took on the responsibility of paying them at 100% of face-value. These were certificates of pay due to the veterans. This is the ill-famed "scandal of the assumption."

England was trying diverse methods of usury and sanctions. The lack of caution on the part of the great property owners of the South reduced them to indebtedness. Slavery became less profitable than the new industrial system, in which the owner did not have to take care of his employees.

Let us note that at the beginning of the Nineteenth Century the "mercantile" concept still retained traces of decency. Adams judged it "hardly mercantile" to do business on borrowed capital. At that time individualism had its own probity, a modest but secure income was called an *"independence."*

History taken as a lesson, and taking into account the difference between certainty and supposition, would be an *ex-*

position of the nature of events, rather than a chronicle of names.

Some events can be known only after centuries. We know, for example, that Parisina d'Este incurred certain expenditures which were paid from the Ducal Treasury of Ferrara, and we also know the date of these payments. Other deeds never become known and must remain buried with the participants. A signed letter proves what the writer wanted the recipient to believe on such and such a day. But the clarity of an idea remains among the ascertained facts. The definition of an idea, as observed by someone who understands the events of the day, may shed more light on the historical process than many volumes.

Sources

The true history of the economy of the United States, as I see it, is to be found in the correspondence between Adams and Jefferson, in the writings of Van Buren, and in quotations from the intimate letters of the Fathers of the Republic. The elements remain the same: debts, altering the value of monetary units, and the attempts, and triumphs of usury, due to monopolies, or to a "Corner."

In order to please those who love to gamble, the Exchange permits Mr. A to sell to Mr. B what Mr. A does not possess; on condition that Mr. A succeeds in buying it and consigning it to Mr. B within a determined time.

The Americans have chosen this game instead of bull-fighting. And naturally, if a group of financiers succeeds in inducing simpletons to sell more than actually exists, or to sell more of it than can be obtained, the late-comers can be made to "pay through the nose." In 1869, Gould, Fisk and others almost succeeded in monopolising the available gold in New York.

The speculators boast about their courage or temerity, but this courage is a different kind of courage from that displayed at roulette, or other games of chance; for, by speculating on wheat and other commodities these gamblers are not just gambling among themselves, they are deciding on the prices the public must pay for its necessities. Civic conscience has not developed in America. It seems to me that this conscience was higher during the first years of the Republic, or, at least, the heroes of that era have left to us monuments of their personal consciences, which seem to have been rather higher than those of today.

From the war of secession up to now, the economic history of the United States has consisted in a series of exchange manoeuvres in New York and in Chicago; attempts to impose monopolies, corners, variations in the prices of the shares of new industries, and of the means of transportation. In the beginning they speculated on the value of land. An inflation in its value was stimulated without bothering about the difficulty, or the impossibility of transporting products from distant fields to the market. Then they speculated on the values of the railroads.

If it is in the interest of the common worker, producer, or citizen to have an equitable and fixed price, this is not at all in the interest of the speculator or broker. "Hell," he says, "I don't want a still market. I couldn't make any money."

Like a patient fisher, the broker waits for the rise or fall of even ¼ or ⅛ per cent, and there is his fifty or one hundred dollars.

He waits for a "break." It may come once in a lifetime; it may be the starting point of a fortune. The great Morgan, during the Civil War, bought on credit a certain quantity of damaged rifles from the War Department in Washington, and sold them to a Military Command in Texas and was paid by the latter before he had to pay the former. He made $75,-000.00 profit. Later he was even sentenced, but that did not prevent his becoming the great Mahatma of Wall Street, and a world politico-economic power. Such is the material of which the economic and human history of the United States is made.

Stratagems and Illusions

The Morgan affair, or trial, will be classified as normal finance and could have happened anywhere in the "old world." But the new land, because of the new conditions, offered several kinds of opportunity for fraud. In order to display the problem of the American mentality and its development, or perversion as a component in the historical process, these frauds should be classified. Take for example, the concession to construct the Northern Pacific Railroad. This concession had a clause in it which conferred on the constructors the right to all the lumber cleared during construction. The route went through virgin forest and the trees were destined to be used as crossties, but the clause did not specify the width of the road to be cut and the company, with perfect legality, cut for itself a strip of land two miles wide. The land and the forests were the property of the nation, but no private citizen felt that he had been swindled.

Similar things are the basis of American humor. These things make for pride and tradition. The fight against the forest, and the difficulties of the desert. Marksmanship and craftiness were being developed. A man in Connecticut succeeded in manufacturing imitation nutmegs out of plain wood and selling them at a profit. This trick sent the whole country into peals of laughter. The centenary of this trick was commemorated at the St. Louis Exposition. Imitation nutmegs were made and sold at 5 cents each. One day, when these souvenirs were exhausted, the man in charge, a true son of Connecticut, pure-blooded yankee, did not hesitate one instant to substitute real nutmegs for them, at the same price. The public heard it, and roared again.

Since the days of the California Gold Rush there have been men who have specialized in "Gold Bricks," that is, a lead brick covered with a layer of gold, or even solid gold in some parts so that the seller can bore through it at known points and show it to be solid gold. After the Alaskan Gold Rush the "gold brick" made its reappearance. The majority of those who had been duped brought their bricks to my father who was an assayer at the Mint. This was the period of free coining of gold, and any one had the right to have his own metal coined. So, the stories of these dupes have been familiar to me, through personal experience, since I was five years old.

I should like to differentiate between two kinds of dishonesty: (1) that of financial frauds and book-keeping; and (2) that arising from particular material opportunities, as in the case of the Northern Pacific.

Tradition

The usual frauds of book-keeping, monopoly, etc., have been known since the beginning of history, and it is precisely for this reason that the usurers are opposed to classical studies. Aristotle, in his *Politics* 1.4/5, relates how Thales, wishing to show that a philosopher could easily "make money" if he had nothing better to do, foreseeing a bumper crop of olives, hired by paying a small deposit, all the olive presses on the islands of Miletus and Chios. When the abundant harvest arrived, everybody went to see Thales. Aristotle remarks that this is a

22

common business practice. And the Exchange frauds are, nearly all of them, variants on this theme—artificial scarcity of grain and of merchandise, artificial scarcity of money, that is, scarcity of the key to all the other exchanges.

Proverbs and Wisdom

The struggle between producers and the falsifiers of book-keeping was clearly seen and understood by the Fathers of the Republic. Their wisdom was recorded in pungent phrases: "The safest place of deposit is in the pants of the people." "Every Bank of Discount is downright iniquity, robbing the public for individuals' gain." An insurance agent once asked a banker why the railroad companies, which are privately owned, must run to him, a banker, in order to sell their bonds. The banker, with ironic sadness, whispered: "Hush."

The Substructure

To understand the American historical process, it is necessary to consider the successive waves of immigration.

1. Those who came through a spirit of adventure or, because of religious convictions and the desire for freedom of conscience, and who were willing to face the difficulties of a savage and uncultivated country;

2. The slaves;

3. Those who arrived when the machinery was being assembled.

Class struggle in the United States is a recent and an almost exotic problem, in the sense that it does not derive from the Founders. Let us take a "typical American family." Two Wadsworth brothers, or two men of that name, arrived in Massachusetts in 1632. In 1882 their descendants had a family reunion and published the history of the family. In the eight

23

generations we find all sorts and conditions—rich and poor. One, at the age of sixteen, sold his hair for a shilling, and "this was the first money he ever did see." Another fitted out a ship with his own money, during the Civil War. On the 250th Anniversary the participants presented equal variety and extremes among them—members of the Stock Exchange, salesmen, doctors, a telegraph operator and two old women for whom a collection was taken up. Under these conditions class warfare, in the true sense of the word, does not exist, even though the differences in wealth and position are undeniably visible.

Colonial Tendencies

The Fathers of the Republic revolted against the English ruling class, the younger brothers against the first-born. Popular hatred of the monarchist idea hampered Adams throughout his life. And all because, at the age of seventeen, he had written a letter in which he foresaw the possibility of an American kingdom capable of resisting any European force. Demagogy seized this phrase to insist that Adams had never been anti-monarchist, but preferred the House of Braintree, that is his own house, to that of Hanover. His father held the plow. His son, John Q. Adams, awaited the results of a presidential election at the plow. Perhaps a classical pose, but he was capable of holding the plow, and was not doing it for the first time in his life.

Let us compare a score of personal cases in order to understand the foundation of American economic history. In the docket of a great-grandfather, Justice of the Peace in New York State, the fines run from $1.30 to about $25.00, and the tribunal's expenses from 8¢ to $1.30.

His daughter, at least once in her life, went to work in a factory, married a man who became a Congressman, super-

24

vised the kitchen, not as a spectator, but in order to prepare meals for about forty lumbermen. At the time of her separation she had $100,000.00 in the bank, but the bank failed. My father, the first white man to be born in that part of Wisconsin, was looked after by a male redskin instead of a nurse. He inspected mines in Idaho, and got a job in the Land Office. One week he had his kindling wood sawed by a certain man for a dollar. Ten days later he asked the man if he wanted to saw a little more wood. "Saw wood? Saw wood? Say Homer do you want to go East and sell a mine? I got $10,000.00 in the bank."

In 1919 I met in Paris a quiet little man, Ambassador at the time, whom my father remembered thirty-five years before in the act of reaching for a revolver to help out his partner. American distances are different from the European, and the statistics do not record all the nuances.

Waves

Religious convictions, anarchic tendencies, love of adventure and then laziness. The American tragedy, in a certain sense, is the tragedy of laziness. The sense of justice surrendered to the sense of laziness. Justice was limited first to the whites, and then to the bosses.

From Europe a flood of workers poured in. The national type was formed from a similarity of tastes and temperaments and not on a racial basis. Those who wanted material gain emigrated to America. Those of a milder nature, the more contemplative, the sentimental, those more attached to their soil and home, remained in Europe. The strong, the restless, the malcontents, the misfits went. The younger sons of the English went in the 1600's, but after 1800 emigrants from England diminished.

The Puritans were bible-crazy, but they did not bring the hebrew scriptures only. The culture of Adams and Jefferson is a latin culture with a mixture of greek. Otis wrote a Greek Grammar, which he destroyed, or which was lost for lack of a competent printer. During the prosperous colonial era the arts of silversmithing, furniture making, and architecture developed. The houses, although made of wood, were a Greek dream. Numbers of them burned down. From Germany came groups of religious sectarians. They brought with them the art of glassmaking, and organised, at least once a year, a Bach festival. Monticello is full of refinement. The polygrapher longed for a complete civilization equal to that of an Italian court, ceremonies omitted, of the Fourteenth Century. He got into debt.

Adams was frugal and used the weatherboards of his attic study as a handy file for his correspondence. For at least a century New England took as an idea: *"Low living, high thinking."*

Usury spoiled the Republic. Usury has been defined as too high an interest on money.* The word finance became fashionable in the bank-paper era. And it is to this that Jefferson alludes in the phrase: "No one has natural right to be moneylender save him who has it to lend." With the "financial" era the word usury disappeared from polite conversation.

There is no greater imbecility than to leave one's own bank-account or one's sources of information in the hands of an enemy, or an irresponsible man.

The struggle betweeen the people and the exploiters in America was waged around these forms of imbecility.

A handful of people who lived on little and did not run into debt brought to, and preserved in America, a rather high, severe culture, and a civic sense nourished by the traditions of

* See definition of usury, p. 210.

26

English legal liberty, that is by a centuries-long conquest in which the traditions of North European tribes and roman law converge.

The Republic was started with a limited suffrage which was gradually extended from the love of justice and because of the good sense of the common people. The frontier aristocracy was, of necessity, a physical aristocracy. The others either died or weakened. My grandfather used to wrestle with his lumber-jacks not only for sport, but to maintain his prestige. Lincoln was the last president of this race and of this tradition. For two centuries the frontier required daring. With the danger gone came the people who know how to suffer and to endure; or those who merely subside.

Up to the time of the Civil War the public seems to have taken some interest in the Congressional debates. The Congressional Record might nourish a civic sense, and the names of the protagonists are recorded in it. Even today it is possible to tell some truths in Congress, but the public has been distracted. The "economic" history of the United States is, on one side, the history of enormous waste of natural resources, waste that took place because no immediate need for thrift was apparent and, in many instances, did not exist.

Land was given to whomsoever wished to settle on it, but no provision was made to protect the nation or the people from the dangers of resettling this land. Often resold for a trifle, it went to form large landed estates which for a long time, and perhaps even today, have not injured anyone.

The Treasure of a Nation Is Its Honesty

The following phases follow one another: Freehold. The need of craftsmen. Slaves. Debts. "Free" craftsmanship in competition with the slave system. In the beginning personal commerce without indebtedness to finance. In many cases direct superintendence by the owners.

No man could be a director of the Salem Museum who had not sailed round both the Cape of Good Hope and the "Horn." The construction of fast clippers was New England's glory a century ago. These clippers had brought the kind of wealth that follows exchange of goods with the orient and the entire world. Even if economic, the history of the United States was, up to the year 1860, romantic. From that period dates the cult of business which continues an Italic tradition, the tradition of the great City Republics of Venice and Genoa, the Superba and the Dominante. Economic affairs need not be wholly sordid. Usury however is a cancer, finance a disease.

Paterson who invented the system of the Bank of England, that is the system of loaning promissory notes, died poor, outcast by his early associates. California gold was discovered on the land of a man who did not profit by it. On the contrary, his farm was ruined and he got no protection from law.

The American tragedy is a continuous history of waste, waste of natural abundance first, then waste of the new abundance offered by the machine, and then by machines no longer isolated but correlated and centuplicating the creative power of human labour.

The improvident Americans killed bison without thought or consideration. Forests were cut down without thought of conservation. This had no immediate effect on the prosperity of the inhabitants, because of nature's abundance. The usurers, now called financiers, plotted against abundance. To understand the scope of the American system, it is necessary to refer to the monopoly of Thales and then take up the thread at the so-called "reform," or protestant schism, seen from the economic angle. The Protestants did not wish to pay ecclesiastical taxes to Rome, and to the priests for their rites. The Bible was invented as a substitute-priest. The Canonical prohibition against usury disappeared. Polite society did not consider usury as Dante did, that is damned to the same circle of Hell as the sodomites, both acting against the potential abundance of nature.

The Catholic economy had proclaimed the doctrine of the just price. Monopoly is a manoeuvre against the just price. One can speculate only on condition of market oscillation.

The employers naturally tried to get their work done for the least possible price. The workingmen, in self-defence, asked for the suffrage. The people won the war against the Bank of the U.S. between 1830 and 1840 but, with the new waves of European work hands, the quality of the electorate declined, and demagogy undertook to corrupt it. The press misled, or distracted, the people from the nature of the economic problem.

Toward the end of the Eighteenth Century the Republic was in revolt against the privileges of "birth," and the whole democratic movement was in revolt against the monopolies held by the guilds; monopolies of the opportunities of working. This explains the bearing of Adam Smith's phrase: "Men of the same trade never gather together without a conspiracy against the general public."

But the monopolies, the sanctions, the restrictions imposed by the guilds were, at least, monopolies of *producers*. The various monopolies which culminate in the monopoly of money itself, key to all the other monopolies were, and are, monopolies of *exploiters*.

The situation is complicated when the same man has his hand both in the production and in the finance. Henry Ford found himself forced into this situation in order to defend himself against Wall Street.

To understand the development of economic ideas in America, it is useful to know European precedents, even if these are little known in Europe itself.

The traces of the Leopoldine Reforms have been lost, as far as I know, but the analogy remains. It can be said with certainty that the same current towards liberation from the shackles of the guilds made its appearance in Tuscany and in the American Colonies. The return to controlled economy in Tuscany was wrecked by the Napoleonic Wars, and nothing has been heard of it in Europe for years. As far as I can discover, it had no echo in America.

John Quincy Adams, almost alone and smeared as an eccentric, supported a doctrine of giving more authority to the state. He wanted to conserve the national lands as property of the nation.

The romance of the covered waggon, clipper of the prairies, finds its analogy in the Italian colonization in Africa. All this emigration had some resemblance to what Italy was doing on her Fourth Shore, but the former was done without the state's doing anything save granting the land without foresight.

The natural abundance existed, but it was wasted. Today, among the few merits of F.D.R. stands, perhaps, a vague idea of reforestation.

Banks

The insidiousness of banking has always followed the same road: abundance, any kind of abundance, tends to create optimism. This optimism is exaggerated, usually with the help of propaganda. Sales increase. Prices of land, or of shares, rise beyond the possibility of material revenue. The banks that favour exaggerated loans, in order to manoeuvre the increase, restrict, recall their loans, and presently panic overtakes the people.

Toward the end of the First World War, C. H. Douglas insisted on the opportunity of potential abundance and demanded national dividends, that is a distribution of family or individual allowances so as to permit the public to buy what the public had produced.

Naturally all that was called insane. The London *Times* and other newspapers in the hands of financiers opposed this suggestion.

The justice of Major Douglas's views was confirmed by the Loeb Report (Report of the National Survey of Potential Product Capacity, New York Housing Authority, 1935). No one has been willing to dispute these statistics. Before entering this war every family of four persons in the United States could have had a $4,000.00 to $5,000.00 a year standard-of-living. Only the iniquity, the imbecility of the monetary-financial system prevented the realization of this material welfare.

War was brought about to impede the utilisation of this abundance. Without scarcity monopoly cannot impose unjust prices.

American money was not socialized. American money had not been democratic for eighty years, as Lincoln had democratized it temporarily, and as Jackson had democratized it, even succeeding in extirpating the national debt.

The American people as late as 1939 had not yet learned the lesson taught by American history, much less that of world history:

it is idiotic to leave the pocket-book of the nation in the hands of private irresponsible individuals, perhaps foreign;

it is idiotic to leave the nation's sources of information in the hands of private irresponsible individuals, sometimes foreign.

This ruin has its roots in greed for lucre, a greed which

separates itself from all commonsense and every sense of proportion, and blindly creates its own undoing.

Man has been reduced not even to a digestive tube, but to a money-receptacle that gradually is losing its own value. This cycle has lasted three centuries; from the arrival of the "Pilgrims" who sought freedom of worship, to the cult of lucre dominating today. This is an economic history. It is the history of a spiritual decadence. Part of this story is technical, monetary, financial.

The aim of finance is to gain by the labour of others. In the last four decades, the aim of finance, in order that the gains of a small group be greater, has been the retention of all the profits of mechanical inventions and the lowering to a minimum of the workers' rewards. And this was done in the open market through free enterprise.

Nowadays, in normal times, the necessity of working as formerly does not exist. Van Buren, a century ago, was interested in reducing the working-day to ten hours. The working day could be limited to four hours now, and everybody could have the opportunity of working. But humanity, or, I should say the working-class is not lazy. The great mass is not touched by an appeal to laziness.

Only the artist for centuries has succeeded in detaching the idea of work from the idea of profit, and not all artists have been capable of this dissociation of concepts.

I do not know whether or not I should cull long or brief citations in regard to financial technique. The former would be a bore, the latter may be incomprehensible.

Van Buren was opposed to imprisoning debtors. The manoeuvres of finance are registered in phrases such as the following:

"The expedient resorted to . . . was nothing less than a largely increased line of discounts. . . . In October 1830 they

32

stood at $40,527,523. Between January 1831 and May 1832 they were increased to $70,428,007: the highest figure ever reached."

Mr. Webster said: "Thirty millions of the capital of the bank are now on loan and discount in the States on the Mississippi. These will all have to be called in within three years and nine months if the charter is not extended."

". . . the annual operations of the bank . . . amounted to three hundred and forty one millions of dollars. . . . The public money subject to the individual control of the President . . . was limited to fifteen or twenty thousand dollars." (Note: The president controlled thousands not millions.)

". . . demoralization of the public mind by means of a pecuniary panic." ". . . this Committee, whose doings were confidential and from whose councils the Government directors were invariably excluded."

". . . funds of the institution, including the money of the Government, as means for operating upon public opinion . . . application of the money over the public press, over influential individuals and over members of Congress."

". . . to derange the credits of the Country and to spread the pecuniary embarrassments over the length and breadth of the land by which the desired panic was produced."

". . . total reduction in thirteen months . . . $17,100,851 upon a discount line of sixty four millions. . . ."

Van Buren had the transitory honour of being called "the liberator of the Treasury," but this decade has disappeared from American memory.

After the assassination of Lincoln, President Johnson did not have the means to maintain fiscal liberty. In 1878 a Congressman expressed or explained his position by saying that he wanted to keep at least part of the non-interest bearing national debt in circulation as currency.

The "Free Silver" movement tried to oppose the interests of the silver owners to the "gold" interests, but did not go to the root. William Jennings Bryan headed this movement, and a few oldsters remember it even now. Once in a while an idealist plays up to the silver men, or is started on his career by them. A silverite, privately, will sometimes confess the truth as in fact Bryan confessed it to Kitson. At the moment I don't remember if Kitson published the details of the interview or communicated them in a personal letter to the undersigned. I am under the impression that I have seen these details in print. Bryan, knowing that he was continuing an honest tradition, and wanting to keep it alive, fought vigorously, taking advantage of whatever means were available to him.

Rottenness

From the "Annual Reports of the Secretary of the Treasury," beginning with June 1932, to June 1939, it can be learned that the Treasury of the United States bought ten billion dollars of gold at thirty-five dollars per ounce instead of $21.65 as in former times. The Treasury does not issue any reports regarding the source of this gold and, even if the Secretary of the Treasury himself wanted to find out where the gold came from, all he could find in his files would be the names of the last sellers. This means that the government, or the American people, paid ten billion dollars for gold that, before the change in price, could have been bought for six billions. This amounts to a gift of four billion dollars to merchants of gold among whom are, as has always been the case, many foreign merchants.

Only God knows how much gold the people have bought during the war, from 1939 to the present time. The trick is simple. Whenever the Rothschild and other gents in the gold business have gold to sell, they raise the price. The public is fooled by propaganda about devaluation of the dollar or other monetary unit according to the country chosen to be victimized. The argument is that the high price of the monetary unit is injurious to the nation's commerce.

But when the nation, that is the people of that nation, own the gold and the financiers own the dollars or other monetary units, the gold standard is restored. This raises the value of the dollar and the citizens of "rich" nations, as well as citizens of other nations, are diddled.

The manipulation follows simple lines. It all fits perfectly into what Aristotle calls the "common practice of commerce." The silver merchants are less important than the merchants of gold. Other metals are monopolized but they do not enter into the monetary game. With these keys you can open the records, or the Congressional Record, whenever you wish, and you will find attempts to resist these swindles, though they are getting weaker and weaker.

Chronological Outline

The chronology of American economic events is, roughly, as follows:

1620-1750: Beginning and development of colonial prosperity based finally upon a system of loans by some of the Colonial Governments to those who tilled the land. This prosperity stimulated gluttony, and the London monopolists tried to impose their monetary monopoly;

1750-1776-1788: Preparation for the Revolution, formation of the American system;

1789: Washington president. Struggle between Hamilton, conservative agent of finance and Jefferson's democratization. "Scandal of the assumption";

35

1801-1825: Jefferson and his disciples in the White House. The Louisiana Purchase. Second war against England;

1829-1841: Jackson and Van Buren in the White House. Fight between the banks and the people. The people won;

1841-1861: Gold discovered in California, in 1849. Debts contracted by the South to New York bankers and elsewhere. Negro slavery, symptoms of the Civil War. From 1861 war of secession, triumph of finance;

1869-1877: Grant president. Scandals. Gold against people;

1890: The silver question. Trusts;

1914: Industrial development. Technocracy. The menace of abundance;

1935: Chart of Potential Product Capacity;

1939: "*War is his only way out*," phrase pronounced by a Congressman to signify that Roosevelt had made such a mess of things that war was his only way of escape. In other words, the only way to hide his past and maintain his political power.

Bibliography

No vast reading is needed to understand this phase of history, if the reader begins at the beginning, that is with the *Politics* and *Economics* of Aristotle, and the Orations of Demosthenes, that against Dionysius, for example. The case of the United States in particular, has been exposed in the books here below listed. As a beginning read the writings of John Adams and Jefferson, Thomas Hart Benton's *Thirty Years' View*, and all the books by Alexander Del Mar that you can lay hands on except *Science of Money*.

C. Bowers: *Jefferson and Hamilton*, for the scandal of the assumption.

Van Buren: *Autobiography*.

Henry Adams: four volumes on the administrations of

Jefferson and Madison. Henry Adams is less interested in a specifically economico-monetary study.

Novelists and playwrights once in a while give one a clearer idea than professors. One can learn more from Ernest Poole's *The Harbour* about fast sailing-ships; and from William Mahl's *Two Plays of Social Comedy* about the attempt at monopolizing gold in 1869, than one is likely to learn from historiographers.

I have already touched on the *Report of the National Survey of Potential Product Capacity*, 1935, New York City Housing Authority.

Irving Fisher was the first man to publish in America *Stamp Scrip*, a book that clearly treats the Gesellist economy. The basic book of this school is *The Natural Economic Order*, by Silvio Gesell.

To get acquainted with the Technocrats' tendencies Dexter Kimball's *Industrial Economics* would be useful.

D. R. Dewey's *Financial History of the United States* could be of help to students already prepared to understand the importance of the facts listed in it. This book lacks, perhaps, total candour. It has been reprinted in various editions beyond the 12th, and it is a favourite textbook in universities. If my memory serves me right, Dewey does not mention any of the above-mentioned writers, except Henry Adams, who is not dangerous.

Chronological Table

Chronological Table regarding other facts, plus a few indications as to the degree of perspicacity existing during the diverse epochs in America.

1684: England suppressed the mint of Massachusetts which had coined silver.

1814: Calhoun opposed the process in which the government was forced to get its own credit on loan.

1819: Crawford issued Treasury bills bearing no interest.

1825: The industrial crisis in England led to dumping on the American market, glutting it with merchandise at bankrupt prices.

1832: Jackson: "The real value of land is due to labour."

1834-5: Jackson eliminates the national debt. The United States was left with no debt whatever.

Upon examining the receipts and expenditures of the government between 1816 and 1833, even Dewey admits that the great decrease of expenditure was due to the reduction and finally to the elimination of the payments of interest on public debt.

Briefly:

    1816: receipts $47,677,000
    1816: expenditure $31,196,000
    1833: receipts $33,948,000
    1833: expenditure $23,017,000
Interest on the public debt:
    1816: $7,823,000
    1833: $ 303,000
and later ZERO.

1836: The National Treasury, having an active balance, distributed this money to the different states. Without going back to the legendary Mohammedan Calif, those who, because of ignorance, shouted that C. H. Douglas's proposal of a National Dividend was a scandal and a novelty, may consider the following facts: Massachusetts distributed its share of the money to the various cities and towns; Boston used it for current expenses; Salem built a Municipal Building; Gro-

38

ton repaired a bridge, and Maine made a per capita distribution.

1863-4: Chase favoured the maximum distribution of the National Loan among the people instead of trafficking with the banks.

1878: The Greenback Party was in favour of the National Bills and against the bankers' monopoly. This party received a million votes.

1884: The end of the Greenback Party.

Note

I should not wish to appear unjust to D. R. Dewey when I say that he lacks candour. He has, perhaps, deceived himself by his own viscid terminology. For example, credit is not directly transformed into wealth. No paper operation can effect such a change, but credit can easily be transformed into buying power with varying terminologies printed on any object, or substance.

A perfect example of instinctive monetary good sense is met today in this small town. The newsvendor, Mr. Baffico, certainly not an erudite man, because he lacked the necessary small change, and not wanting to use postage stamps as they lose their freshness and paste in a series of exchanges, has had some little tags printed which he now gives to his patrons as change. I found Signor Baffico indignant because other merchants had begun to accept his tags as money and he had to have another supply printed.

Any form of transferable memory-aid serves, and has served, to simplify book-keeping, and to liberate us from the necessity of keeping every debit and every credit written in a ledger.

In order that money, admonitions, symbols, or certificates of debt become valid means of exchange, all that is necessary is that whoever issues them have the means to honour them.

BUREAUCRACY THE FLAIL OF
JEHOVAH ⋙ 1928

BUREAUCRATS are a pox. They are supposed to be *necessary*. Certain chemicals in the body are supposed to be necessary to life, but cause death the moment they increase beyond a suitable limit.

The time has come when we should begin to study Lenin qualitatively and analytically, and not merely polemically. He is, after all, an historic figure, and we should consider him calmly, as we consider Cardinal Richelieu, Mazarin, or any other man indubitably effective in public action. It is highly probable that we will find him a more interesting and far less disagreeable character than either of these so distinguished french prelates.

And it now begins to appear that, considering his setting, Lenin was a very moderate person . . . surrounded by fanatical and emotionally excitable persons—swayed often by aimless bitterness. Apart from the social aspect he was of interest, technically, to serious writers. He never wrote a sentence that has any interest in itself, but he evolved almost a new medium, a sort of expression half way between writing and action. This was a definite creation, as the Napoleonic code was creation. Lenin observed that bureaucracy was an evil, and "meant" to eliminate it as fast as possible. Giving it as nearly as possible in the words Steffens used on his return from Russia, Lenin

40

had said: "All that is the political department and it is to be got rid of as soon as we can."

No country produces two Napoleons or two Lenins in succession; so we may expect Russia to be reasonably slow in producing Utopia, but we have fairly straight testimony as to one man's perception of a law of state. That is: as soon as any group of men found a government, or an order, bureaucrats begin to destroy it.

It makes no difference whether it is an autocracy, tyranny, democracy, or even one of these projected horrors based on the mutually merging imbecility of the stupidest; the minute the state exists the bureaucrat begins parasitic action for himself and against the general public. He is in perpetual session, he acts continuously.

The ideal bureaucracy is the smallest possible one, and one with functions reduced to a minimum. Kipling in his third intelligent moment defined proper function of governments as "dealing with the traffic, and all that it implies."

One can cite delightful anecdotes of the incompetence of Taft's efficiency experts, but the point is that this idea of activity as a merit is, when applied to bureaucrats, as deadly as the idea of activity among tuberculous baccillae. Whereas in time past they slacked, and left the nation in comparative peace, they, under Taft, began to justify their existence by working, and by discovering things to work on. The necessity being to work, as distinct from finding work which was of use to the public or which contributes to the general convenience.

It is not convenient to have one's nose blown by another, and we therefore blow our own noses, after the age of two.

That is the view point of the sane citizen. But the point of view of the fonctionnaire is: I must have a function. I must do something. I must keep busy. And moving along that line there is absolutely nothing he is not ready to do to or for the "people," regardless absolutely and utterly of whether the "peepul" want it done, or derive any benefit or any augmented convenience from it.

Hence he, the fonctionnaire, becomes first a mild nuisance, then an aggravated nuisance, and finally an unending curse, everywhere present, nowhere desirable, and daily increasing in pomposity, stupidity, ingenuity and a conviction of the divinity of his mission, he becomes, in his own eye, the life-blood of the state.

As to the ingenuity in inutility to which bureaucracy can attain in well bureau'd states, one has the incident reported to us by Mr. Antheil: before the war all foreigners were registered in Germany; wanting to find a friend who had changed his address Mr. A was told that "they" wd. know at the Stadt-sverwhichumwhach, whither he repaired. Oh yes they were all registered, there were slips for everyone who had come to the city since 1813, but the records had only been *made up* as far as A.D. 1848. That is to say there were slips, all right enough, for everyone who had come to the town, but those that cd. be found without having to examine each slip of the myriad stopped in that year, A.D. 1848.

That is the type of harmless bureaucracy, under tyranny. It corresponds with pre-Taft America where the treasury still bought wads of red string of a given length for the purpose of tying up sacks of two cent pieces. No two cent pieces having been made since, let us say some time in the sixties. Let us say gov't. waste of about 60 dollars a year. That is innocuous.

The actions of one efficiency expert inebriated by the above discovery, take me into pure comedy and away from the subject. They are perfectly factual.

All it comes to is that everyone must observe constant vigilance; knowing that the official is paid "by the people," that he is definitely their employee, they must insist on his behaving with the same sort of serviceability that a waiter shows when bringing their dinner.

There must be no ambiguity whatsoever in this matter. The waiter is not there to juggle plates, to wash the dishes in the diningroom, to bring dishwater for soup, etc. or to inspect the private lives of the clientele.

You don't, on the other hand, expect a good waiter at half price.

We must have bureaucrats? If we must have bureaucrats by all means let us treat them humanely; let us increase their salaries, let us give them comforting pensions; let them be employed making concordances to Hiawatha, or in computing the number of sand-fleas to every mile of beach at Cape May, but under no circumstances allow them to do anything what bloody ever that brings them into contact with the citizen. The citizen should never see or meet an official in the exercise of its functions. Treat the bureaucrat with every consideration, and when he ultimately dies do not replace him.

A VISITING CARD ⋅⊰ 1942

The State

THE REVOLUTION, or the revolutions of the nineteenth century, defined the idea of liberty as the right to do anything that does not injure others. But with the decadence of the democratic—or republican—state this definition has been betrayed in the interests of usurers and speculators.

In the beginning was the word, and the word has been betrayed.

The introduction to any ordered discourse is composed of conscious or unconscious quotations. For 2,500 years Europe has been quoting Aristotle, wittingly or unwittingly. In China every dynasty that lasted as long as three centuries was based on the *Ta Hsueh* or "Great Digest" of Confucius and had a group of Confucians behind it. The Master Kung collected the Odes and historical documents of the ancient kings, which he considered instruments worthy of preservation.

We find two forces in history: one that divides, shatters, and kills, and one that contemplates the unity of the mystery.

"The arrow hath not two points."

There is the force that falsifies, the force that destroys every clearly delineated symbol, dragging man into a maze of abstract arguments, destroying not one but every religion.

But the images of the gods, or Byzantine mosaics, move the soul to contemplation and preserve the tradition of the undivided light.

Translated from Italian by John Drummond

44

Brooks Adams

This member of the Adams family, son of C. F. Adams, grandson of J. Q. Adams, and great-grandson of J. Adams, Father of the Nation, was, as far as I know, the first to formulate the idea of *Kulturmorphologie* in America. His cyclic vision of the West shows us a consecutive struggle against four great rackets, namely the exploitation of the fear of the unknown (black magic, etc.), the exploitation of violence, the exploitation or monopolization of cultivable land, and the exploitation of money.

But not even Adams himself seems to have realized that he fell for the nineteenth-century metaphysic with regard to this last. He distinguishes between the swindle of the usurers and that of the monopolists, but he slides into the concept, shared by Mill and Marx, of money as an accumulator of energy.

Mill defined capital "as the accumulated stock of human labour."

And Marx, or his Italian translator: "commodities, in so far as they are values, are materialized labour,"

so denying both God and nature.

With the falsification of the word everything else is betrayed.

Commodities (considered as values, surplus values, food, clothes, or whatever) are manufactured raw materials.

Only spoken poetry and unwritten music are composed without any material basis, nor do they become "materialized."

The usurers, in their obscene and pitch-dark century, created this satanic transubstantiation, their Black Mass of money, and in so doing decieved Brooks Adams himself, who was fighting for the peasant and humanity against the monopolists.

shareholders, "the bank hath benefit of the interest of all moneys which it creates out of nothing."

This swindle, calculated to yield interest at the usurious rate of sixty percent, was impartial. It hit friends and enemies alike.

In the past the quantity of money in circulation was regulated, as Lord Overstone (Samuel Lloyd) has said, "to meet the real wants of commerce, and to discount all commercial bills arising out of legitimate transactions."

But after Waterloo Brooks Adams saw that "nature herself was favouring the usurers."

For more than a century after Waterloo, no force stood up to the monopoly of money. The relevant passage from Brooks Adams is as follows:

"Perhaps no financier has ever lived abler than Samuel Lloyd. Certainly he understood as few men, even of later generations, have understood, the mighty engine of the single standard. He comprehended that, with expanding trade, an inelastic currency must rise in value; he saw that, with sufficient resources at command, his class might be able to establish such a rise, almost at pleasure; certainly that they could manipulate it when it came, by taking advantage of foreign exchange. He perceived moreover that, once established, a contraction of the currency might be forced to an extreme, and that when money rose beyond price, as in 1825, debtors would have to surrender their property on such terms as creditors might dictate."*

I'm sorry if this passage should seem obscure to the average man of letters, but one cannot understand history in twenty

* Brooks Adams, *The Law of Civilization and Decay*, New York, 1896. New York: Vintage Books, 1955.

minutes. Our culture lies shattered in fragments, and with the monetology of the usurocracy our economic culture has become a closed book to the aesthetes.

The peasant feeds us and the gombeen-man strangles us—if he cannot suck our blood by degrees.

History is written with a knowledge of the despatches of the ambassador Barbon Morosini (particularly one dated from Paris, 28 January, 1723 (Venetian style), describing the Law affair), together with a knowledge of the documents leading up to the foundation of the Monte dei Paschi, and the scandalous pages of Antonio Lobero, archivist of the Banco di San Giorgio of Genoa.

We are still in the same darkness which John Adams, Father of the Nation, described as "downright ignorance of the nature of coin, credit, and circulation."

Money

Money is a title, quantitatively determined, exchangeable at will against any kind of commodities offered on the market. In this respect it differs from a railway ticket, which is a specific title without any general application.

State or imperial money has always been an assertion of sovereignty. Sovereignty carries with it the right to coin or print money.

Misunderstandings about money have been, and continue to be, intentional. They derive neither from the nature of money nor from any natural stupidity of the public. The cultural tradition with regard to money, which should never have become separated from the main stream of literary culture, may be traced from Demosthenes to Dante; from Salmasius to M. Butchart's *Money* (an anthology of opinions of three centuries); from the indignation of Antoninus Pius, that people should attempt to exploit other people's misfortunes (e.g., shipwrecks), to

> . . . il duol che sopra Senna
> induce, falseggiando la moneta. (*Par.* XIX, 118-19).

Credit is a social product. It does not depend on the individual alone. The confidence you have that I will pay you 100 lire in ten years' time depends on the social order, the degree of civilization, the probabilities and possibilities of the human congeries.

To say that the state cannot take action or create something because it "lacks the money" is as ridiculous as saying that it "can't build roads because it's got no kilometres."

It is nature, the actual existence of goods, or the possibility of producing them, that really determines the capacity of the state. Yet it resides above all in the will and the physical force of the people. And the will becomes concentrated in the few.

Said Machiavelli, "gli uomini vivono in pochi."

It is within my power to think when I want to think. I will not go into the mystery of the transformation, or transit, from thought to the mobilization of other people's activities.

As a Cavourian I long neglected the writings of Mazzini. The economists of the last thirty years did not read Mazzini. Their propaganda has not, therefore, been based on the following passage from the last chapter of the *Duties of Man.*

"The establishment of public storehouses or depots from which, the approximate value of the commodities deposited having been ascertained, the Associations would issue a document or *bond*, similar to a banknote, capable of circulating and being discounted, so that the Association would be able to

49

continue its work without being thwarted by the need of quick sales, etc."

He speaks, moreover, of a "fund for the distribution of *credit*," thus anticipating the theories of the Scotsman, C. H. Douglas.

"The distribution of this credit," Mazzini continues, "should not be undertaken by the Government, nor by a National Central Bank; but, with a vigilant eye on the National Power, *by local banks administered by elective Local Councils*."

And at this point he enters into questions of administration which do not concern me.

What counts is the direction of the will.

The nineteenth century: the century of usury. Mazzini wrote, ". . . the history of the last half-century, and the name of this half-century is *Materialism*."

C'Est Toujours le Beau Monde Qui Gouverne

Or the best society, meaning the society that, among other things, reads the best books, possesses a certain ration of good manners and, especially, of sincerity and frankness, modulated by silence.

The Counsellor Tchou said to me, "These peoples (the Chinese and Japanese) should be like brothers. They read the same books."

Le beau monde governs because it has the most rapid means of communication. It does not need to read blocks of three columns of printed matter. It communicates by the detached phrase, variable in length, but timely.

Said the Comte de Vergennes, "Mr. Adams, the newspapers govern the world."

And Adams in his old age:

50

Every bank of discount is downright corruption
taxing the public for private individuals' gain.
    and if I say this in my will
the American people wd/ pronounce I died crazy.
                      (Canto LXXI)

The democratic system was betrayed. According to Adams, Jefferson, Madison and Washington, it rested on two main principles of administration, local and organic. The basis was roughly geographical, but it also represented different ways of life, different interests, agrarian, fisheries, etc. The delegates of the thirteen colonies formed, more or less, a chamber of corporations.

And the nation controlled the nation's money—in theory at least until 1863, and occasionally even in fact. This essential basis of the republican system of the U.S.A. is today a dead letter, though it can still be seen printed in the text of the U.S. Constitution.

"The Congress shall have Power . . . To coin Money (and) regulate the Value thereof."

Wörgl

In the early 1930's the small Tyrolean town of Wörgl sent shivers down the backs of all the lice of Europe, by issuing its own Gesellist money (or rather the Gesellist variety of Mazzinian money). Each month every note of this money had to have a revenue stamp affixed to it of a value equal to one per cent. of the face-value of the note. Thus the municipality derived an income of twelve per cent. per annum on the new money put into circulation.

The town had been bankrupt: the citizens had not been able to pay their rates, the municipality had not been able to pay the schoolteachers, etc. But in less than two years everything had been put right, and the townspeople had built a new stone bridge for themselves, etc. All went well until an ill-starred Wörgl note was presented at the counter of an Innsbruck bank. It was noticed, all right—no doubt about that. The plutocratic monopoly had been infringed. Threats, fulminations, anathema! The burgomaster was deprived of his office, but the ideological war had been won.

Senator Bankhead proposed an emission of dollar bills up to a limit of a milliard dollars (Bankhead-Pettengill, 17 February, 1933), but the stamps were to be affixed at the insane rate of two cents per week, equal to an interest of 104 per cent. per annum. Incomprehension of the principle of the just price could not have been carried to absurder lengths. And the Social Creditors in Alberta committed equally gross stupidities: the prescribed stamp was impracticably small and provided with a very unadhesive gum.

A Principle

The state can lend. The fleet that was victorious at Salamis was built with money advanced to the shipbuilders by the State of Athens.

The abuse of this state prerogative was demonstrated during the decadence of the Roman Empire. The state lent money to unworthy borrowers who did not repay it. With stamp scrip the reimbursement is automatic. Anyone who does not want to pay up watches his purchasing-power being gradually annulled.

The Colony of Pennsylvania lent its colonial paper money to the farmers, to be repaid in annual instalments of ten per cent., and the prosperity that resulted was renowned throughout the western world. Equally renowned was the system of the Jesuits in Paraguay.

52

Cancellation

Among all the so-called mysteries of economics none is so little understood as that of the cancellation of superfluous money or credit.

Under the Gesellist system this becomes so simple as to be practically understandable by a child.

Every given sum of money emitted cancels itself in 100 months (eight years and four months), and therefore acts, to a certain extent, as a safeguard against inflation.

Note that inflation occurs when commodities get consumed quicker than money, or when there is too much money about. It seems to me stupid that in order to furnish the state its purchasing power, money should be collected as it is by regular taxation, in accordance with the superstitions of the mercantilist and usurocratic epochs. As ridiculous as it would be for someone who possessed a tin mine to go about collecting old tin cans.

To sum up: The Gesellist system means an advantage of 17 per cent. per annum to the state compared with the system of government loans. For loans cost the government approximately 5 per cent. per annum, which has to be collected from the public in the form of additional taxation. Stamp scrip, on the other hand, if issued by the state for any kind of service useful to the state, would lessen pre-existing taxation to an amount equal to 12 per cent. of the quantity of Gesellist money spent by the state.

Saving

We need a medium for saving and a medium for buying and selling, but there is no eternal law that forces us to use the same medium for these two different functions.

Stamp scrip might be adopted as an auxiliary currency, and not as the sole form of money.

The proportion of normal money to stamp scrip, if judiciously and accurately estimated, could be used to maintain a just and almost unvarying ratio between the amount of available and wanted commodities and the total quantity of the nation's money, or at least to bring its fluctuations within tolerable limits.

Bacon wrote: "money is like muck, no good except it be spread."

Jackson: "The safest place for deposits is in the pants of the people."

Age-old economic wisdom does not hide itself behind university faculties.

The Roman Empire was ruined by the dumping of cheap grain from Egypt, which sold at an unjustly low price. And usury corrodes.

From the day when the T'ang Emperors began to issue their state notes (in about A.D. 656 it is thought) the use of gold in the manufacture of money was no longer necessary and in most cases became a matter of ignorance or a means of usury. These notes kept their original form from the year 656 down to 841-7, and the inscription is substantially the same as that to be seen on an Italian ten-lire note.

All these facts fit into the system. We may write or read explanations, or we may reflect and understand by ourselves, without wasting optical energy deciphering printed pages.

The Iconoclasts

The power of putrefaction aims at the obfuscation of history; it seeks to destroy not one but every religion, by destroying the symbols, by leading off into theoretical argument.

54

Theological disputes take the place of contemplation. Disputation destroys faith, and interest in theology eventually goes out of fashion: not even theologians themselves take any more interest in it.

The power of putrefaction would destroy all intrinsic beauty. It is spread like the bacilli of typhus or bubonic plague, carried by rats wholly unconscious of their role.

Suspect anyone who destroys an image, or wants to suppress a page of history.

Latin is sacred, grain is sacred. Who destroyed the mystery of fecundity, bringing in the cult of sterility? Who set the Church against the Empire? Who destroyed the unity of the Catholic Church with this mud-wallow that serves the Protestants in the place of contemplation? Who decided to destroy the mysteries within the Church so as to be able to destroy the Church itself by schism? Who has wiped the consciousness of the greatest mystery out of the mind of Europe, to arrive at an atheism proclaimed by Bolshevism?

Who has received honours by putting argumentation where before had been faith?

Communications

Who, what is more, attacks, continuously, the nerve centres, the centres of communication between nation and nation? How is it that you know only a chance selection of the books by your foreign contemporaries, but almost never any of their principal or key works? Who controls and impedes the commerce of perception, of intuition, between one people and another?

I demand, and I shall never cease to demand, a greater degree of communication. It is already too late for you to know eighty per cent. of the English and American books that I could have suggested to you in 1927, for translation or for reading in the original.

Joyce is familiar to you, but not Wyndham Lewis or E. E. Cummings. You were introduced to Eliot without too serious a time-lag, but you do not know Ford Madox Ford, nor W. H. Hudson. The copying of the France of 1920 continues, but you do not know Crevel. And so on. The crap has been delivered in abundance—in superabundance.

Nicholas V considered every book translated from the Greek as a conquest. The better the book, then, the greater the conquest?

The conquest of a Wodehouse is not as great as that of a Hardy, or, say, of Trollope's *The Warden*. To conquer a chance work by a good writer means less than to conquer a masterpiece by the same author or by another equally great.

The Critic

The worth of the critic is known not by his arguments but by the quality of his choice. Confucius has given us the best anthology in the world, which has already lasted 2,400 years. He collected the documents of a history already ancient in his own time, as were the *Odes*.

Criticism may be written by a string of names: Confucius, Ovid, and Homer. Villon, Corbière, Gautier.

One does not discuss painting with a man who is ignorant of Leonardo, Velasquez, Manet, or Pier della Francesca. In my efforts to establish the distinction between the first and second degree of poetic intensity, it's no good my arguing; one cannot condense a score of volumes into a few pages. I have edited several anthologies. Even my anthology of nineteenth-century French poets* contains observations that I cannot state more concisely. But with a score of books I could

* In *Make It New*, Yale University Press, 1935.

give you a basis for fruitful discussion—at least I believe so.

I have translated *Moscardino* by Pea: the only time in my life that I have wanted to translate a novel.

Controversy is valuable only insofar as it influences action, and the *Book of Mencius* is the most modern book in the world.

The pedlar brings you plenty of stuff in his pack. *News is what one hasn't heard.*

Wealth comes from exchange, but judgment comes from comparison.

We think because we do not know.

The History of Literature

Yeats said: "They don't like poetry; they like something else, but they like to think they like poetry."

There are at least three kinds of people who practice the art of writing: the instinctives, almost unconsciously; the inventors; and the exploiters.

Philologists, writers of theses, etc., frequently mistake the clamour of exploitation for inventive work. Eliot would recognise, I imagine, a greater influence of Lanman and Woods, his professors of Sanskrit, than the superficial influence of the French poets. And I consider the hours spent with Layamon's *Brut*, or copying a prose translation of Catullus by W. MacDaniel; Ibbotson's instruction in Anglo-Saxon, or W. P. Shepard's on Dante and the troubadours of Provence —more important than any contemporary influences. One who really understood the question of clear expression was Ford Madox Ford.

Literary criticism gets bogged in useless arguments if the following categories are not accepted:

1. what is read by the young serious writer for the purpose

of learning his profession, i.e., to learn to know a masterpiece and to form his own critical standards;

2. what is read as a narcotic, easy reading for the lazy, for the illiterate and dilettante public;

3. what may be usefully introduced from one country into another in order to nourish the intellectual life of the latter. The first and third of these categories may overlap, but they do not necessarily have the same boundaries.

Paideuma

A culture is an organism made up of:

1. a direction of the will;

2. certain ethical bases, or a general agreement on the relative importance of the various moral, intellectual, and material values;

3. details understood by specialists and members of the same profession.

To replace the marble goddess on her pedestal at Terracina is worth more than any metaphysical argument.

And the mosaics in Santa Maria in Trastevere recall a wisdom lost by scholasticism, an understanding denied to Aquinas. A great many images were destroyed for what they had in them.

> Ma dicon, ch'è idolatra, i Fra Minori,
> per invidia, che non è lor vicina.

In his *After Strange Gods* Eliot loses the threads of Arachne, and a new edition of Gabriele Rossetti's *Mistero dell' Amor Platonico* (1840) would be useful.

Of Wanderers

It is amusing, after so many years, to find that my disagreement with Eliot is a religious disagreement, each of us accus-

58

ing the other of Protestantism. Theophile Gautier and Swinburne are members of my church. But what Eliot says about Confucius is nonsense, or nearly so. He has renounced America ever since the time of his first departure, but if he would consider the dynasty of the Adamses he would see that it was precisely because it lacked the Confucian law that this family lost the Celestial Decree.

In five generations we have had a president, another president, an ambassador, and two writers; and now one or two almost anonymous officials, absolutely outside public life—with the nation in the hands of the enemy.

Style

In one's youth one discusses style—or one should. The poetical reform between 1910 and 1920 coincided with the scrutiny of the word, the cleaning-up of syntax. This should be tackled in addition to, almost apart from, the question of content: one should seek to define the image, to discover the truth, or a part of the truth, even before one has learned that it may not be the whole truth.

I repeat: the art of poetry is divisible into *phanopoeia*, *melopoeia*, and *logopoeia*. Verbal composition, that is to say, is formed of words which evoke or define visual phenomena, of words which register or suggest auditory phenomena (i.e., which register the various conventional sounds of the alphabet and produce, or suggest, a raising or a lowering of the tone which can sometimes be registered more accurately by musical notation), and, thirdly, of a play or "dance" among the concomitant meanings, customs, usages, and implied contexts of the words themselves.

In this last category Eliot surpasses me; in the second I surpass him. Part of his *logopoeia* is incompatible with my main purpose.

59

We have collaborated in literary criticism, we have made decisions and taken measures against certain diseases of writing. The problem of the word cannot be exhausted in a single lifetime. It consists of at least two parts:

1. the word of literary art which presents, defines, suggests, the visual image: the word which must rise afresh in each work of art and come down with renewed light;

2. the legal or scientific word which must, at the outset, be defined with the greatest possible precision, and never change its meaning.

As for ethics, I refer the reader to the *Great Digest* of Confucius.

Of religion it will be enough for me to say, in the style of a literary friend, "ogni ravennate che si rispetta, viene procreato, o almeno riceve spirito o alito di vita, nel mausoleo di Galla Placidia" (G.B.V.)—"every self-respecting Ravennese is procreated, or at least receives spirit or breath of life, in the Mausoleum of Galla Placidia."

Dante perhaps said too much in the *Paradiso* without saying enough. In any case the theologians who put reason (logic) in place of faith began the slithering process which has ended with theologians who take no interest in theology whatsoever.

Tradition *inheres* in the images of the gods, and gets lost in dogmatic definitions. History is recorded in monuments, and *that* is why they get destroyed.

Terminology

One should distinguish between the fraud of enjoying interest on money created out of nothing, and the swindle of raising the value of the monetary unit through the manipulation of some monopoly, so forcing debtors to pay double in terms of the commodities or property they got at the time of the loan.

Whence one descends or returns to another ancient fraud,

that of forcing a nation to purchase commodities (often use-less) for twice as much as they are worth.

I would say that every book of value contains a bibliography declared or implied. The *De Vulgari Eloquio* refers us to Richard of St. Victor, Sordello, Bertran de Born, and Arnaut Daniel. Dante was my Baedeker in Provence. Here I may mention *Il Giusto prezzo nel medio Aevo* by the Sac. L. P. Cairoli.

Terminology is not science, but every science advances by defining its terminology with ever greater precision.

With a clear and exact definition of money, a clear under-standing of the nature of money, years of economic be-wilderment and stupidity will be avoided. Add definitions of credit and circulation, and you will practically arrive at an economic erudition that can be recorded in a few pages and really understood in a few months of study.

Without understanding economics one cannot understand history. John Adams was amazed that very few men had studied systems of government. Between his time and that of Aristotle political literature is scarce enough. And Salmasius? *De Modo Usurarum* appears not to have been reprinted since 1639 or 40.

The emphasis given to economics by Shakespeare, Bacon, Hume, and Berkeley does not seem to have been enough to have kept it prominent in the Anglo-Saxon public conscience. After the arch-heretic Calvin, it seems, discussion of usury has gone out of fashion. A pity! As long as the Mother Church concerned herself with this matter one continued to build cathedrals. Religious art flourished.

Kulturmorphologie

To repeat: an expert, looking at a painting (by Memmi, Goya, or any other), should be able to determine the degree of tolerance of usury in the society in which it was painted.

Art is a means of communication. It is subject to the will of the artist, yet goes beyond it.

"The character of the man is revealed in every brush-stroke" (and this does not apply only to ideograms).

Text-Books

The text-book for anyone who wants to study the art of metric, the art of making verses, remains the *De Vulgari Eloquio*, but no one can become an expert without knowing Bion ("Death of Adonis"), the troubadours mentioned by Dante, and the technical development in France during the nineteenth century, including a score of poets without great importance for the matter they had to communicate (see *Make it New*).

We can already understand Chinese *phanopoeia* up to a point, both in the original and in good translations, but their art of sound and metric must remain a closed book to the West until the advent of a really impassioned sinologue.

To learn what poetry is one cannot dispense with a score of authors who did not write in the language of Petramala:

"Quoniam permultis ac diversis idiomatibus negotium exercitatur humanum ..." (*D.V.E.*, I, vi).

Unless you know Homer, Sappho, Ovid, Catullus, Propertius, Dante, Cavalcanti, a few songs of the troubadours together with a few of von der Vogelweide or Hans Sachs, Villon, and Gautier, you won't know European poetry. And your understanding will not be complete unless you take a look at Anglo-Saxon metric.

The appellation "anseres naturali" is not mine (see *D.V.E.* II, iv).

No one who is unprepared to train himself in his art by

comparative study of the culture today accessible, in the spirit of the author of the *De Vulgari Eloquio,* can expect to be taken seriously. The matter to be examined is more extensive —that is all.

Confucius was an anthologist—the greatest.

Dante was content to cite the first lines of certain *canzoni.*

The convenience of printing allows us to make things easier by giving an entire poem.

In the latter half of the nineteenth century technical and metrical development was centred in France. After 1917 it was continued in the English language. It was my intention that there should have been two classes of Imagists: Hellenists and modernists. Mercantilism intervened. The development continued. Practically no one has succeeded in producing satisfactory English translations from the Greek: only a few fragments have come through successfully.* Perhaps the most beautiful books of poetry in the English language are Arthur Golding's translations of Ovid's *Metamorphoses,* printed in 1567, and Gavin Douglas's *Eneados,* done half a century earlier, in a Scots dialect that no one can read today without a glossary. No one has succeeded in translating Catullus into English, yet technical development has made progress since Eliot, and E. E. Cummings achieves a Catullian ferocity in his untranslatable:

DIRGE

flotsam and jetsam
are gentleman poeds
useappeal netsam
our spinsters and coeds)

* Since this was written Pound has translated Sophocles' *Women of Trachis,* N.Y., 1957.

thoroughly bretish
they scout the inhuman
itarian fetish
that man isn't woman

vive the millenni
um three cheers for labor
give all things to enni
one buggar thy nabor

(neck and senektie
are gentleman ppoyds
even whose recta
are covered by lloyds

In his *tour de force* L. Zukofsky gives a phonetic representation of an American chewing chewing-gum. We must distinguish between the masterpieces of world poetry and a certain few poems which are necessary to keep us informed of what our contemporaries are doing elsewhere.

Twenty years ago Guy Charles Cros and Vlaminck wrote a few verses; ten years ago Basil Bunting wrote some too. Of these, and of the novel *Les Pieds dans le Plat* by the late René Crevel, it may be said that they are better than the foreign crap currently displayed on the bookstalls.

En Famille

No one, perhaps, has ever built a larger tract of railway, with nothing but his own credit and 5,000 dollars cash, than that laid down by my grandfather. The credit came from the lumbermen (and in face of opposition from the big U. S. and foreign steel monopolists) by printing with his brother the

64

paper money of the Union Lumbering Co. of Chippewa Falls, bearing the promise to "pay the bearer on demand . . . in merchandise or lumber."

It was only when my father brought some old newspaper clippings to Rapallo in 1928 that I discovered that T. C. P. had already in 1878 been writing about, or urging among his fellow Congressmen, the same essentials of monetary and statal economics that I am writing about today.

Social

Credit is a social phenomenon. The credit of the nation belongs to the nation, and there is not the slightest reason why the nation should have to pay rent for its own credit.

Money is a title and a measure. If it is metallic it is subject to assay to ensure that the coin is of specific fineness and weight. The use of such money still falls under the classification of barter. When people begin to understand the function of money as a title, the desire to barter disappears. When the state understands its duties and powers it does not leave its sovereignty in the hands of private interests that are irresponsible or arrogate to themselves unwarranted responsibilities.

The beauty of the designs on ancient coins rightly symbolizes the dignity of sovereignty inherent in royal or imperial responsibility. The disappearance of numismatic art coincides with the corruption of the governments concerned.

The Rothschilds financed the Austrian armies against Venice and Romagna. Naturally. The Rothschilds financed the armies against the Roman Republic. Naturally. They tried to buy over Cavour. Naturally. Cavour accomplished the first stage towards Italian unity, allowing himself to be exploited

65

according to the custom of his times, but he refused to be dominated by the exploiters.

```
R O M A
O     M
M     O
A M O R
```

Above all this, the substantiality of the soul, and the substantiality of the gods.

Dichten = Condensare

The German word *Dichtung* means "poetry." The verb *dichten—condensare.**

In our intellectual life—or "struggle," if you prefer it—we need facts that illuminate like a flash of lightning, and authors who set their subjects in a steady light.

The writings of Frobenius contain flashes of illumination. From nineteenth-century philology, relegating everything to separate compartments, creating specialists capable of writing monographs or articles for encyclopaedias without the least understanding of their import or relation to the total problem, Frobenius advanced to Kulturmorphologie. He brought the living fact to bear on the study of dead documents. It began—*incipit vita nova sua*—with his hearing that certain railway contractors were in conflict with some local tradition. A king and a girl had driven into the ground where there was a certain hillock: they ought not to make a cutting through the sacred place. The materialist contractors took no notice and went ahead—and unearthed a bronze car with effigies of Dis and Persephone.

* The two words *dichten* (to draw in, tighten) and *dichten* (to write poetry) appear to have different roots. Whether the poet's intuition has seen deeper than philology, remains to be determined. Ed.

66

Later he wrote, "Where we found these rock drawings there was always water within six feet of the surface."

The oral tradition, surviving rites, and also the practical import of archaeological findings are all part of his total perception. He saw nothing ridiculous in a child's wanting to know if the last letter of the word *Katz* stood for the cat's tail, and the first one for its head. But to the school teacher, who cared little for intelligence or lively curiosity, the child just seemed stupid.

To live we need facts, and opportunities for comparison. We want no foreign dumping, neither of material goods nor of pseudo-literary produce. But samples for comparison, certainly. To know the best model, and to improve on it. To know the masterpieces, and then achieve self-sufficiency. Conquests in the manner of Nicholas V.

A reform of the universities could be effected, in my opinion, by the infusion of certain known facts condensable into a few pages. Confucius, Mencius, the anthology compiled by Confucius of poems already ancient in his time. A dozen Chinese poets, and a general idea, at least, of the nature of the ideogram as a means of verbal and visual expression. This vitalizes.

A proper sense of the maxima of poetry. Homer not to be neglected. The study of metre will require an odd half-hour or so with Bion, the troubadours, and French poetry between 1880 and 1910. A certain snobbery, dating back to the Renaissance, has perhaps unduly boosted the Greek authors at the expense of Ovid, Propertius, and Catullus.

Do not overburden the student, do as one would in taking him to a picture-gallery containing a few paintings by the greatest masters. Quality, not quantity.

In teaching history: a synthesis not inferior to that of Brooks Adams.

67

Our friend T. E. Hulme truly said: "All a man ever *thought* would go onto a half sheet of notepaper. The rest is application and elaboration."

Without strong tastes one does not love, nor, therefore, exist.

De Modo Usurarum

Getting into debt is one way of having a career in politics. The Mandarin Wu Yung tells us that when he was appointed Governor, the bankers pressed him to borrow money from them. He insisted that he would never have been able to repay them out of his salary. That was a mere detail that didn't worry them in the least.

This anecdote has its bearing on the life of an usher I knew at a library in Venice, who hanged himself after forty years faithful service. The note of hand

"... rompe i muri e l'armi."

and a policy of unjustly low salaries can favour the usurers' game. The emphasis is on the adverb "unjustly." Such a policy derives from an imperfect understanding of the nature of money, and of the power of the state. The state monetary authorities can supply the needs of the people and provide for all work useful to the state, up to a limit imposed by the availabilities of raw materials and the people's brain-power and muscle-power, without having to ask permission of the usurer or have recourse to the Cavourian alternative.

Money A Warning

It is not yet sufficiently understood that every sound economic system, every economic procedure, depends on justice.

Money is a warning or notification of the amount the public owes to the bearer of the coin or note. "Not by nature, but by custom, whence the name *nomisma*."

In producing these metallic discs, or pieces of paper, which serve as a means and a measure of exchange, the state is doing work; and it would be perfectly just that the employees and officials of the state were remunerated for doing this work rather than that the state should collect taxes on the products of other people's work. The ethical and intellectual work that goes into determining the measure of the just price deserves its due reward. This is the ethical basis of the Gesellist idea, though Gesell may not have said so himself.

There is no reason why an inventor should understand all the implications of his invention. Gesell saw his system from the point of view of the merchant who wants a rapid, and always more rapid, exchange of goods. "Wealth is exchange." Rossoni, when Italian Minister for Agriculture, saw at once the advantage it would bring to the state: "Then the state will get something out of it too," he said.

It is unjust that money should enjoy privileges denied to goods.

Monetary theory is worthy of study because it leads us to the contemplation of justice.

Should the circulation of capital be automatic? We must distinguish between capital and purchasing power. Striving for a clear terminology one might limit the term capital to the sense of "productive undertaking," or the securities of such an undertaking, i.e., securities that presuppose a material basis which yields a product that can be divided periodically, paying interest (share interest in monetary form) without creating inflation, which is superfluity of paper money in relation to available goods.

University

The modern university was founded at Frankfurt by Leo Frobenius, or at least it was the first approach to the modern university. If I had been thirty-five years younger I would have wanted to enroll myself as a student. If I wish to know, for example, if J. S. Mill is right in saying that certain African tribes have a money of account—a money which, according to him, was a concept of value, having a name that meant nothing other than this indication of the value of a means of exchange—I write to Frankfurt. In this particular case I received, within ten days, a list of all the tribes that used, or had used, the "makute." It had become an abstract measure, though it had originally meant one of the mats or circles of plaited straw that the natives carry slung behind them as protection against damp, thorns, etc., when they sit down.

It was an article of commerce that served to calculate the prices of other goods, such as salt, or knives—until the Portuguese began to coin metal "makutes," and to counterfeit them.

When I wanted to know how the primitive telegraph, tapped out on wooden drums worked, I wrote to Frankfurt. I believe that Frobenius has marked the transition from the stage of "comparative philology" to that of "Kulturmorphologie," but in any case one cannot fully understand modern thought without some awareness of Frobenius's work. *Gli uomini vivono in pochi.* The books that change our understanding are few. Several Germans tell me that they make no distinction between "Der Kundige" and "Der Kenner."

The foreigner is liable to acquire some queer ideas about other peoples' languages, but I'm not sure that he's always wrong.

The communication system is slow and imperfect. I want a

printer who, at least once a month, will print what I want him to print, *pro bono publico* and not for immediate gain.

As long as the really interesting books are in the hands of only a hundred—even a dozen—individuals, how is one to find keen and competent translators? A young friend wanted to read Galdos, but we couldn't find any editions. Eventually I had to send to London, but I received only secondary works, not the principal masterpieces.

The amount of matter to be introduced from abroad is quantitatively small. It is the quality that counts in this commerce, not the bulk. We need to import every year say twenty, perhaps even fifty, books that are not crap and filth. Moral filth is perhaps less poisonous than intellectual filth, when it comes to considering the printed page. Moral filth, in print, poisons the reader; intellectual filth can be toxic to a whole race. The means a nation chooses (or lets be chosen) for the distribution of books and printed matter are of importance. For the last hundred years few have worried about them. Flaubert published his *sottisier*. But half a century later the study of what was actually printed and offered for sale on the bookstalls was considered eccentric on the part of the present writer. I made an analysis in eighteen numbers of the *New Age*, but no publisher has wanted to reprint the series, which was, in any case, cut short by the protests of the readers of the said journal. Yet a whole system is collapsing, and for want of having paid attention to the symptoms of its own defilement.

We must distinguish between the intellectual construction of Europe, and poison. Perhaps in re-reading the *Divina Commedia* we may find this dissociation of ideas. I cannot say. Geryon is biform. He takes you lower down. And after the eighth canto of the *Paradiso*, who understands the meaning?

It seems that only a few persons occupied about the temples at least at Rome, were enough to keep alive the cult of the old gods. The preservation of verities, the process of history, the rise and fall of a dogma, whether or not affected by contingent events, are a great deal more interesting than is commonly supposed.

Italy has lived more fully than other nations because she has kept up the habit of placing statues in gardens. The grove calls for the column. *Nemus aram vult.*

Good Government

I believe the most useful service I could do would be to put before you, every year, a few lines of Confucius, so that they might sink into the brain. One reads a phrase of Confucius, and it seems nothing. Twenty years later one returns to think over its meaning. When I was thirty I read a French translation, then an English one, and then gradually I have profited from Fenollosa's notes. One cannot get the full meaning without analysing the ideograms. Legge translates a certain ideogram with the word "beclouding," but the basic idea it conveys is one of wild vegetation which encroaches upon and grows over everything, creating a dense and tangled confusion, which would imply "overgrowing" in English. This ideogrammatic component of wild vegetation with broken water, meaning "swamp," is frequently encountered in ideogram lexicons.

Here is a piece of Confucian dialogue.

Tze-Lu: The Lord of Wei is waiting for you to form a government, what are you going to do first?

Kung: Settle the names (determine a precise terminology).

72

Tze-Lu: How's this, you're divagating, why fix 'em?

Kung: You bumkin! Sprout! When a proper man don't know a thing, he shows some reserve. If words (terminology) are not (is not) precise, they cannot be followed out, or completed in action according to specifications.

It all seems too easy? The more responsibilities you have the more you will understand the meaning.

And I have to thank Dante for having drawn our attention to a treatise by Richard of St. Victor, *De Contemplatione*, in which the three words *cogitatio, meditatio* and *contemplatio* arc defined.

Towards order in the state: the definition of the word. But if I have made any contribution to criticism I have done so by introducing the ideogrammic system. True criticism will insist on the accumulation of these concrete examples, these facts, possibly small, but gristly and resilient, that can't be squashed, that insist on being taken into consideration, before the critic can claim to hold any opinion whatsoever.

Let us consider certain facts of literature; let us mark out the categories whenever it may be convenient or possible, but *not* before knowing the facts (i.e., the masterpieces, either of the highest intensity or superior in particular aspects). When we know them we can discuss them—but not painting without a knowledge of Mantegna or Manet, not poetry if we dare not make comparisons.

Italian songs include "Ahi ritorna l'età dell'oro" and the stornelli of Romagna. Good, so-called "popular" songs often have this value: the music renders the words without deforming them. There is no snobbery that the critics won't lick from the boots of an established reputation.

After ten days' struggle, Gino Saviotti was reduced to

"there are days when one feels the need of a peppermint cream" (*Difesa della Poesia di Francesco Petrarca,* last chapter).

After Cavalcanti and Dante the Italian writers are those who have had something precise to relate. The stylists declined from the moment they wanted to write Latin instead of Italian.

And anyone who wrote in Latin then went and imitated his own watered-down style in the so-called vulgar tongue (cf. *De Vulgari Eloquio*).

France began to become tongue-tied with the *Pleiade.* She recovered again after Stendhal, who wrote badly. Gautier did not write badly—when he wrote verse.

Thought is organic. It needs these "gristly facts."

The idea is not well planned until it is capable of going into action. The idea goes into action by means of the word. It is completed from the time it goes into action. The idea that does not go into action is a truncated idea. It lacks some essential small part. This does not mean, of course, that it has to go into action half an hour after it's born.

We think because we do not know.

```
R O M A
O     M
M     O
A M O R
```

POSSIBILITIES OF CIVILIZATION:
WHAT THE SMALL TOWN
CAN DO ⌇ 1936

It is our strength as Americans that those of us who are any good at all start out to make a record. Whistler set out to beat every European painter. If Henry James didn't think of himself as the Babe Ruth among novelists it was possibly because he was born first and left his native habitat before the King of Swat emerged.

This "great desire for excelling" was and perhaps still is absolutely necessary as an antidote to local self-complacency and falsification of standards.

The great outpouring of print that can only be classified as "swill" by any honest inspector of mental health is due in part to commercial pressure, and in part to inferiority complex. A considerable number of names will occur to the reader without my dragging in personal reference to writers who have put up smoke screens, who have striven all their lives to usurp high places, who have striven all their lives to prevent the great honest mass of the public from reading better books, and to keep the average reader ignorant of the best that has been and is being written.

After a quarter of a century's effort I am not yet hardened against that sort of infamy. I had it vividly lighted up for me two years ago on the sea walk beneath my terrace. A very bashful young man whom I had seen on a bathing raft during the previous weeks, finally approached me: did I mind his speaking to me? He had never spoken to an author. There then followed some very naive questions; very naive but wholly honest. That kid *wanted* very sincerely to read good books, and he had, most unfortunately, believed the sort of stuff that gets printed in the normal way of publishers' commerce. He knew almost nothing of first rate books, and was earnestly ploughing through a lot of jam. Commercial jam, marmalade made less from oranges than from turnips.

Against the product of local vanity, honest American energy simply *had* to insist on the *best*, nothing but the best. No truce with the second rate, no truce with pretenders. The pretender is born sometimes of intellectual cowardice. Men and ladies who start for the top, for the first bracket, and can't make it, are often ashamed to confess.

It is at this point that we can learn from older countries. In France after the war there were almost no first rate writers. Those who were first rate were so highly specialized that they had almost no contact with the general public.

But Paris still beat us in high class work of the second order. Cocteau came out against jim-cracks and demanded music "like tables and chairs." He had Franch tradition behind him in the sort of proverb: "My glass isn't very large but I don't try to grab other peoples'."

There is all the difference in the world between the man who does his job well, and the lunatic who thinks he is Napoleon.

The American small town has something to learn from Italian civilization as it now exists. I mean the small town in distinction from New York and Chicago. These big cities have tried to *buy out* Europe. They have got, probably, the most expensive music in the world. They are the Paradise for orchestral conductors, because the conductors are cocks of the walk and there have been no great composers to keep 'em in order.

It is as childish as tennis on the French Riviera after the war. The colonels made the courts insufferable for the plain man *until* a general arrived to keep 'em in order. As soon as General G. got into a set the colonels behaved like human beings.

There are hundreds of towns in America that cannot bribe the best performers to leave European orchestras. There are hundreds of towns that cannot outbid London and Paris, but that is no reason for their doing nothing whatever. A very wise man whom I suspect of having been a woman remarked long ago: the manners of the aristocracy are good because they are their own. All others are bad because they are an imitation.

I have seen various manners in my time; the first three examples that really impressed me as perfect were those of a Russian Prince, of a Japanese Daimyo and thirdly of a huge red-bearded peasant at Born. He was engaged in a job of amateur cobbling, mending one of his children's shoes, when I lost the road between Perigord and Excideuil and came into his cottage in search of an omelet. Gentleness and dignity: tie between him and the Daimyo.

I have no regret at having spent my first ten years in Europe hounding down the best living writers and artists. Knowing what I did, it would have been gross neglect of duty to have omitted this action. It is just as much up to a writer to know the best as it is up to a biologist to know as much biological truth as possible.

But when you have placed the great inventors, that doesn't mean you have come to the end of your job. An Italian can be of some use without being a greater author than Gabriele d'Annunzio. The thing is not to be a pseudo-d'Annunzio. Italians know this in a more thorough way than we Americans in general know it.

There is on the other hand, a false modesty, a species of bragging modesty that is just as corrosive as and harder to deal with than megalomania. It does perhaps more harm, and prevents more real work than the silliest vanities.

The Latin sense (which concords with Confucius' philosophy) consists in sizing up the possible job, the job that can be done only in a given place; that can sometimes be done better in one place than another, or at least as well in the place a man is, as anywhere else.

We in America have no families who have been living father to son in the same house for 2000 (two thousand) years. That doesn't matter. We have few families who have lived in the same town for three generations, and among them a certain number can contain no other ideas save that of familial tradition.

It might however be useful to observe what an Italian can occasionally do with a specifically limited opportunity.

It will probably never be the kind of opportunity that would occur in a small American city, but it might set a small town group thinking.

My research into the life of Sigismundo Malatesta took me to Cesena and from the library to a concert, managed by the librarian. The program was composed of music of the highest quality and a local lawyer was adding more interest to it (from the piano) than the professional musicians who had been imported for the occasion. Cesena is not numbered among the ten largest cities of Italy; I should say not among the largest 40 or 60. Szigeti had played there a few weeks before.

Both that concert and the librarian have taught me a good deal. M. T. Dazzi is probably less known to the outer world than Dazzi the sculptor; his name does not appear in heavy advertising. Let me take his record as showing what a man can do outside a big city and without any pretentions to upsetting the history either of his age or of letters.

Firstly: M. T. Dazzi has probably rectified learned opinion of Mussato. At any rate Dante's contemporary, a dramatist and historian, is better known because Dazzi started being interested in him some years ago, and is still editing him for a very learned and encyclopedic collection.

Secondly: The Malatestine Library in Cesena, a unique monument to the culture of the best decades of the Renaissance, is in better condition because Dazzi was once its librarian.

Thirdly: Cesena showed me how to have first rate music in a small town.

Fourthly: If you look in your Baedeckers you will find a few lines, or maybe only a line or two given to the "Querini Stampalia." This also is a unique Italian (Venetian) possession; the last heir of the two noble families left his books, his house and his pictures to Venice. A monument of taste and, what is rarer, a monument to great common sense and thoughtfulness for humanity.

The library is open in the evening; it opens in the afternoon a bit before the other libraries shut. No student is cramped for paper. Naturally most students use note books or bring their own paper, but the Querini foundation has provided for those who forget to bring paper and for whom even that expense might have caused trouble.

When I first saw the picture gallery it was a mess, it might have been a secondhand junk shop. Enter Dazzi. The Querini has a few first rate pictures. They are where you can see them. It had a little good furniture which is now so placed as to give an air of life to part of the gallery, but the creative act of the curator has been directed to the second rate painting. Perhaps

79

Longhi is not a second rate painter, though no one has quite tried to place him among the world's greatest. The Querini now has its Longhis all together in two or three rooms. That offers one a unique experience.

Settecento portraits that had been scattered and were without any interest as single paintings, have been assembled. The visitor is now aware of an "existence"; of something definite having occurred in XVIIIth century Venice.

And there is a whole room of Venetian life—I suppose 60 scenes—showing the whole habits, celebrations, modes of living in a Venice where bears were baited so that after you have seen San Marco and the Palace of the Doges and Santa Maria Miracoli and the Carpaccios in S. Giorgio dei Schiavoni it is now almost a toss up whether you should go to the Accademia or to the Querini or to the Museo Correr.

And all this has been done without ostentation and on the basis of recognizing what the Querini is, and what it could be, and not trying to do the impossible. To the best of my knowledge the main expense was buying a few Longhis that were in Venice, but that might have been scattered instead of being concentrated into that gallery. There has been no attempt to *rival* the matchless galleries of Milan and Perugia. There was no attempt to get something out of the Accademia into the Querini.

The man built with what he had in his charge. That spirit may not be needed in cities of two million and five million inhabitants, but it could be enormously useful wherever a few or a few dozen people want a life of more interest, where they want to see, hear or read better pictures, music or printed volumes.

I read Dazzi novels, printed and still in typescript. I respect the language and technique of his poems. I can't get up on my hind feet and shout to the world that he is a greater novelist than . . . XXuxus, YuYuks, and Zeekus or that no one else ever emitted such poesy, but I can take off my hat to a man who knows how to live where fate set him and in the years Chronos has provided.

When I start thinking of other Italian "figures" it's not that I don't "know where to draw the line," it is that the whole state of mind which leads to line drawing is irrelevant to the kind of culture I am trying to write about.

L. C. has written several volumes and essays and translated some Henry James and some Hudson; G. M. writes stories that would probably evaporate in translation. E. D. has translated enough Blake to fill a volume (printed a decade ago).

Gino Saviotti has written novels, the last one on S. Antonio contains a long chapter on usury; he has summarized Croce; he has written a history of Italian Literature in Seven Volumes which is said to have disturbed the curricula. This *kind* of activity seems to proceed here without trying to force itself out of its frame. Perhaps no one can improve on an epigram made years ago by Maurice Vlaminck: intelligence is international, stupidity is national, art is local.

It may need international intelligence to recognise authenticity; that is why vagabond critics are not wholly useless. They may be indeed very useful in stirring up the animals, dispossessing forgers and pretenders, but at the other end of the seesaw there is ample room for the man who can build in his own ambience. And in this latter activity we have not yet learned all we can from Italy, peninsula of many small cities.

The lesson is: figure out what you can do with the local plant:—local printing press, local musicians. Find out something that is not being done in New York or London. Find out what the big commercial people can't do, or won't do.

Men who have set out with the intention of losing money by doing something real, have even found that they just couldn't *lose*. The great example of this is the Abbey, now the Irish National Theater, but it is by no means the only example. It put a town on the map.

No organization can do an artist's work for him, but the isolated artist often envies the unused potentialities of an organization.

MURDER BY CAPITAL ✺§ 1933

I

TWENTY-FIVE years ago "one" came to England to escape Ersatz; that is to say, whenever a British half-wit expressed an opinion, some American quarter-wit rehashed it in one of the "respectable" American organs. Disease is more contagious than health. England may be growing American in the worst sense of that term. The flagrant example is that of receiving Spengler instead of Frobenius. I can't conceive of Spengler's being the faintest possible *use* in any constructive endeavour. Frobenius is a bitter pill for the Anglo-Saxon. He believes that when a thing exists it probably has a cause.

His most annoying tendency is to believe that bad art indicates something more than just bad art.

Twenty years ago, before "one," "we," "the present writer" or his acquaintances had begun to think about "cold subjects like economics" one began to notice that the social order hated *any* art of maximum intensity and preferred dilutations. The best artists were unemployed, they were unemployed long before, or at any rate appreciably before, the unemployment crises began to make the front page in the newspapers.

Capitalist society, or whatever you choose to call the social organization of 1905 to 1915 was *not* getting the most out of its available artistic "plant."

"I give *myself* Work," said Epstein when he was asked if he had any.

The best writers of my generation got into print or into

books mainly via small organizations initiated for that purpose and in defiance of the established publishing business of their time. This is true of Joyce, Eliot, Wyndham Lewis and of the present writer, from the moment his intention of break with the immediate past was apparent. My one modern volume issued by Mathews was sent to the ineffable printer before dear old Elkin had read it. He wanted a "book by" me. In the case of *Quia Pauper Amavi*, he again wanted a book by me, and suggested that I omit the *Propertius* and the *Moeurs Contemporaines*.

The story of getting *Lustra* into print is beyond the scope of this essay, it belongs to stage comedy not even to memoirs. If a new England or a new generation is being born, it can only know the wholly incredible island of those years *if* some genius who remembers them can be persuaded to devote himself wholly and exclusively to developing a comic technique.

You might put the question in the following form: What drives, or what can drive a man interested almost exclusively in the arts, into social theory or into a study of the "gross material aspects" videlicet economic aspects of the present? What causes the ferocity and bad manners of revolutionaries?

We know that Lenin was annoyed by the execution of his older, admired brother. We mostly do not know or remember that George Washington greatly admired an elder brother who was, roughly speaking, sacrificed to official imbecility and ultimately died of it, i.e., after-affects of the "war of Jenkins's ear."

Why should a peace-loving writer of Quaker descent be quite ready to shoot certain persons whom he never laid eyes on? I mean to say, if it ever should come to the barricades in America (as England is not my specific business).

What specific wrong has the present order done to writers and artists *as such,* not as an economic class or category, but

84

specifically *as artists*? And why should some of them be "driven" to all sorts of excessive opinion, or "into the arms of" groups who are highly unlikely to be of use to them? If Frobenius saw the inside of Schönbrunn he was not surprised by the fall of the Habsburgs.

I do not believe that any oligarchy can indefinitely survive continuous sin against the best art of its time. I certainly did not look forward to the Russian Revolution when I wrote my monograph on Gaudier-Brzeska, but I pointed out that the best conversation was to be found, 1912 to 1914, in *quadriviis et angiportis*, under a railway arch out by Putney, in cheap restaurants and not in official circles or in the offices of rich periodicals. The cleverness and quickness "in society" was probably even then limited to the small segment actually concerned in governing. I mean to say that those who govern, govern *on condition* of being a *beau monde* of one sort or another. Their rule cannot indefinitely survive their abrogation of "culture" in the decent sense of that word, if any decent sense still remain in it.

II

Hatred can be bred in the mind, it need not of necessity rise from the "heart." Head-born hate is possibly the most virulent. Leaving aside my present belief that economic order is possible and that the way to a commonly decent economic order is known. What has capital done that I should hate Andy Mellon as a symbol or a reality?

This article is *per far ridere i polli* among our Bolshevik friends. Many of them are, alas, as far from understanding as are the decadents.

I have grown, if not fat under the existing order, at least dangerously near it. I have no personal grievance. They tried to break me and didn't or couldn't or, at any rate, chance and destiny, etc., gave me "a fairly good break." I was tough enough to escape or to stand the pressure. Personally. Why then have I blood lust?

I have blood lust because of what I have seen done to, and attempted against, the arts in my time.

A publishing system existed and was tolerated almost without a murmur, and its effect, whether due to conscious aim or blind muddling fear, was to erect barriers against the best writing. Concurrently, there rose barriers against the best sculpture, painting and music. Toward the end of my sojourn in London even an outcast editor of a rebellious paper, Mr. Orage of the *New Age*, as it then was, had to limit me to criticism of music as no other topic was safe. Contrary to general belief I did not arrive hastily at conclusions, but I observed facts with a patience that I can now regard as little short of miraculous. As a music critic I saw the best performers gradually driven off the platform. I saw a few desperate attempts and a still smaller number of successful attempts to put over something a bit better than was "wanted." A few years later the French musicians were parading the streets wanting work. This is not due to radio, and it was still less due to radio a decade and more ago.

It is perhaps only now that all these disagreeable phenomena can be traced to maladministration of credit. Artists are the race's antennae. The effects of social evil show first in the arts. Most social evils are at root economic. I, personally, know of no social evil that cannot be cured, or very largely cured, economically.

The lack of printed and exchangeable slips of paper corresponding to extant goods is at the root of bad taste, it is at the root not of bad musical composition, but at the root of the non-performance of the best music, ancient, modern

86

and contemporary; it is at the root of the difficulty in printing good books *when* written.

The fear of change is very possibly a contributing cause. I don't mean an honest and perspicacious fear of change, but a love of lolling and a cerebral fixation. But with a decent fiscal system the few hundred people who want work of first intensity could at any rate have it, whether it were supposed to leaven the mass or not.

The Unemployment Problem

Mussolini is the first head of state in our time to perceive and to proclaim *quality* as a dimension in national production. He is the first man in power to publish any such recognition *since*, since whom?—since Sigismond Malatesta, since Cosimo, since what's-his-name, the Elector of Hanover or wherever it was, who was friendly with Leibnitz?

The unemployment problem that I have been faced with, for a quarter of a century, is not or has not been the unemployment of nine million or five million, or whatever I might be supposed to contemplate as a problem for those in authority or those responsible, etc., it has been the problem of the unemployment of Gaudier-Brzeska, T. S. Eliot, Wyndham Lewis the painter, E. P. the present writer, and of twenty or thirty musicians, and fifty or more other makers in stone, in paint, in verbal composition.

If there was (and I admit that there was) a time when I thought this problem could be solved without regard to the common man, humanity in general, the man in the street, the average citizen, etc., I retract, I sing palinode, I apologize.

One intelligent millionaire *might* have done a good deal —several people of moderate means have done "something"; i.e., a poultice or two and bit of plaster hither or yon.

The stupidity of great and much-advertised efforts and donations and endowments is now blatant and visible to anyone who has the patience to look at the facts. The "patron" must be a live and knowledgeable patron, the entrusting of patronage to a group of bone-headed professors ignorant of art and writing, is and has been a most manifest failure. There is no reason to pity anyone. Millions of American dollars have been entrusted to incompetent persons, whose crime may not be incompetence but consists, definitely, in their failure to recognize their incompetence. I suppose no pig has ever felt the circumscription of pig-ness and that even the career of an Aydelotte cannot be ascribed to other than natural causes.

This is what American capitalism has offered us, and by its works stands condemned. The British parallel is probably that lord and publisher, X, who objected to colloquial language.

For the purpose of, and the duration of, this essay, I am trying to dissociate an objection or a hate based on specific effects of a system *on* a specific and limited area—i.e., I am examining the effects on art, in its social aspect; i.e., the opportunity given the artist to exist and practice his artistry *in* a given social order, as distinct from all questions of general social justice, economic justice, etc.

Autobiography if you like. Slovinsky looked at me in 1912: "Boundt, haff you gno bolidigal basshuntz?" Whatever economic passions I now have, began *ab initio* from having crimes against living art thrust under my perceptions.

It is no answer to say that "my" programme in art and letters has gradually been forced through, has, to some extent, grabbed its place in the sun. For one thing, I don't care about "minority culture." I have never cared a damn about snobbisms or for writing *ultimately* for the few. Perhaps that is an

88

exaggeration. Perhaps I was a worse young man than I think I was.

Serious art is unpopular at its birth. But it ultimately forms the mass culture. Not perhaps at full strength? Perhaps at full strength. Yatter about art does *not* become a part of mass culture. Mass culture insists on the fundamental virtues which are common to Edgar Wallace and to Homer. It insists on the part of technique which is germane to both these authors. I believe that mass culture does not *ultimately* resist a great deal that Mr. Wallace omitted. I think it ultimately sifts out and consigns to the ash-can a great deal that the generation of accepted authors of Mr. Arnold Bennett's period put in. I do not believe that mass culture makes any such specific and tenacious attack on good art as that which has been maintained during the last forty years of "capitalist, or whatever you call it," ci—or whatever you call it—vilization.

Mass culture probably contains an element present also in Christianity, I mean the demand for that which is hidden. This sometimes pans out as demand for colloquial; i.e., living language as distinct from the ridiculous dialect of the present Cambridge school of "critics" who believe that their books about books about writing will breed a "better taste" than would familiarity with the great poets.

You can probably do nothing for a man who has arrived at the cardboard cerebration of supposing that you read Homer and Villon in order to "collect a bag of tricks," or that you "train a sensibility" by reading a book about Villon rather than by reading Villon himself. And when such men write criticism and tell you to read other critics we are carried back to the scarcity economist Mr. Smith, who remarked that men of the same trade never gather together without a conspiracy against the general public.

The bureaucracy of letters is no better than any other bureaucracy, it injects its poison nearer to the vital nerves of the State.

Mr. Yeats's criticism is so mixed up with his Celticism that it may be more confusing to cite it than not, but he gave a better reason for reading great poets.

When you read Homer you do not read him for tricks, but if you are engaged in the secondary activity of building up a critical faculty you might read him in order not to be fooled by tricks, by second-hand sleight of hand derivations.

To Recapitulate

The effects of capitalism on art and letters, apart from all questions of the relations of either capitalism, art, or letters, to the general public or the mass, have been: (1) the non-employment of the best artists and writers; (2) the erection of an enormous and horrible bureaucracy of letters, supposed to act as curators, etc., which bureaucracy has almost uninterruptedly sabotaged intellectual life, obscuring the memory of the best work of the past and doing its villainous utmost to impede the work of contemporary creators.

As for proposed remedies, C. H. Douglas is the first economist to include creative art and writing in an economic scheme, and the first to give the painter or sculptor or poet a definite reason for being interested in economics; namely, that a better economic system would release more energy for invention and design.

INTEGRITY OF THE
WORD ✎§ 1939

Definition

WE will never see an end of ructions, we will never have a sane and steady administration until we gain an absolutely clear conception of money. I mean an absolutely not an approximately clear conception.

I can, if you like, go back to paper money issued in China in or about A.D. 840, but we are concerned with the vagaries of the Western World.

1. MEASURE OF PRICE. Let us be quite clear. Money is a measured title or claim. That is its basic difference from unmeasured claims, such as a man's right to take all you've got under wartime requisition or as an invader or thief just taking it all. Money is a measure which the taker hands over when he acquires the goods he takes. And no further formality need occur during the transfer, though sometimes a receipt is given. The idea of justice inheres in ideas of measure, and money is a measure of price.

2. MEANS OF EXCHANGE. Money is valid when people recognise it as a claim and hand over goods or do work up to the amount printed on the face of the "ticket," whether it is made of metal or paper. Money is a general sort of ticket, which is its only difference from a railway or theatre ticket. A railway ticket is a measured ticket. A ticket from London to Brighton differs from one for London to Edinburgh. Both are measured,

but in miles that always stay the same length. A money ticket, under a corrupt system, wobbles. For a long time the "public" has trusted people whose measure was shifty. You will hear money called a "medium of exchange," which means that it can circulate freely, as a measure of goods and services against one another, from hand to hand.

3. GUARANTEE OF FUTURE EXCHANGE. We will have defined money properly when we have stated what it is in words that can NOT be applied to anything else and when there is nothing about the essential nature of money that is omitted from our definition. When Aristotle calls money "a guarantee of future exchange" that merely means that it is an undated ticket that will be good when we want to use it. Tickets have sometimes stayed good for a century. When we do not hand over money at once for goods or services received we are said to have "credit." The "credit" is the other man's belief that we can and will some time hand over the money OR something measured by money.

Purpose

Most men have been so intent on the individual piece of money as a measure that they have forgotten its purpose, and they have got into inextricable muddles and confusions regarding the total amount of money in a country.

A perfectly good hammer is useless to pick your teeth with. If you don't know what money is for, you will get into a muddle when using it, and still more will a government get into a mess in its "monetary policy."

Statally speaking, that is from the point of view of a man or a party that wants to govern justly, a piece of money is a ticket, the country's money is a mass of tickets for getting the country's food and goods justly distributed.

The job for a man today who is trying to write on money is not to say something new, it is simply to make a clear statement about things that have been known for 200, and often for 2,000 years.

You have got to know what money is for.

The aim of a sane and decent economic system is to fix things so that decent people can eat, have clothes and houses up to the limit of available goods.

Measure

Take money in such a system as a means of exchange, and then realise that to be a just means of exchange it must be measured.

What are you going to use to measure the price of anything? An egg is an egg. You can eat it (until it goes bad). Eggs are not all the same size, but they might serve among primitive people as an approximate measure.

Unterguggenberger, the Austrian monetary reformer, used work as a measure, "Arbeitswert," 10 schillings' worth of work. That was o.k. in a mountain valley where everyone could do pretty much the same kind of work in the fields.

Charlemagne had a grain measure, so many pecks of barley, wheat or rye worth a denar, or put it the other way on. The just price of barley was so much the peck.

In 796 A.D. it was 2 denars.

And in 808 A.D., it was 3 denars.

That means that the farmer got more denars for the same quantity of barley. Let us hope that he could buy more other goods with those denars.

Unfortunately the worth of all things depends on whether there is a real scarcity, enough or more than can be used at a given time.

A few eggs are worth a great deal to a hungry man on a raft.

Wheat is worth more in terms of serge in some seasons than in others. So is gold, so is platinum.

A single commodity (even gold) base for money is not satisfactory.

State authority behind the printed note is the best means of establishing a just and honest currency.

The Chinese grasped that over 1,000 years ago, as we can see from the Tang state (not bank) note.

Sovereignty inheres in the power to issue money and to determine the value thereof.

American interests hide the most vital clause in our constitution. The American government hasn't, they say, the right to fix prices. But it has the right to determine the "value" of money and this right is vested in Congress. This is a mere difference in legal formalities and verbal arrangements. The U.S. government has the right to say "a dollar is one wheat-bushel thick, it is one serge-foot long, it is ten gallons of petrol wide."

Roosevelt and his professors were on the right line with their commodity dollar. But they hooeyed and smoke-screened and dodged the problem of having enough tickets to serve the whole people, and of keeping those tickets moving.

Distribution

There is nothing new in creating money to distribute wealth.

If you don't believe the Emperor Tching Tang issued the first national dividend in B.C. 1766 you can call it something else. It may have been an emergency dole, but the story will at least clear up one muddle. The emperor opened a copper mine and issued round coins with square holes and gave them

94

to the poor "and this money enabled them to buy grain from the rich," but it had no effect on the general shortage of grain.

That story is 3,000 years old, but it helps one to understand what money is and what it can do. For the purpose of good government it is a ticket for the orderly distribution of what is available. It may even be an incentive to grow or fabricate more grain or goods. But it is not in itself abundance.

Inflation

The term "inflation" is used as a bogey to scare people away from any expansion of money at all.

Real inflation only begins when you issue money (measured claims) against goods or services that are undeliverable (assignats of the French Revolution issued against the state lands) or issue them in excess of those wanted.

That amounts to saying: two or more tickets for the same seat at the same time, or tickets in London for a theatre performance tonight in Bombay, or for a dud show.

Money can be expended as long as each measured claim can be honoured by the producers and distributors of the nation in goods and services required by the public, when and where they want them.

Terms

It is useless to talk of economics or to listen to talk about economics or to read books on the subject until both reader and writer know what they mean by the half-dozen simplest and most necessary terms most frequently used.

The first thing for a man to think of when proposing an economic system is: What is it for?

And the answer is: to make sure that the whole people

95

shall be able to eat (in a healthy manner), to be housed (decently) and be clothed (in a way adequate to the climate).

Corrosion

The Left claim that private ownership has destroyed this true purpose of an economic system. Let us see how ownership was defined at the beginning of a capitalist era during the French Revolution.

OWNERSHIP "is the right which every citizen has to enjoy and dispose of the portion of goods guaranteed him by the law. The right of ownership is limited, as are all other rights, by the obligation to respect the rights of others. It cannot be prejudicial to the safety, nor to the liberty, nor to the existence, nor to the ownership of other men like ourselves. Every possession, every traffic, which violates this principle is illicit and immoral."—Robespierre.

The perspective of the damned XIXth century shows little else than violation of these principles by demoliberal usurocracy. The doctrine of capital, in short, has shown itself as little else than the idea that unprincipled thieves and anti-social groups should be allowed to gnaw into the rights of ownership.

This tendency "to gnaw into" has been recognised and stigmatised from the time of the laws of Moses and he called it *neschek*.

And nothing differs more from this gnawing or corrosive than the right to share out the fruits of a common cooperative labour.

Indeed USURY has become the dominant force in the modern world.

"Moreover, imperialism is an immense accumulation of money capital in a few countries, which as we have seen, amounts to 4 or 5 thousand million pounds sterling in securities. Hence the extraordinary growth of a class, or rather a stratum, or *rentiers*, i.e. persons who live by 'clipping coupons,' who take absolutely no part in any enterprise, and whose profession is idleness. The exportation of capital, one of the most essential economic bases of imperialism, still further isolates this *rentier* stratum from production, and sets the seal of parasitism on the whole country living on the exploitation of labour of several overseas countries and colonies." (V. I. Lenin, quoting Hobson, in *Imperialism the highest stage of Capitalism.*)

The only people who do not seem to have read and digested this essay are the British Labour Party and various groups of professing communists throughout the Occident.

Some facts are now known above parties, some perceptions are common heritage of all men of good will.

THE ENEMY IS IGNORANCE
⋐§ 1944

To the memory of Aurelio Baisi

Until you have clarified your own thought within your-
self you cannot communicate it to others.

The Way of Utopia

ON THE 10th of September last, I walked down the Via Salaria
and into the Republic of Utopia, a quiet country lying eighty
years east of Fara Sabina. Noticing the cheerful disposition
of the inhabitants, I enquired the cause of their contentment,
and I was told that it was due both to their laws and to the
teaching they received from their earliest schooldays.

They maintain (and in this they are in agreement with
Aristotle and other ancient sages of East and West) that our
knowledge of universals derives from our knowledge of particulars, and that thought hinges on the definition of words.

In order to teach small children to observe particulars they
practise a kind of game, in which a number of small objects,
e.g., three grains of barley, a small coin, a blue button, a coffee
bean, or say, one grain of barley, three different kinds of but-
tons, etc., are concealed in the hand. The hand is opened for
an instant, then quickly closed again, and the child is asked

Translated from Italian by John Drummond.

to say what it has seen. For older children the game is gradually made more elaborate, until finally they all know how their hats and shoes are made. I was also informed that by learning how to define words these people have succeeded in defining their economic terms, with the result that various iniquities of the stock market and financial world have entirely disappeared from their country, for no one allows himself to be fooled any longer.

And they attribute their prosperity to a simple method they have of collecting taxes or, rather, their one tax, which falls on the currency itself. For on every note of 100 monetary units they are obliged, on the first of every month, to affix a stamp worth one unit. And as the government pays its expenses by the issue of new currency, it never needs to impose other taxes. And no one can hoard this currency because after 100 months it would have lost all its value. And this solves the problem of circulation. And because the currency is no more durable than commodities such as potatoes, crops, or fabrics, the people have acquired a much healthier sense of values. They do not worship money as a god, they do not lick the boots of financiers or pests of the market-place. And, of course, they are not menaced by inflation, and they are not compelled to make wars to please the usurers. In fact, this profession—or criminal activity—is extinct in the country of Utopia, where no one is obliged to work more than five hours a day, because their mode of life makes a great deal of bureaucratic activity unnecessary. Trade has few restraints. They exchange their woollen and silk fabrics against coffee and groundnuts from their African possessions, while their cattle are so numerous that the fertilizer problem almost solves itself. But they have a very strict law which excludes every kind of surrogate from the whole of their republic.

Education for these people is almost a joy, and there are no

99

redundant professors. They say that it is impossible to eliminate idiotic books, but that it is easy to distribute the antidote, and they do this by means of a very simple system. Every bookseller is obliged to stock the best books; some of outstanding merit must be displayed in his window for a certain number of months each year. As they become familiar with the best books, the disgusting messes served up periodically by *The Times* or the *Nouvelle Revue Française* gradually disappear from the drawing-rooms of the more empty-headed young ladies of both sexes.

They attach the importance to skill in agricultural tasks that I attached in my youth to skill at tennis or football. In fact, they have ploughing contests to see who can drive the straightest furrow. As for myself, I felt I was too old for such activities, and recalled the case of a young friend who had also been seized by this archaic passion: he wrote that his first acre "looked as if a pig had been rooting about all over it."

After I had heard these very simple explanations of the happiness of these people, I went to sleep under the sabine stars, pondering over the astonishing effects of these reforms, apparently so trifling, and marvelling at the great distance separating the twentieth century world from the world of contentment.

Inscribed over the entrance to their Capitol are the words:

THE TREASURE OF A NATION IS ITS HONESTY.

Particulars of the Crime

It is no use assembling a machine if a part is missing or defective. One must first have all the essential parts. Fully to understand the origins of the present war it will be useful to know that:

The Bank of England, a felonious combination or, more precisely, a gang of usurers taking sixty per cent interest, was founded in 1694. Paterson, the founder of the bank, clearly stated the advantages of his scheme: "the bank hath benefit of the interest on all moneys which it creates out of nothing." In 1750 the paper currency of the Colony of Pennsylvania was suppressed. This meant that this confederacy of gombeen-men, not content with their sixty per cent, namely, the interest on the moneys they created out of nothing, had, in the fifty-six intervening years, become powerful enough to induce the British Government to suppress, *illegally*, a form of competition which had, through a sane monetary system, brought prosperity to the colony.

Twenty-six years later, in 1776, the American colonies rebelled against England. They were thirteen independent organs, divided among themselves, but favoured by geographical factors and European discords. They conquered their perennial enemy, England, but their revolution was betrayed by internal enemies among them.

The economic facts behind the American "Civil" War are extremely interesting. After the Napoleonic wars, after the "Civil" one, after Versailles, the same phenomena may be observed.

Usurocracy makes wars in succession. It makes them according to a pre-established plan for the purpose of creating debts.

For every debt incurred when a bushel of grain is worth a certain sum of money, repayment is demanded when it requires five bushels or more to raise the same sum. This is accompanied by much talk of devaluation, inflation, revaluation, deflation, and a return to gold. By returning to gold, Mr. Churchill forced the Indian peasant to pay two bushels of grain in taxes and interest which a short time before he had been able to pay with one only.

C. H. Douglas, Arthur Kitson, Sir Montagu Webb give the details. The United States were sold to the Rothschilds in 1863. The Americans have taken eighty years to discover facts that are still unknown in Europe. Some of them were made known in Congress by Charles A. Lindbergh, the aviator's father, and later included by Willis A. Overholser in his *History of Money in the United States.*

A letter from the London banking firm of Rothschild Bros., dated June 25, 1863, addressed to the New York bank of Ickleheimer, Morton & Van der Gould, contains the following words of fire:

"The few who understand the system . . . will either be so interested in its profits, or so dependent on its favours that there will be no opposition from that class, while, on the other hand, the great body of people, mentally incapable of comprehending the tremendous advantages that Capital derives from the system, will bear its burden without complaint, and perhaps without even suspecting that the system is inimical to their interests. . . ."

The favourite tricks of the usurocracy are simple, and the word "money" is not defined in the clerks' manual issued by the Rothschilds, nor in the official vocabulary "Synonyms and Homonyms of Banking Terminology." The tricks are simple: taking usury at sixty per cent and upwards, and altering the value of the integer of account at moments advantageous to themselves.

Ignorance

Ignorance of these tricks is not a natural phenomenon; it is brought about artificially. It has been fostered by the silence of the press, in Italy as much as anywhere else. What is more, it has been patiently and carefully built up. The true basis of credit was already known to the founders of the Monte dei Paschi of Siena at the beginning of the seventeenth century.

This basis was, and is, the abundance, or productivity, of nature together with the responsibility of the whole people.

There are useful and potentially honest functions for banks and bankers. One who provides a measure of prices in the market and at the same time a means of exchange is useful to the nation. But one who falsifies this measure and this means is a criminal.

A sound banking policy aims, and in the past has aimed, as Lord Overstone (Samuel Lloyd) has said, "to meet the real wants of commerce, and to discount all commercial bills arising out of legitimate transactions."

Nevertheless, at a certain moment about the beginning of the century, Brooks Adams was moved to write:

"Perhaps no financier has ever lived abler than Samuel Lloyd. Certainly he understood as few men, even of later generations, have understood, the mighty engine of the single standard. He comprehended that, with expanding trade, an inelastic currency must rise in value; he saw that, with sufficient resources at command, his class might be able to establish such a rise, almost at pleasure; certainly that they could manipulate it when it came, by taking advantage of foreign exchange. He perceived moreover that, once established, a contraction of the currency might be forced to an extreme, and that when money rose beyond price, as in 1825, debtors would have to surrender their property on such terms as creditors might dictate."

So now you understand why the B.B.C., proclaiming the liberation of Europe, and of Italy in particular, never replies to the question: *And the liberty of not getting into debt—how about that?*

And you will understand why Brooks Adams wrote that after Waterloo no power had been able to resist the force of the usurers.

War is the highest form of sabotage, the most atrocious form of sabotage. Usurers provoke wars to impose monopolies in their own interests, so that they can get the world by the throat. Usurers provoke wars to create debts, so that they can extort the interest and rake in the profits resulting from changes in the values of the monetary units.

If this is not clear to the novice, let him read and meditate the following sentences from the Hazard Circular of the year 1862:

"The great debt that (our friends the) capitalists (of Europe) will see to it is made out of the war must be used to control the volume of money. . . . It will not do to allow the greenback, as it is called, to circulate . . . for we cannot control them" (i.e., their issue, etc.).

Italy's ambition to achieve economic liberty—the liberty of not getting into debt—provoked the unleashing of the ever-accursed sanctions.

But the great Italian publishing houses, more or less open accomplices of the perfidious Italian press, have not published the works of Brooks Adams and Arthur Kitson in which these facts are given. The press has been perfidious and the great publishing houses have been more or less accomplices according to their capacity. One cannot hope to prevail against bad faith by making known the facts, but one might against ignorance. The publishers have received their information through certain channels; they have taken their tone from the

Times Literary Supplement and from books distributed through Hachette and W. H. Smith & Son, or approved by the *Nouvelle Revue Française*.

Nothing, or practically nothing, has arrived in Italy that has not been picked over by the international usurers and their servitors. And the result is to be seen in an artificially created ignorance and snobbery. Neo-malthusianism needs looking into. In Italy, as elsewhere, crime fiction has served to distract attention from the great underlying crime, the crime of the usurocratic system itself. If this may seem of no importance to politicians and men of action, it has nonetheless created a vast blockage of passive inertia in the very so-called "literary" or "cultured" circles which set the tone of printed matter. They read, they write, and the public gets the sweepings. And from this dishwashing process derives the credulity that has contaminated a great part of the public with the "English disease," namely, a pathological disposition to believe the fantastic tales put out from London and disseminated gratis by indigenous simpletons.

Of the liberals (who are not always usurers) we would ask, Why are usurers always liberals?

Of those who demand the dictatorship of the proletariat we would ask, Must the proletariat of one country impose dictatorship on the proletariat of another?

To those who inveigh against the concept of autarchy, saying it costs too much; that grain should be bought in the cheapest market—we would recall that it was precisely the importing of cheap grain from Egypt that ruined Italian agriculture under the Roman Empire. And if this fact appears too remote from our own times, it may be noted that those who speak of this kind of free trade usually end up by talking about the export of *labour*, that is, the export of workers, the export of human beings, in exchange for commodities.

Many are beginning to understand that England, in her sadistic attempt to destroy Italy, is destroying herself, though the public still fails to understand the origin of this mania for destruction. Deny, if you like, that the purely and exclusively economic man exists, yet the analysis of economic motives is useful for an understanding of avarice. The greed for monopoly is a fundamental evil. It may be seen in the transgression of the unjust price, condemned by the economic doctrine of the Church throughout the period of its greatest splendour.

It must be understood that the whole of current taste in literature and the entire journalistic system are controlled by the international usurocracy, which aims at preserving intact the public's ignorance of the usurocratic system and its workings.

Liberalism and Bolshevism are in intimate agreement in their fundamental contempt for the human personality. Stalin "disposes" of forty truckloads of human "material" for work on a canal. We find the liberals talking about the export of "labour."

Liberalism conceals its baneful economics under two pretexts: the freedom of the spoken and written word, and the freedom of the individual, protected, in theory, by trial in open court, guaranteed by the formula of *habeas corpus*. Enquire in India, or in England, to what extent these pretexts are respected. Ask any American journalist what freedom of expression is left him by the big advertisers.

Some further items of useful knowledge:

1. We need a means of exchange and a means of saving, but it does not follow that the means must be the same in each case.

2. The state can LEND. The fleet that was victorious at Salamis

106

was built with money lent to the shipbuilders by the Athenian state.

3. To simplify both government and private management, a system which can operate at the counter, whether of a government or private office, is preferable.

A NATION

THAT WILL NOT

GET ITSELF INTO DEBT

DRIVES THE USURERS

TO FURY

The Pivot

All trade hinges on money. All industry hinges on money. Money is the pivot. It is the middle term. It stands midway between industry and workers. The pure economic man may not exist, but the economic factor, in the problem of living, exists. If you live on clichés and lose your respect for words, you will lose your "ben dell' intelletto."

Trade brought prosperity to Liguria; usury lost it Corsica. But in losing the ability to distinguish between trade and usury one loses all sense of the historical process. There has been some vague talk in recent months about an international power, described as financial, but it would be better to call it "usurocracy," or the rule of the big usurers combined in conspiracy. Not the gun merchant, but the traffickers in money itself have made this war; they have made wars in succession for centuries, at their own pleasure, to create debts so that they can enjoy the interest on them, to create debts when money is cheap in order to demand repayment when money is dear.

But as long as the word "money" is not clearly defined, and

as long as its definition is not known to all the peoples of the world, they will go blindly to war with each other, never knowing the reason why.

This war is a chapter in the long and bloody tragedy which began with the foundation of the Bank of England in far-away 1694, with the openly declared intention of Paterson's now famous prospectus, which contains the words already quoted: "the bank hath benefit of the interest on all moneys it creates out of nothing."

To understand what this means it is necessary to understand what money *is*. Money is not a simple instrument like a spade. It is made up of two elements: one which measures the prices on the market, one which bestows the power to purchase the goods. It is this twofold aspect the usurers have taken advantage of. You know well enough that a watch contains two principles, a mainspring and a hairspring, with a train of wheels between the two. But if someone asks you what money is, you don't know what the ten-lire notes and the twenty-centisimi pieces, which you have in your pockets, are.

Until the seventh century after Christ, when an Emperor of the T'ang Dynasty issued state notes (*state* notes, not bank notes, mind you), the world was practically compelled to use as money a determined quantity of some commonly used commodity, such as salt or gold according to the degree of local sophistication. But since A.D. 654, at least, this metal has no longer been necessary for trading between civilized people. The state note of the T'ang Dynasty, of the year 856, which is still in existence, has an inscription almost identical with the one you read on your ten-lire notes.

The note measures the price, not the value; or in other words, prices are calculated in monetary units. But who supplies these notes? And, before the present war, who controlled the issue of international money? If you want to discover the causes of the present war, try and find out who controlled *international* money, and how it came under such control.

The Enemy

The enemy is ignorance (our own). At the beginning of the nineteenth century John Adams (Pater Patriae) saw that the defects and errors of the American government derived not so much from the corruption of government officials as from ignorance of coin, credit, and circulation.

The situation is the same today. The subject is considered too dry by those who do not understand its significance. For example, at about the end of last December a banker boasted to me that at a certain period he could remember Italian paper money was worth more than gold. One concludes that in that particular "golden age" the Rothschilds were wanting to purchase gold cheap, in order to send its price rocketing later.

In the same way the Sassoons and their accomplices profited from the slump in silver. At one period, in fact, silver fell to 23 cents per ounce, and was later bought by certain American idiots at 75 cents per ounce, in order to please their masters and to "*save India*," where, with the return to gold, Mr. Churchill, as we have remarked, forced the peasants to pay two bushels of grain in taxes and interest which a short time before could have been paid with only one.

To combat this rigging of the gold and silver markets we must know what money is. Today money is a disk of metal or a slip of paper which serves to measure prices and which confers, on its possessor, the right to any goods on sale in the market up to a price equal to the figure indicated on the disk or slip of paper, without any formality other than the transfer of the money from hand to hand. Thus money differs from a special coupon, such as a railway or theatre ticket.

This universal quality confers special privileges on money which the special coupon does not possess. Of these I will speak another time.

Besides this tangible money, there is also intangible money, called "money of account," which is used in accounting and banking transactions. This intangibility belongs to a discussion of credit rather than a treatise on money.

Our immediate need is to clarify current conceptions with regard to the so-called "work-money," and to make clear that money cannot be a "symbol of work" without any other qualification. It could be a *certificate of work done* on condition that the work is done within a system. The validity of the certificate would depend on the honesty of the system, and on the authority of the certifier. And the certificate would have to refer to some work useful—or at least pleasurable—to the community.

An item of work not yet completed would serve as an element of credit rather than as a basis for money properly understood. Speaking metaphorically, one might call credit the "future tense of money."

The elaborate assay procedure of mints has been developed to guarantee the quality and quantity of the metal in coined money; no less elaborate precautions would be necessary to guarantee the quality, quantity, and appropriateness of the work which will serve as the basis for what is to be called "work-money" (meaning "certificate-of-work-done-money").

The same frauds of *accounting* practised by the gombeen-men of the past in order to swindle the public under a metallic monetary system will, of course, be attempted by the gombeen-men of the future in their attacks on social justice, irrespective of the kind of monetary system that may be established. And they will be just as likely to succeed unless the nature and workings of these practices have been fully understood by the public—or at least by an alert and efficient minority.

It is only one plague-spot that the creation of work-money would eliminate. I mean that the advantages of the gold-standard system lauded by the bankers are advantages for the bankers only—for *some* bankers only, in fact. Social justice demands equal advantages for all.

The advantage of work-money mainly derives from one fact alone: work cannot be monopolized. And this is the very reason for the bitter opposition, for the uproar of protest, natural and artificial, which issues from the ranks of the gombeen-men, whether they be exotic or indigenous.

The idea that work might serve as a *measure* of prices was already current in the eighteenth century, and was clearly expounded by Benjamin Franklin.

As for monopolizability: no one is such a fool as to let someone else have the run of his own private bank account; yet nations, individuals, industrialists, and businessmen have all been quite prepared—almost eager—to leave the control of their national currencies, and of international money, in the hands of the dregs of humanity.

As for the validity of primitive forms of money such as a promissory note written on leather, we have C. H. Douglas's memorable comment that it was valid enough as long as the man who promised to pay an ox *had* an ox.

The Toxicology of Money

Money is not a product of nature but an invention of man. And man has made it into a pernicious instrument through lack of foresight. The nations have forgotten the differences between animal, vegetable, and mineral; or rather, finance has chosen to represent all three of the natural categories by a single means of exchange, and failed to take account of the

111

consequences. Metal is durable, but it does not reproduce itself. If you sow gold you will not be able to reap a harvest many times greater than the gold you sowed. The vegetable leads a more or less autonomous existence, but its natural reproductiveness can be increased by cultivation. The animal gives to and takes from the vegetable world: manure in exchange for food.

Fascinated by the lustre of a metal, man made it into chains. Then he invented something against nature, a false representation in the mineral world of laws which apply only to animals and vegetables.

The nineteenth century, the infamous century of usury, went even further, creating a species of monetary Black Mass. Marx and Mill, in spite of their superficial differences, agreed in endowing money with properties of a quasi-religious nature. There was even the concept of energy being "concentrated in money," as if one were speaking of the divine quality of consecrated bread. But a half-lira piece has never created the cigarette or the piece of chocolate that used, in pre-war days, to issue from the slot-machine.

The durability of metal gives it certain advantages not possessed by potatoes or tomatoes. Anyone who has a stock of metal can keep it until conditions are most favourable for exchanging it against less durable goods. Hence the earliest forms of speculation on the part of those in possession of metals—especially those metals which are comparatively rare and do not rust.

But in addition to this potentiality for unjust manipulation inherent in metallic money by virtue of its being metallic, man has invented a document provided with coupons to serve as a more visible representation of usury. And usury is a vice, or a crime, condemned by all religions and by every ancient moralist. For example, in Cato's *De Re Rustica* we find the following piece of dialogue:

"And what do you think of usury?"

"What do *you* think of murder?!"

And Shakespeare: "Or is your gold . . . ewes and rams?"

No! it is not money that is the root of the evil. The root is greed, the lust for monopoly. "Captans annonam, maledictus in plebe sit!" thundered St. Ambrose—"Hoggers of harvest, cursed among the people!"

The opportunity of dishonest dealing was already offered to the possessors of gold at the dawn of history. But what man has made he can unmake. All that is needed is to devise a kind of money that cannot be kept waiting in the safe until such time as it may be most advantageous for its owner to bring it out. The power to swindle the people by means of coined or printed money would thus disappear almost automatically.

The idea is not new. Bishops in the Middle Ages were already issuing money that was recalled to the mint for recoining after a definite period. The German, Gesell, and the Italian, Avigliano, almost contemporaneously, devised a still more interesting means of achieving a greater economic justice. They proposed a paper-money system by which everyone was obliged, on the first of the month, to affix a stamp on every note he possessed equal to one per cent of the note's face value.

This system has given such praiseworthy results in certain restricted areas where it has been put into operation, that it is the duty of any far-sighted nation to give it serious consideration. The means is simple. It is not beyond the mental capacity of a peasant. Anyone is capable of sticking a stamp on an envelope, or on a receipted hotel bill.

From the humanitarian point of view, the advantage of this form of taxation over all others is that it can only fall on persons who have, at the moment the tax falls due, money in their pockets worth 100 times the tax itself.

113

Another advantage is that it doesn't interfere with trade or discourage building activity; it falls only on superfluous money, namely on money that the holder has not been obliged to spend in the course of the preceding month.

As a remedy for inflation its advantages will be seen immediately. Inflation consists in a superfluity of money. Under Gesell's system each issue of notes consumes itself in 100 months—eight years and four months—thus bringing to the treasury a sum equal to the original issue.

The expense of numerous departments whose present function is to squeeze taxes out of the public would be reduced to a minimum and practically vanish. Office workers don't go to the office to amuse themselves. They could be given the chance of spending their time as they liked, or of raising the cultural level of their social circle, while still receiving their present salaries, without the need of diminishing the material wealth of a country by a single bushel of grain, or by a litre of wine. Those who are not studiously inclined would have time to produce something useful.

A cardinal error of so-called liberal economics has been to forget the difference between food and stuff you can neither eat nor clothe yourself with. A republican realism should call the public's attention to certain fundamental realities.

Philip Gibbs, writing of Italy for Anglo-American readers, cannot see that anything can be done with a product except sell it. The idea of *using* it does not penetrate the Bolshevik-Liberal psychology.

The Error

The error has been *pecuniolatry*, or the making of money into a god. This was due to a process of denaturalization, by which our money has been given false attributes and powers that it should never have possessed.

Gold is durable, but does not reproduce itself—not even if you put two bits of it together, one shaped like a cock, the other like a hen. It is absurd to speak of it as bearing fruit or yielding interest. Gold does not germinate like grain. To represent gold as doing this is to represent it falsely. It is a falsification. And the term *"falsificazione della moneta"* (counterfeiting or false-coining) may perhaps be derived from this.

To repeat: we need a means of exchange and a means of saving, but it does not follow that the means must be the same in each case. We are not forced to use a hammer for an awl.

The stamp affixed to the note acts as the hair-spring in the watch. Under the usurocratic system the world has suffered from alternate waves of inflation and deflation, of too much money and too little. Everyone can understand the function of a pendulum or hair spring. A similar mental grasp should be brought to bear in the field of money.

The distinction between trade and usury has been lost. The distinction between debt and interest-bearing debt has been lost. As long ago as 1878 the idea of non-interest-bearing debt was current in the United States—even of non-interest-bearing *national* debt. The interest that you received in the past has been largely an illusion: it has functioned on a short-term basis leaving you with a sum of money arithmetically somewhat greater than that which you had "saved," but expressed in a currency whose units had lost part of their value in the meantime.

Dexter Kimball collected statistics of American rail bonds issued over a period of half a century, and made interesting discoveries as to the proportion of these obligations that had simply been annulled for one reason or another. If my memory doesn't betray me, the figure was as high as seventy per cent.

That industrial concerns and plants should pay interest on their borrowed capital is just, because they serve to increase production. But the world has lost the distinction between production and corrosion. Unpardonable imbecility, for this distinction was known in the earliest years of recorded history. To represent something corrosive as something productive is a falsification, a forgery. Only fools believe in false representations. Give money its correct potential; make it last as long as things last in the material world; give it, above all, its due advantage (i.e., that of being exchangeable for any goods at any moment, provided the goods in question exist); but do not give money, beyond this advantage, powers that correspond neither to justice nor to the nature of the goods it is issued against or used to purchase. This is the way that leads to social justice and economic sanity.

Definition of Words

To cultivate competence in historiography in future generations one must begin in the schools with observation of particular objects, as introduction to the apprehension of particular facts in history. The individual does not need to know everything on an encyclopaedic scale, but everyone with any kind of public responsibility must have knowledge of the essential facts of the problem he has to deal with. It begins with the game of the objects shown to the child for an instant in the hand that is quickly closed again.

Thought hinges on definition of words. Aristotle and Confucius bear witness. I would conclude the compulsory studies of every university student with a comparison, even a brief one, between the two major works of Aristotle (*Nichomachean Ethics* and *Politics*), on the one hand, and, on the other, the Four Books of China (i.e., the three classics of the Confucian tradition—the *Great Digest, The Unwobbling Pivot,* and the *Analects*—together with the *Works of Mencius*).

Anyone who is familiar with the masterpieces, especially those of Aristotle, Confucius, Demosthenes, together with Tacitus, will not be taken in by the nasty messes now offered to the public.

Money can cause injury, and economic knowledge is today about as crude as was medical science when it was realized that a broken leg was damaging but when the effects of germs were unknown. Everywhere there is the hidden work of interest, gnawing away, corroding. This is not the interest paid to the private individual on his bank account, but interest on money that does not exist, on a mirage of money; interest equivalent to sixty per cent and over, as opposed to money that represents honest work or goods useful to mankind.

To repeat: the distinction between production and corrosion has been lost; and so has the distinction between the sharing-out of the fruits of work done in collaboration (a true and just dividend, called *partaggio* in the Middle Ages) and the corrosive interest that represents no increase in useful and material production of any sort.

And we would ask the Mazzinians why they never read those pages of the *Duties of Man* which deal with banks.

子孟 1.

MANG TSZE: THE ETHICS
OF MENCIUS ◂§ 1938

I AM convinced that the most fantastically foolish or at best crassly inadequate notions both of Kungfutsu and of Mang tsze are current not only among the weak minded but among that class which, if it can't quite be considered an intelligentzia has at least a greater domesticity with books than has the average reader.

A chinese female in the U.S. has been lamenting in print that although chinamen greatly outnumber the chinese girls in America these girls have the deuce of a time finding husbands. The men go back to China for wives, they say the girls with an American "education" are brainless.

And this I take it arises from our occidental habit of never looking at anything. I may be inattentive. I have no doubt whatsoever that my long-suffering friends consider me inattentive, but on the other hand I am not a distracted infant, and I have on occasion seen more than was meant for me, or even, in the case of Gaudier's sculpture and Wyndham Lewis's drawings back in 1911 to 1914 more than some others did.

Nevertheless we occidentals do not see when we look.

Kim had an education. I doubt if we occidentals ever receive one. Having drawn an ideogram, quite a simple one, three times WRONG, I am humbled but not in any dust of the occident. It was a simple picture, a bureaucrat (or minister) faced by a member of the public, thereby forming the verb "to sleep," occurring in the sentence: Mencius put his head on his stool (or head rest) and slept. It was not difficult to write, and it looked wrong when done wrong. I committed the same error three times running before I found out what was wrong, and whatever be my "low" for idiocy I find traces of at least similar failure in sinologues. This note is the result of an experiment, necessarily personal but which I must describe if the reader is to judge its results. During August and the first half of September 1937, I isolated myself with the chinese text of the three books of Confucius, *Ta Hio*, *Analects* and the *Unwavering Middle*, and that of Mencius, together with an enormously learned crib but no dictionary. You can't pack Morrison or Giles in a suit case.

When I disagreed with the crib or was puzzled by it I had only the look of the characters and the radicals to go on from. And my contention is that the learned have known too much and seen a little too little. Such of 'em as knew Fenollosa profited nothing.

Without knowing at least the nature of ideogram I don't think anyone can suspect what is wrong with their current translations. Even with what I have known for some time I did not sufficiently ponder it. The *Ta Hio* is of textures far more mixed than Pauthier's version. I see no reason to doubt the statement that it was a family possession, and that the actual bamboo tablets had got out of order and some of them lost, any more than I doubt the ethnographic evidence of the portrait of Confucius, as likely to be authentic as any bust of Caesar.

This diversity is not due to any failure of unity in the meaning of the *Ta Hio*. No one has brought out the contrasts of style from the magnificence of citation to the terseness and lucidity of Kung's statements. Kung was an anthologist and a shortener.

With Pauthier under my hand for 23 or more years and the Confucian matter in that form long familiar I had never read through Pauthier's Mencius. In the french he seemed merely prolix and inferior. The original gives ample reason for the four books appearing together, and my title is for a reason. Mencius nowhere turns against Kung, all of Mencius is implicit in Kung's doctrine. This doctrine is one, indivisible, a nature extending to every detail as the nature of being oak or maple extends to every part of the oak tree or maple. Mencius has gone into detail as, let us say, Van Buren goes into detail from a Jeffersonian basis.

By taking the "ethics of Mencius" I include the ethics of Kung. Yet if I tried to ascribe some of the opinions here about to be exposed, to Kungfutsu I might be accused of trying to modernize them or of seeing too much in the original text. In Mencius several cardinal lines are explicit, the most squirmy Ersatz-monger will have difficulty in worming away from them.

What I mean by not looking at the text can be shown by the very nice little story of Kung in discouragement saying— "It's no go. We aren't getting anywhere. I think I'll get a raft and float about at sea for a little. And the one of you chaps who will go along, will be Yu."

The elected disciple throws out his chest at the compliment, and Kung continues, "Yu likes danger better than I do. But he wouldn't bother about getting the logs."

Implying I think that logs are used to make rafts. Nevertheless the translator in question talks about "exercise of judgment," losing we believe the simple and Lincoln-like humour of the original. (See ideogram 2.)

For the LOGS are there in the ideogram very clearly. Whatever later centuries may have done about political platforms etc., and the raft ideogram appears to show a log and claw and a child (see ideogram 3) hinting sylvan (if riparian) origin.*

材 2.　　　桴 3.

I am not denying certain ambiguities in the text or in certain statements in ideogram but there are also certain utterly unambiguous uses of ideogram. You must distinguish between the inclusive and the ambiguous.

Ambiguity and inclusiveness are far from the same.

The specialist will often want a more particular statement inside the inclusive one, but the including statement can be perfectly categoric, in the sense of having its frontiers clearly defined. And this is not in the least the same as straddling the category's fence.

In ascribing ideas to Mang tsze I shall limit myself to what seem to me utterly clear cases of statement. Any borderline cases will be noted as such, and where I am stumped I shall ascribe no meaning.

I do, on the other hand, object to under-translation. I do *not* think that I have a better mind than Confucius. Mencius' great merit is that *he* did not think he had a better mind than Confucius. (There are numerous cases recorded of Confucians refusing to be had by such suggestions re themselves.) When I get a good idea from the ideograms I do not think it is my idea. If by any chance my ideas are better than those of the Man of Tsau's offspring, then, of course, my tablet

* Note similar process in meaning in the greek ὕλη uncut forest, and the stuff of which a thing is made, matter as a principle of being.

should be placed in the Temple and my views replace those of earlier sages. But I consider it unlikely that occasion for this will arise. What matters is the true view. If my views are better than those in the ideogram, pray do accept them, but accept also the burden of proving it.

The ethics of Mencius are Confucian. The spelling *Mencius* is all right if you take count of the way some people pronounce latin. Kung-fu-tsu. Chung Ne, Kung, Confucius all refer to the man of Tsau's son. Nobody now in anglo-saxon countries pronounces a *c* as *tsz*.

Serious approach to Chinese doctrines must start with wiping off any idea that they are all merely chinese. Mencius had an holy fear of cranks and idiots, and nearly all the most recent forms of idiocy had already pullulated in his time, among sectaries of one sort or another. As to subversiveness, the editor of the *Criterion* may for all I know still be waiting for me to review a volume of chinese philosophy which I found too rancid to mention. After finding the text too rancid for use I turned to the introduction. (The translator has merits of efficiency, his english must have been as slippery as the original, and in this introduction he delighted me with the statement that all except the most hard-boiled Confucians had swallowed his author.)

Thanks to nature, destiny, or Kung fu tsu, I did not swallow him.

Nevertheless before we can have any serious discussion of chinese philosophy we must agree on terminology. We must decide more clearly than has, I think, yet been done, which ideograms correspond to what terms of good latin. *Directio voluntatis*. Dante's view upon rectitude rimes certainly with that of Mencius.

Here (Analects IV, IV) is luminous doctrine reiterated in *Tsin Sin*, part 1, XXXIII, 2, Mencius. I cannot think that the

尚
志 4.

translators have been careful enough in correlating their
terms either with those having great contents and elaborate
precisions in Christian (catholic) theology,* or with those of
greek philosophy. Apart from latin (and greek) theologians I
doubt if we have any occidental theologians. We have a word
"sincere," said to date from Roman luxury trade in faked
marble. The chinese have a sign which is translated by this
word of english. But the chinese sign implicates quite definitely
naming the emotion or condition.

誠 5.

Which you can tie up if you like to the first chapter of Leone
Vivante's *Originalità nel pensiero*. There are two ideograms,
one middle-heart,

忠 6.

which might be translatable by sincere in its now current
meaning, and this other sign: the *word* and the action of fixing
or *perfecting* (just given, ideogram 5).

All of which comes out of the Confucian answer when
asked about the first act of government: "call things by their
right names."

* Since writing this, though not necessarily altering the mentioned
condition of things, Routledge announces "Soothill and Hedous' Dictionary of Chinese-Buddhist terms," and Motoschiro's Greek-Japanese
dictionary has been published.

正名 7.

There is a third sign recurring and again recurring, of the man who stands by his word.

信 8.

The conditions of my experiment, if you will consider them, implied not being distracted or led off into the mazes of the dictionary with its infinite (i.e. unbounded) interest and interests. Having been three times through the whole text and having perforce to look at the ideograms and try to work out the unfamiliar ones from their bases, I should have now a better idea of the whole and the unity of the doctrine, at any rate I believe that I have, and that the constants have been impressed on my eye.

Clearly what they translate virtue is the greek *arete*

it is not mediaeval *virtu*, though it is radically *virtus* from *vir*. It is, in chinese, the whole man and the whole man's contents. This is or should be impressed on the eye.

The sick part of our philosophy is "greek splitting," a term which I will shortly re-explain. The Confucian is totalitarian. When the aims of Shun and Wan were set together, though after a thousand years interval, they were as two halves of a tally stick. (Even the greatly learned translator has translated this "seal" in the text with a foot-note to say "tally-stick.")

符 10.

That things can be known a hundred generations distant, implied no supernatural powers, it did imply the durability of natural process which alone gives a possibility for science.

I take it the Mencian affirmation is of a permanent human process. There is no reason for me to tone that down with the phrase "I take it." The doctrine is clear. But the effects of the doctrine are startling when Mr. D. tells me he suspects Soothill of modernizing his version of *Analects*.

Mencius distinguishes a tax from a share, he is for an economy of abundance. Riches are due to exchange. The man who wants to lower the standard of living should end as an earthworm. Simple-lifers are half wits. All this is perfectly clear and utterly non-semitic in the original text.

The semitic is excess. The semitic is against ANY scale of values. The Church in the middle ages evolved an hierarchy of values.

It is mere shouting for the home team to pretend that the so-called Christian virtues were invented A.D. 1 to A.D. 32 in Judea.

"If a man died in a ditch Shun felt it as if he had killed him." This of the Emperor Shun.

"Is there," said Mang Tsze, "any difference between killing a man with a club and a sword?"

"No," said King Hwuy.

"Is there any difference between killing him with a sword and with a system of government?"

This is not the Chemin de Velours. There are perfectly good reasons why this philosophy does not get more publicity.

The cabinet ministers who can face it? I know of none in London or Paris.

Greek philosophy was almost an attack upon nature. That sentence cannot stand as it is, but may serve to disturb excessive complacencies.

The school of Kung included intelligence without cutting it from its base.

You can no more fake in this company than you can fake in a science laboratory. But you are not split into fragments. The curse of European thought appeared between the Nichomachean notes and the Magna Moralia. Aristotle (as recorded in the earlier record) began his list of mental processes with TeXne, τέχνη, and the damned college parrots omitted it. This was done almost before the poor bloke was cold in his coffin.

Greek philosophy, and european in its wake, degenerated into an attack on mythology and mythology is, perforce, totalitarian. I mean that it tries to find an expression for reality without over-simplification, and without scission, you can examine a living animal, but at a certain point dissection is compatible only with death. I believe Leibnitz felt this, and that Gemisto Plethon felt it.

Without knowing the Book of Rites it would be foolish to talk on Mencius' position in this regard further than to note what is actually said in his writing. There is an allusion to banishing the spirits of the fields and grain and electing others. I doubt if this is compatible with pejorative superstition. The point relevant to my title is that at no point does the Confucio-Mencian ethic or philosophy splinter and split away from organic nature. The man who pulled up his corn because it didn't grow fast enough, and then told his family he had assisted the grain, is Mencius' parable. The nature of things is good. The *way* is the process of nature, *one*, in the sense that the chemist and the biologist so find it. Any attempt to deal with it as split, is due to ignorance and a failure in the direction of the will.

Whence the Mencian does not try to avoid concrete application. Marx and Hegel break down when their ideas come to be worked out in conduct. My contention is that you can quite clearly judge what Mencius would have thought of specific situations in our time, and to support this I shall now quote, first from his talks with King Hwuy of Leang:

"Your dogs and swine eat the food of men and you do not make any restrictive arrangements.

"Your people are dying from famine on the roads and you do not know how to issue stores for them. When they die you say it is owing to the year. How does this differ from killing a man and saying it was not I but the weapon?"

and a few lines lower:

"Is there any difference between killing a man with a sword or with a system of government? Beasts devour one another . . . there are fat horses in your stables (while people die of famine) . . . this is called leading on beasts to devour men."

In another place he defines "leading on the earth to devour men," that is in a prince's wars for more territory. "In the *Spring and Autumn* there are no righteous wars, some are better than others." Spring and Autumn is the title of Confucius' history text book.

I have found very curious opinions as to Kung's formalism. L. Vivante recently showed me "a horrible reference book" as he called it, where the condensing ass had cited nothing but details of Kung's behaviour and several rules of formality.

Anyone who had read the text of Kung and Mencius in even a passable translation would know that at no point and on no occasion do such rules ask one to overstep common sense. There are times for politeness and times for prompt action. Discretion in perceiving the when is basic in Confucianism.

There are two elements in the "rules of propriety."

A. the expression of finer feelings and a resultant standard of behaviour on occasions when no graver and more impelling circumstance demands their abrogation. This is the permanent part. There is (B) the part relative to the times of Confucius. Certain ceremonies served, I think, as passports, such as the complicated Guard's salute. Today a man not a guardsman would give himself away if he tried it without preparation.

When you hadn't a telegraph, some of these ceremonies would have served to show the authenticity and also the nature of the man who turned up at the frontier.

The three years mourning is scarcely in the New England blood. It was not universal in China. Mencius justifies it as being more civil and human than allowing one's dead to lie in ditches and be chewed by stray animals. From which he dates the idea of having any burial customs at all. There is no doubt that latins and nordics differ greatly in their feeling for funerals. This is not my prime concern, nor do I introduce it save to protest against taking the chinese texts on the subject out of focus and out of the Mencian sense of their origin. His ideas on where to begin improving the social order are more to my point and our time.

"Therefore an intelligent ruler will regulate the livelihood of the people, so as to make sure that they shall have sufficient to serve their parents, and sufficient wherewith to support their wives and children: that in good years they shall be abundantly satisfied, and in bad years shall escape danger of perishing.

"Only men of education can maintain a steady heart without a fixed livelihood."

The steady or fixed heart is part of the *directio voluntatis*. The commendable have it, and work inside themselves, the uncommendable look out for lucky chances. Permit me a longer quotation from (Book VII) *Tsin Sin*, i, Chap. 22 & 23.

"At fifty warmth cannot be maintained without silks and at seventy flesh is necessary to satisfy the appetite. Persons not kept warm and supplied with food are said to be starved and famished, but among the people of King Wan there were no aged who were starved and famished.

"Let it be seen that their fields of grain and hemp are well cultivated, and make the taxes on them light . . . so that the people may be made rich.

"Let it be seen that the people USE (caps. mine) their resources of food seasonably and expend their wealth on the ceremonies, and they won't be able to exhaust it at that."

The "ceremonies" here would cover the equivalents for greek drama, and the outlay for latin processions at the feast of the Madonna, etc. They are of the amenities.

"People cannot live without water and fire. Knock at a door in the dusk of evening and no one will deny you water and fire. . . .

"When pulse and grain are as abundant as water and fire, how shall the people be other than humane."

(Here the ideogram for ARETE, entire man.)

仁 9.

The question of tax is here specified. Other passages clearly define the root difference between share and impost. "Nothing is worse than a fixed tax." A fixed tax on grain is in bad years a tyranny, a tithe proper, no tyranny. If, as he brings out against the simple lifers, a country cannot do without potters it certainly cannot do without governors. As for an emperor tilling his fields, it is mere shop front, no one ever expected him to make his own clothes as well, in fact, "is," he asks, "the imperial function the only business compatible with doing one's ploughing, potters and carpenters being exempt?"

In the conditions of 500 and 400 B.C. if you cut the tithe lower than 10 per cent you could live only as the "dog and camp-fire people." If you raised it above 10 per cent for traders and people in the centre of empire and above the NINE FIELDS share system for rurals and border folk, you would have tyranny.

The analogy of the nine fields system to Rossoni's *ammassi* in present-day Italy is notable.

It is OF the permanence of nature that honest men, even if endowed with no special brilliance, with no talents above those of straightness and honesty, come repeatedly to the same answers in ethics, without need of borrowing each other's ideas.

Shun and Wan had a thousand years between them and when their wills were compared they were as two halves of a tally stick.

節 11.   符 10.

From Kung to Mencius a century, and to St. Ambrose another six or so hundred years, and a thousand years to St.

130

Antonio, and they are as parts of one pattern, as wood of a single tree.

The "Christian virtues" are THERE in the emperors who had responsibility in their hearts and willed the good of the people; who saw that starvation can gnaw through more than the body and eat into the spirit; who saw, above all, that in so far as governing the people went, it begins with a livelihood, and that all talk of morals before that livelihood is attained, is sheer bunkum and rotten hypocrisy.

The level of civilization recorded in these ideograms is higher than anything in the near eastern tradition.

It is only in the evolved Roman sense of proportion that we find equal sanity.

There is a root difference between an immoderate demand or a law which takes no account of the nature of things and the Mencian hierarchy of values.

"Our" hierarchy of values shines from the *Divina Commedia,* or one can at least use that work as a convenient indicator of it. Both the catholic mediaeval and the chinese hierarchies and senses of proportion are infinitely removed from semitic immoderation. When Europe flopped from the state of mind of St. Ambrose and St. Antonio into pre-Christian barbarisms we suffered a not inconsiderable set-back. The thing we flopped back to is unpleasant. It was and still filthily is usurer's measure. Let us try to avoid words that could give rise to partisanship and say, you can no more consider Western civilization without the Roman component than you can consider the Orient and leave out the Chinese Imperial order, which already in Kung's time recognized an historic process, including the alternating periods of order and confusion.

The ethic of Kung and Mencius is not registered in words of irresponsible fanatics. The semitic component in Christianity is anarchic and irresponsible. Take the record on its face value, it is of a sect in a rebellious and irresponsible province, and for a kingdom, specifically in the words of its founder, not of this world but the next.

The Christian ideal has been recognized as something different, something NOT evolved without Constantine and Justinian and those who built it with them. Civilization consists in the establishment of an hierarchy of values, it cannot remain as a mere division between the damned and the saved . . . with alternate wailing and hysterical merriment.

Mencius' sense of responsibility is omnipresent. It is in man to himself. Governing of the Empire was specifically NOT among the sage's desires, or at least not regarded by him as a simple pleasure. Out of office he attends to his own internal order, in office to that of as much of the state as is entrusted to him. But at no moment is he irresponsible. His desideratum: to gather and teach the most intelligent of his contemporaries, unless by good fortune he find a sage from whom he can learn, but in any case not to start teaching prematurely and not to teach his own ignorance.

The alibi of the irresponsible is often a false one, those who say they can do nothing because they lack talent, could at least refrain from deleterious action. This phase of Mencian doctrine has, I think, been grossly exaggerated in our superstition as to the nature of Confucianism. It is set out as the MINIMUM and universal requirement, not as a maximum.

The earlier *politica* of *ammassi* was as follows: in a square divided in nine equal parts, the central one was cultivated by the eight surrounding families, and its produce went to the administration, this was commuted to a ten per cent. on central or as you might say in the metropolitan areas where "things aren't as simple as all that." In irregular country a just equivalence of what would be equal measuring of flat acreage.

Marketing customs similarly equitable. The profit motive is specifically denounced. I mean that you will get no more accurate translation of the ideograms in Mencius' talk with King Hwey than "profit-motive."

Mercantilism is incompatible with Mencius. Cheap evasion and evasiveness are impossible anywhere near him.

Naturally men love life. Mencius professes a taste for fish and bears' trotters, but there is an order of preference. Some things are worth more than others. Life is not above rectitude.

If anyone in calm mind will compare the Four Classics with the greatly publicized hebrew scriptures he will find that the former are a record of civilized men, the latter the annals of a servile and nomadic tribe that had not evolved into agricultural order. It is with the greatest and most tortuous difficulty that the Sunday School has got a moral teaching out of these sordid accounts of lechery, trickery and isolated acts of courage, very fine and such as could be paralleled in the annals of Mohawks and Iroquois. Any sort of objectivity, taking the record as it stands, must arrive at something like this conclusion.

Jehovah is a semitic cuckoo's egg laid in the European nest. He has no connection with Dante's god. That later concept of supreme Love and Intelligence is certainly not derived from the Old Testament.

Numerous invasions of China have destroyed several strata of civilisation, but this in no way detracts from the Mencian wisdom, nor does even Mr. Lin Yutang's brilliant picture of Chinese folly, which latter is a portrayal of universal stupidity.

In every country idiots treat the branch as the root. If you deprive Confucianism of its essentials among which are the sense of proportion and timeliness, if you take isolated remarks and cut them off wholly and utterly from the rest of the four books, naturally the text can be quoted in defence of five hundred follies.

The Rules of Propriety are to be observed under certain circumstances and at the proper times, obedience and respect have their limits.

Some sort of time focus must be applied.

It may quite well be that Confucius and Mencius are a hormone that could be more vitally effective in the West today than in a China busily engaged in livening up the business of the Acceptance Houses. Apropos which I understand that a living Kung has stated in private conversation that his Most Illustrious Ancestor is now more regarded here than in Pekin. Foreign loans for munitions do not enter the *Analects*.

When Pih Kwei stated that his irrigation system was better than the Emperor Yu's, Mencius pointed out that the latter had led off the excessive flood water to the sea "according to the natural law of waters," whereas Pih Kwei had merely dumped his into a neighbouring state. Mencius declined to regard this bit of *scaltrezza* as an improvement.

I have no doubt that if the Acceptance Houses succeed in piling up a sufficiency of Chinese debt to Europe and then induce hefty or half-starved occidentals to try to collect it, even China might wake and the great final and definitive armageddon, yellow peril, etc. become as actual as our American civil war was, because of the South's debts to our (N.Y.) city.

Naturally if you neglect the root of the Doctrine the rest will wither, and a neglect of its basic wisdom is undoubtedly apparent among the less wise Chinese.

134

Neither that country nor any other has ever suffered a glut of sages.

"Dead!" said Mencius on hearing that P'wan-shing Kwoh had received a high government post in Ts'e. After execution, a disciple asked M. "How did you know this would happen?" "He was a busy fellow," said Mencius, "with a little talent. Just enough to get himself condemned to the scaffold."

The "busy" exists in the four classics with just the shade that has given it a derogative sense in the argot of Edgar Wallace's crooks. Not meaning "cop" in chinese but indicating why the crook calls the policeman a busy. A better word than busybody and more aromatic.

If the reader jumps every verb meaning CHANGE or MOVE, if he remains blind to the verbs meaning RENEWAL and neglects every allusion to "changing what is not good," naturally he can reduce the rest of Mencius and Confucius to a static and inactive doctrine, inactive enough to please even the bank of Basel and our western monopolists. But this would mean excising a great deal of the original text.

In fact it can't be done. You cannot so ignore the bright ideogram for the highest music,

12.

the sign of metamorphosis,

13.

or the constantly recurring radical symbol which looks like the back of boat with rudder,

14.*

and might lead one to think that it emerged from association with river traffic. Danger ever present to the autodidact, as it comes from representation of a foot, with foot prints.

This constant pageant of the sun, of process, of the tree with its "small, white, small" (ideogram 12) does not give any clear-headed spectator the feeling of deadness and stasis.

There are categories of ideogram not indicated as such in the dictionaries, but divided really by the feel of their forms, the twisted as evil, the stunted, the radiant.

The mountain itself has a "nature" and that nature is to come forth in trees, though men cut and sheep nibble.

Tsin Sin, pt. 1, xxxiii, 2, is our solidest join with Dante. "What is the scholar's aim?" (Scholar here being also officer.) There follows one of the shortest verses, *"Mang tse said,"* then the sign for *"raise"* and the sign for *"will."* (Vide ideogram 4.) They translate it "exalt the aim." This is definitely Dante's *directio voluntatis*, with no ambiguity possible. The top of the *will* sign is the scholar-officer sign, and its base the heart. The lifting up is structural.

Nevertheless Dante's "god above" exists in an ideogram. No one with any visual sense can fail to be affected by the way the strokes move in these characters.

The "above," Plato's power above the heaven; lateral motion; the tree trunks; the man who stands by his word; the qualities of these signs are basic and no one who does not perceive them can read ideogram save as an ape.

Man, man, man, humanity all over the page, land and trees.

The people who take up one point and spoil the totality "neglecting a hundred other points" are un-Mencian. They

* Used in composition as part of a sign.

"lift up and grind one, and hang up and cover a hundred."

Condensing from the Third book of Mencius (the T'ang Wan Kung) and from other passages, I find the belief that "without government services distribution and use of resources will be insufficient." I find definite statement as to what conduces to borrowing, and its results. I find an interesting series of five characters, the meaning of which someone may say that I force.

The first contains the knife radical, plus pearls or precious shell, and certainly means draw an outline, make a pattern of (it is used also as a particle "derivative from that"). It is followed by wealth, use, not enough.

It might apply to production, but it appears to me to apply equally to the distribution. The "use" is utterly undodgeable. It does not mean exhaust.

"If he levy a ground tax and *do not* tax goods or enforce proper regulations *without* levying tax . . . Merchants will store goods in his market." I.e. one OR the other not both.

All through there is the sense of need of a proper (not an improper) income for administrative expenses.

"No tax out of season." "No better system than mutual aid, none WORSE than a fixed tax." A tithe is another matter.

Government's job is to feed the people, that is its FIRST job. (This not to be confused with Kung's "get the right names." That "Ch'ing Ming" is the first step toward conditioning the government to do its work.)

Anyone who mistakes Kung or Mencius for a materialist is a plain unadulterated idiot. Their philosophy is not in the least materialist, it is volitionist.

(1) Arms and defences, (2) food, (3) the faith of the people, if they must be given up, be it in this order.

"Let Mulberry trees be planted about the homesteads with

137

their five *mow* (land measure) and persons of fifty may be clothed with silk. In keeping fowls pigs and swine let not their times of breeding be neglected, and persons of seventy may eat flesh. Let there not be taken away the time that is proper for the cultivation of the farm with its hundred mow, and the family of 8 mouths that is supported by it shall not suffer from hunger. Let there be careful attention to education in schools. . . ."

All this is on an infinitely higher level than Mosaic lex talionis. It is all out, over, and above the balderdash that was inflicted on my generation of christians.

I am not inveighing against the best Christian ethic or against the quality of Western mind shown in Bishop Grosseteste's treatise on light. I am against the disorderly tendencies, the anarchy and barbarism which appear in poor christian teaching, fanaticism and superstition; against the lack of proportion and failure of objectivity when dealing with texts extant, and, naturally, against the insularity which credits Byron with having invented a kind of writing that had been used by Pulci.

But if we are ever to communicate with the orient, or cohabit a planet rapidly becoming more quickly circumnavigable, had we not better try to find the proportions, try perhaps to collect some of our own better writers (of the ages) to present to our oriental comtemporaries, rather than offer them an unmixed export of grossness, barbarities, stove pipes and machine guns? Several young men in Tokio seem pleased to meet Cavalcanti. I have no doubt that even the Ten Remnants* could have found something admirable in our tradition had it been more tactfully shown them.

* (Ten Remnants. A title given to several elderly gentlemen of the Empress Dowager's time, now, alas, disappearing.)

Lady Hosie's introduction in a recent reprint tells us that the Four Classics "have been relegated to University study and are no longer the main preoccupation of Chinese schools." She dates the essay 1937, which year has brought the natural consequence of unusual idiocy in the form of Japanese invasion. If China had got to this point, naturally there would be an invasion, and quite naturally some Chinese would, as they do, hold the view that such an invasion is to be welcomed.

Lady Hosie, M. A. Cantab., regards the degradation as temporary. Tuan Szetsun is old. Certainly a nucleus of sanity exists in China. The West needs the Confucian injection.

The Four Books have survived Ch'in Shih Huang (the gorilla who ordered these books to be destroyed) and China was not effaced by that pimple.

The blots of my correction are not dry on this quotation from Lady Hosie before a still later bulletin confirms an old belief to the effect that any order in China proceeds from a Confucian centre. Chang Kai Shek "the Christian general" and the one man who got a little order out of chaos took to using Confucian slogans a little too late, thereby confirming another text of the philosopher.

I am not in this essay trying to give a modern chinese feeling about the effects of such Confucianism as survived in China in 1900, and Mr. Lin Yutang will probably admit that the citizen of a chaos which has long lacked a certain code of ideas and perceptions is bound to see that code differently from the citizen of a chaos wherein such ideas have long been abused.

I am putting the original text against semitic insanity and against Socrates. If the shoving of it into University study in China were intended to bring it with fresh impact on to more thoughtful minds ??? . . . if . . . but was it? and is, in any case, the adolescent any fitter to receive it than the child?

Obviously Mr. Yutang knows its worst side—Obviously certain practices come to us dated China 500 B.C. and we brush very lightly over them. They have not affected our lives and cannot. Seven inch planks for one's coffin or cremation is all pretty much one to us.

In any case there are or were practices. Soaking our occidental selves in the quite clearly illuminated principles of Confucius would hardly bring *us* out into certain chinese forms. In fact, for us to take up odd rites would be, as it were, "sacrificing to a spirit which does not belong to us," and therefore against Mencian and Confucian good taste, anyhow.

I do not see the abuse as inherent in the principle of Confucius, whereas the semitic is schizophrenic essentially. People, who talk about "something deeper in their nature" which laid the chinese open to Buddhism, seem to me to have failed lamentably to LOOK at the Mencian text.

In any case I am dealing with ethics and not with cosmology, imaginary, pneumatic, or "scientific," granting that Mencius hadn't the Western female to deal with and that the captious may think he over simplifies in this domain, or rather avoids it, though he can't be said to deny its importance. But the abuses of the "system," mentioned by descriptive writers, are incompatible with the root. This I don't propose to argue save with someone who has passed the Pythagorean time of silence. The putting order inside oneself first, cannot be omitted from Confucian-Mencian practice if that is to be valid. Any other course is sheer fake.

Faith without works is fake, and the Mencian suggestion is that one should act right before formulating the axiom tried in act, and thereafter follow it.

The ethic of Confucius and Mencius is a Nordic ethic, a Nordic morale, if it has been boggit in laissez faire and tropical indolence that cannot be blamed on its shape. It is not

140

quietistic. It is concentrated in the Mencian parable: "An Archer having missed the bullseye does NOT turn round and blame someone else. He seeks the cause in himself."

Mencius is very difficult to summarize, yet as Legge cannot be suspected of collusion with credit cranks and new ortho-logic economists I add a few sentences and phrases from his version:

"Resources arising from government," that is to say the increment of association. So far as I know this is the earliest clear formulation of it.

"If a man can prevent the evils of hunger and thirst from being any evils to his mind. . . ."

"Hostile states do not correct one another."

"The way of the people is this: if they have a certain liveli-hood they will have a fixed heart. If they have not a fixed live-lihood . . . there is nothing they will not do in the way of . . . moral deflection."

"What leisure have they to cultivate propriety and right-eousness?"

"Only men of education are able to maintain a fixed heart without a certain livelihood."

To treat the needy as criminals is not governing decently, it is merely trapping them.

AN IMPACT ৵§ 1935

"The earth belongs to the living."
T. Jefferson

Definitions

Increment of association: Advantage men get from working together instead of each on his own, e.g., crew that can work a ship whereas the men separately couldn't sail ships each on his own.

Cultural heritage: Increment of association with all past inventiveness, e.g., thus, crops from improved seed; American wheat after Carleton's researches; a few men hoisting a locomotive with machinery.

I

I. An epic is a poem including history.

No one can understand history without understanding economics. Gibbon's History of Rome is a meaningless jumble till a man has read Douglas.

My generation (that born in the 1880's) was dragged up in black ignorance of economics, an ignorance in part the product of malice, in part of sheer sloth and incompetence.

To say that "every man in high office in England is a thieves' accomplice, and that they are mostly too ignorant to understand what I mean by this term," would lay me open to the charge of intemperate language. Yet how many men knowing, really, the facts, can draw gentler conclusion?

II. In our time, everything that we eat, use or wear, has become cheap, cheap with an unspeakable cheapness if its cost be measured by the physical effort needed to produce it, or the material difficulty in procuring it, as compared with such difficulties in earlier epochs.

Douglas' "just price" is a recognition of this material cheapness. The parts of his system, all those details which deal with price adjustment are, fundamentally, a recognition and registration of realities, of the real cost (in effort) of forks, spoons, automobiles, grain fit to eat, eggs promptly delivered, and not carried liquid from China.

III. A thousand volumes a year ooze from dead minds all rendered dull, tangled, useless by the failure to make a few rudimentary dissociations, to distinguish, that is, between capital and property, between gold as deposit, and gold as measure, between demand meaning wish for, and demand meaning power to get it.

Property is not capital. The increment of association is not usury.

Historians have been too lazy to seek the facts, and too bull-witted to understand them.

The state has credit. Distribution is effected by little pieces of paper. The best facts of history are not in the school books. The job of this generation is to teach growing children; to make it impossible for any child to arrive at the threshold of manhood, ignorant as my generation arrived there.

The state has credit.

Distribution is effected by little pieces of paper.

If you don't watch these, you will be slaves. If you don't know how they are made; who makes them; who controls them; you will be diddled out of your livings, as millions of dead men have been diddled, and as millions of live ones are being. The sword can "protect the furrow," ... etc. ... against foreign invasion, but not against the usurer's cunning. Against usury it has availed never at all.

Usury and sodomy, the Church condemned as a pair, to one hell, the same for one reason, namely that they are both against natural increase.

Dante knew this and said it. It is registered in the *Merchant of Venice*, where Shylock wants no mere shinbone or elbow, but wants to end Antonio's natural increase. You can find it in Lombard Chronicles, the laws against making eunuchs.

Van Buren's memoirs, the records of the American bank war, the death struggle between the bank and the people, were written around 1860, and never got printed till 1920.

The knowledge of true coining, the principles of honest issue of money have been known, over and over again, and forgotten. It is our generation's job so to hammer a few simple truths into the human consciousness that no Meyer Anselm can efface them.

Certain facts must stand in the common tongue. These root facts must go to the people, they must go into the one everlasting repository, the mind of the people. They must go into the folk-lore, into men's proverbs.

The necessities of mankind are now cheap. Effort can be unbounded only in the dimension of quality. In that road there is room enough for all discipline. No man has out distanced Homer.

But for everything that is not great art, participant in that form of undyingness, for all that is used and used up, all that is worn, worn out, dwelt in, we must know the new cheapness, we must know that its cost in effort, in toil, in sweat, in difficulty, has dwindled, and dwindles.

144

We must let no man cozen us out of this knowledge.

"And all this costs the Khan nothing," said Marco Polo of Kublai Khan's stamped paper money.

Peter Simple prints touching poems about the poor old soldier, neglected, dank, cold in the gutter . . . for want (Peter doesn't quite say), of a few pieces of paper.

The English are degrading their empire, murdering their home population for the sake of a fixed idea as to the nature of money.

The American New Deal to date (December 1934—January 1935) has shown no comprehension of fundamentals, no perception of the basic relations of currency system, money system, credit system to the needs and purchasing power of the whole people.

Coffee in France, gone to hell; coffee offered free by Brazil —too expensive for the poor of Vienna. Wallace ploughing grain under; Perkins too bull-witted to know that work is not a commodity.

Work is not a commodity, in the sense of goods for traffic.

Money is not a commodity in this sense.

The people of two populous countries tolerate rulers too whey-headed to understand or to say this.

IV. Amoral technocrats have gathered the statistics of production. Gesell observed that Marx found no fault with money; "nothing to criticize in money"; just took it for granted.

Douglas for seventeen years has been working to build a new England and to enlighten England's ex- and still annexed colonies. The corporate state has invented a representative body that should function in the age of correlated machinery

145

better than the old representation of agricultural districts.*

There are between honest economists, sincere differences of opinion as to policy, but against the underlying fact there is no intellectual answer. You cannot borrow yourself out of debt.

The increment of association exists. The cultural heritage, in Douglas' sense of the term, is an extension of the increment of association; a hook-up with the accumulation of all past inventiveness.

The earth belongs to the living. Chattel slavery has gone. Slavery to a printed fetish, to stamped paper and embossed discs of metal, must follow it. There is an increment of statal well-being over and above the well-being of the individual. "Over and above" does not mean "counter to" or "against."

Money is a form of agreement; it implies an agreed order. It implies an honesty and an ability.

"Fiat money" is a poor term; it is camouflage made of half Latin. The old Este mandates were valid. "Give to" or "I promise," or "we promise to give to," is the correct reading of the inscription, whether spelled out or implied.

"Fiat" is bad only if it means "let there be grain, or wood, where grain is not, or where there is nothing."

Intended in that sense, fiat money would be an evil. Like every other economic term it has been used as a scarecrow, and used with two or more meanings.

You can issue valid money against any commodity (or against services) up to the amount people want. The commodity must be there; services must be available.

* Pound believes that in twentieth-century industrialized communities it is better for people to be represented by one of their own trade or profession, rather than by geographic area. He believes also that trade unions should become a responsible part of the state machinery, with division of powers inside them—judicial, executive and rule-making—comparable to the national mechanism as intended by Adams and Jefferson in the framing of the United States Constitution.—Ed.

You should not confuse a bill with a mortgage. You cannot soundly monetize land, but only its produce.

Two kinds of banks have existed: the Monte dei Paschi and the devils. Banks differ in their intention. Two kinds of bank stand in history: banks built for beneficence, for reconstruction; and banks created to prey on the people.

Three centuries of Medici wisdom went into the Monte dei Paschi, the only bank that has stood from 1600 till our time.

Siena was flat on her back, without money after the Florentine conquest. Cosimo, first duke of Tuscany, had all the Medici banking experience behind him. He guaranteed the capital of the Monte, taking as security the one living property of Siena, and a certain amount of somewhat unhandy collateral.

That is to say, Siena had grazing lands down toward Grosseto, and the grazing rights worth 10,000 ducats a year. On this basis taking it for his main security, Cosimo underwrote a captial of 200,000 ducats, to pay 5 per cent to the shareholders, and to be lent at 5½ per cent; overhead kept down to a minimum; salaries at a minimum and all excess profit over that to go to hospitals and works for the benefit of the people of Siena. That was in the first years of the 17th century, and that bank is open today. It outlasted Napoleon. You can open an account there tomorrow.

And the lesson is the very basis of solid banking. Credit rests *in ultimate* on the abundance of nature, on the growing grass that can nourish the living sheep.

And the moral is in the intention. It was not for the conqueror's immediate short-sighted profit, but to restart the life and productivity of Siena, that this bank was contrived.

The hell banks have, from as far as the record takes us, started as gangs of creditors, associated to strangle the last ounce of profit out of their debtors. This they have done with splendour, boasts and parade. They have stood for exactitude in accounting. Once the dice have been loaded, they have counted up every point, every decimal. Chief and most glorified was the Banca S. Giorgio, the pitiless company of Genoese creditors, the model bank among bankers, against which I am, for all I know, the first to utter detraction.

"About the year 1200 there existed in Genoa, divers societies. . . .

"In 1252 they united. . . .

"In 1451, 9th April. The commune of Genoa vested in perpetuity its dogana (that is the collection of all import tax), in the Banca S. Giorgio." That means that the bank got all the proceeds.

"1539. The Doge, governors and procurators confirmed and anew conceded and assigned to the protectors of S. Giorgio all the proceeds of the salt tax . . . approving the addition of the taxes on oil and grain, meat, wine, etc. . . . with the right to sell the same if they chose.

"1749 the bank got the right to tax church property also, but at a fourth less than the secular.

"The revolution of 1797 disorganized its collection of taxes, the provisional government leaving the bank (of S. Giorgio) provisionally its internal administration and the collection of customs, took from its directors their *absolute civil and criminal jurisdiction* as incompatible with unity of the republic, and the sovereignty of the people."—*Memorie sulla banca di S. Giorgio*, Genoa, 1832. Compiled by their keeper of archives, Antonio Lobero.

Lobero seems rather indignant at this infringement of bankers' omnipotence, his spirit appears reincarnate in our day in Paul Einzig.

This shows what bankers will placidly do if you let 'em.

148

The great company of St. George could be both plaintiff and judge in a civil or criminal suit against its interests.

The arts did not flourish in Genoa, she took almost no part in the intellectual activity of the renaissance. Cities a tenth her size have left more durable treasure.

II

You can issue sound money to express the will of the people, which amounts to saying that you can issue it against services wanted. You cannot issue sound money against land, or against anything undeliverable. You cannot issue sound money save against something wanted.

The soundness of money is not limited to its being state money. Countless examples of valid private and valid local money exist: Scovil metal dollar, 1842; Lockport Mills,* 1851; my grandfather's money against "lumber or merchandise"; Larkin & Co. "merchandise bonds" issued before the recent American bank holiday. States fail or fall into hands of ignorant men or of scoundrels. The banks have tried to throttle communities over which they have bloody and armed power

* I am not advocating a "return" to private money in place of Government money. There are indubitable advantages in having a uniform money for the whole nation, backed by the whole nation. But the nation should learn from the history of private monetary issues. Neither banks nor governments are a necessary preliminary to the existence of money. Banks have not produced a uniform or stable currency. In fact they have done their utmost to destroy such uniformity and stability for the sake of their own paunches and moved by intemperate greed, gross ignorance and an inhuman callousness to every human need, to every form of human misery and in contempt for every amenity, for every art and for every science.

The last half of the nineteenth century in America saw the gross mug of the profit-seeker predominant. Papers with vast circulations defiled literature and cried down every human motive save avarice, every human ability save that of absorption.

of militia or police armed with machine-guns, fire-hoses and gas-bombs; sane men and free merchants have issued their own paper or metal implements of exchange and accountancy, and will do so wherever the light of reason penetrates or the spirit of manhood co-exists with a minimum of necessary knowledge.

"Peace on his lying lips, and on his hands Blood."

"They make a wilderness and call it peace."

"Avenge, O Lord."

No rhetoric and no denunciatory poem launched against a military tyrant is too strong for the devils of finance, in whose hands lie the tyrants and for whose fist military prowess is merely a knuckleduster.

They make a desert. "Free coffee too dear for Vienna"; Austrian Charity League asks for Brazilian surplus, but finds it will cost three shillings and ninepence a pound even if Brazil GIVES 'em the coffee instead of destroying it. This situation is the glory and boast of Messrs. Norman and Rothschild. It is the certificate of efficiency. Deterding, Herbert Lawrence, Duff Cooper, Sarvazy, Sieff, De Wendel, Robert Protot, the brothers Schneider of Creusot, and ten thousand fatted bankers proclaim the virtues of "orthodox" economics, assisted by 500 curs, and titled straw men, waiting for something to break.

There will be no red revolution in England. Englishmen will go on patiently dying; they will go on as they have gone on for 200 years on progressively pejorated diet. France is losing its bread and wine, its coffee went to hell after the war. The Germans have been fed on Ersatz, having been broken to it during the war, and are thankful for an occasional let up.

Well-meaning Englishmen assure me that they personally "cannot attack the banks." Douglas for seventeen years has been showing them how not to annihilate banks. Freedom has been used to camouflage almost every known form of folly and infamy. The local cry for freedom (Rapallo), is specifically for the right to leave tubercles free in the milk. By God, they just won't keep any cows, if they can't have the ancient right of poisoning the consumers of cow-juice, which is a mild and intelligent desire if compared with the acts of contemporary commerce in its assault on English and American provender. With millions spent on medical research, we find that the biologists in the fight against pellagra, searched for years for a "medicine cheaper than food."

The state has credit. "Just as I have credit at the Albergo Rapallo. I could eat there for three months without the proprietors presenting a bill or feeling any uneasiness. I do not have to go to the Bank of Chiavari and borrow money and pay the bank usury on that money, in order to lunch and dine."

For a hundred years states have done little with their credit save sabotage it, save use it for less than its value, save pay private companies tribute. A government of hypnotized rabbits could not behave with greater imbecility, and there can, in the long run, be no greater treason to the people.

All this is known, all this has been known ten times over. It was known to Jackson and Van Buren. The American Civil War shelved the knowledge. Not only did the Americans pay with their blood (a million dead), for negro freedom, but they paid with the death of knowledge. America paid by her loss of memory, she came out of her Civil War with unspeakable shell-shock and a dead loss of cultural heritage of which she was utterly and unspeakably unconscious. The war of the 1830's is not to be found in the school books. Jackson is regarded as a tobacco-chewing half-wit, or a tuppeny militarist, the murderer of a few indians, and the victor of New Orleans; Van Buren either vilified or forgotten. Only abnormal Englishmen have ever heard of such presidents.

No system of inter-communication exists. Lights, as they are considered, of the American intellectual world, pass their days shut in a village, and get their news fifteen years late, faded and colourless.

The intelligentsia, or a part of it, delayed Marxian, tries to start a "union," on the supposition that writing is a commodity, and not a system of communication; failing to recognise that the value of a printed page depends not on the amount of its verbiage, but on its efficiency as communication. Both speed and clarity count; both reliability and exactness.

III

We need in economics: 1. simplification of terminology; 2. articulation of terminology ("distinguish the root from the branch").

We need: 3. less intolerance towards converging movements; 4. to hammer on root ideas.

Prosperity comes of exchange; a high standard of living comes of exchange of goods; a monetary system, a banking system which sabotages exchange, and impedes it, is evil. Its sustainers are enemies of the people.

No day passes without my coming on pages that are foolish from lack of simple dissociations, already cleared in my ABC.*

Four things are necessary in any modern or civilized economic system:

1. the labourer; 2. the product; 3. the means of transport; and 4. the monetary carrier.

Inadequate monetization has made "inaccessable islands" of fields lying adjacent one with the other; it has created barriers between garden and factory.

Two men have ended the Marxist era. Douglas in conceiv-

* *ABC of Economics* by Ezra Pound, 1933.

ing that the cultural heritage, the increment of association with all past inventiveness, is the great and chief fountain of value. Gesell in seeing that "Marx never questioned money. He just took it for granted."

It is the devil capital, sheltering himself behind property, that has played hell with the world. Capital is a lien on other men's services.

To reward another man for needed help, we must give him something more useful than a noose round his neck. And when we give help to our neighbour we must show more intelligence than to stick our own head through a halter.

You cannot monetize land, but only its deliverable products. All the errors regarding land have parallels in industry. Many men have been land poor; they can now be factory poor, "plant poor."

The nature of property is radically (at the root, in the root), different from the nature of capital. The inherited terminology of false economics has served both fools and devils. All such phrases as "capital in the form of" are misleading. Properly understood capital is liquid. The great division is between whatever is a lien on the other men's services, and what is either completely neutral and passive, or constitutes a potential responsibility, whereof the weight leans on the owner. Land can lie fallow, houses decay at various speeds, industrial plants depreciate both from decay and standing still while invention goes past them. The increment of association is not usury. To see clearly one must divide capital from everything that is not capital. The moment money is spent, whatever thing is purchased is no longer capital, it is property; it has but three possibilities: you may keep it, use it, or lose it. Many vast and heavy books have ended in muddle from failure to see that property and capital are *radically* different. Property does not imply the enslavement of others.

There is a difference between durable and perishable goods, in fact there are all degrees of durability, from that of fresh-plucked fruit to that of the art works of Chaldea.

The reason for growing food is to feed the people. The reason for weaving cloth is to clothe them. The function of a monetary system is to get the goods from where they are to the people that need them.

A man's understanding of any subject should be like a city with enough cross-streets. He should be able to get about it in any direction, and without traffic blocks.

Economics are like Euclid or like physics in that if you don't understand a few simple principles you will fall into error after error, but if you have a few very simple perceptions you can construct soundly without any very great learning.

Money has been treated not only as if it were goods, but it has been given privileges above all other goods. This was flagrant injustice. Free men will not tolerate it for one hour after they understand it.

Men living under the domination of catchwords live in a hell of their own making. Terms like "fiat money" scare people blue. If the printed paper means "let there be wheat or goods where there is none," it is a bluff and unsound. The Este "mandati" were of a different nature, as I have emphasised in my Cantos. These slips of paper were orders; give to a man something that exists and is there in charge of the agents.

If the American government owned crops sufficiently to order their destruction, it owned them quite enough to order their delivery.

Free coffee too dear for Vienna. Brazil would have *given* the coffee for the Viennese poor. Because of brute habit, Austria saw no way to get it without paying IMPORT tax.

154

IV

The poor in mind, the sidlers and avoiders of truth, the confused economists fail to see problems in their proper order and ratio. Let the purchasing power be first adequate. After that, the lechers after total security can calculate their decimals and their millesimals.

"Would you call it inflation to print tickets for every seat in a theatre, regardless of the fact that the house had hitherto been always two-thirds empty simply because no tickets had been printed for the greater number of seats?" (A. R. ORAGE.)

"Inflation" occurs when you issue more money than can be honoured in wanted goods or in wanted services.

The safest place for reserve purchasing power is in the pockets of the people.

Agglomerates of protoplasm, listed as professors in the 'phone book, still bleat that money is just false teeth, metal and spectacle frames. Professors! they started as boys who said "yes" to their teachers 30 years ago, and therefore got taken on as assistants.

The strength of Douglas' position comes from the fact that he was not drifting about in vapid theory, or trying to get himself noticed in the papers. He observed a concrete fact on the books of the airplane factory which he was running and for which he was responsible.

He observed that *that* company was creating prices faster than it gave out the power to buy.

Having the concrete case before him, he considered its

155

consequences. And if that happens in every other factory, every other industry? It needs no fancy algebra to prove that the purchasing power of the whole people can never catch up with the price of the goods that they bring into being. There is one way for any serious man to refute this, he can show us the books of two, three or one prospering company where such is not the case.

Why England should be the slowest and last country to utilize ideas invented in London must be left to local pathologists.

I never make out what Englishmen think their government is. I believe it is a constitutional accumulation of indefinite hand-me-downs. But if a man were a royalist he would believe (I mean the theory he would think he believed would imply), that the King is boss of the coinage. If he were a "democrat" he would believe that the power to issue money is delegated *by* the people *to* its representatives. Neither of their beliefs can sanction the mere leaving it in the hands of irresponsible men.

IN THE WOUNDS: MEMORIAM
A. R. ORAGE ✍§ 1935

NEITHER the great public, nor the very small public that can afford to pay 7s. 6d. a shot for its magazines will understand the significance of Orage's death, or be able to answer the question: "Who was Orage?" until they understand the ideas to which he devoted the last fifteen years of his life:

A. In themselves.

B. In relation to the living economic ideas of this decade and the known and undeniable facts of history.

C. In relation to the gross ignorance in which my generation and yours and our fathers' generation have been reared and in which the generation that followed mine was very largely killed off.

Plenty of people know in vague way that Orage "started as a guild socialist," but clear ideas of what guild socialism was when O. started are uncommon. He found it advisable to move on.

Sometime in 1918 or thereabouts an ex-engineer, ex-head of Westinghouse's Indian branch, then managing an airplane factory noticed that his factory was creating prices faster than it emitted the power to buy.

Say that in a month the factory produced £20,000 "worth" of airplanes, but distributed only £17,000 as purchasing power, in wages, dividends, etc. Douglas saw that if his factory was doing so, all other successful factories must be doing so in greater or lesser degree. If factories don't, they go "bust."

The Major's first observation is on a par with the observation of the falling apple or of the kettle lid lifted by steam: a point of departure.

No one, so far as I know, has attempted to disprove this part of Douglasism either to Douglas, to Orage or to the present writer by the simple presentation of the accounts of a firm.

Douglas's perception was that under the present accounting system the actual money available can never buy all the available goods.

Orage's last words over the radio, emerging for Rapallo from the crackle of Alpine thunder were: "in the gap between Price-values and Income is enough gunpowder to blow up every democratic Parliament."

Adnuit. That was a fine sentence to die on.

Anyone who thinks out the results of the accounting system will see that the deficiency of purchasing power is not static, but that the gulf is constantly widening. The idiocy of mere spasmodic dumping of purchasing power, ought to be visible. Douglas proposes an irrigation system.

The main complaint is: where will the state get the money to pay dividends? Why isn't it merely "persistent, never-ending inflation"?

For Douglasism (itself part of a thought-heritage) proposes to distribute purchasing power to the public via national dividends. And this strikes some people as absurd, or at least impossible.

These same people often receive dividends from their "investments in industrial or national bonds." They often read in newspapers that "government subsidies have been granted" or that "doles," etc., etc. are being provided or that "relief" is being provided. But the spectacle of nations pouring our purchasing power by the million through specific grants, emergency measures and as "charity" causes no mental cohesion, or no mental activity based on convergence and interaction of thoughts.

Apart from deliberate cheats and fools, men of goodwill and partial enlightenment often do honestly wonder whence the state could draw its power to pay continual dividends (i.e. distribute pieces of engraved paper with a certain regularity) without going bankrupt.

It was a black day for Europe when the distinction was lost, between usury and the "increment of association." It was also a dull day for England when Insularity raged so that Gourmont's writings on the Dissociation of Ideas failed to receive proper attention, simply as method in thinking.

When small merchants could not fill each his own ship, they banded together, and shared in marine adventure, both peril and profit. When savages hunted, they now and again hunted in bands. A group of men acting together can, in some circumstances achieve more than the sum of the possible attainments of the same hundred men acting each on his own.

The difference between these sums is the "increment of association."

That increment is essential in the comprehension of the Douglas plan, for which Orage gave his life.

Five thousand Basutos cannot sling a Baldwin locomotive forty feet into the air, and put it down gently on the other side of a factory.

When men associate not only with other live men, but with the aggregate of all acquired skills and inventions, the increment of association with all these skills and inventions adds another dimension to the "increment of association," an increment so enormous that popular imagination is still incapable of understanding it, and many people are still scared, as of a bogey man.

The new increment is the "cultural heritage" of Douglas's economics.

The fundamental material reality underlying the Douglas solution of poverty, slums, industrial tyranny, is that the cost of production is consumption.

That is to say a nation during a year is out of pocket, or out of possession, those things it consumes, destroys, sends abroad.

Douglas aims high, and wants economic justice. It may be an engineer's blueprint of a state unattainable. Radio and flying were once "unattainable."

At any rate Orage writing "for God" insisted on, or at any rate emphasized justice, though we won't see it in action this summer.

Orage was so built as to feel indignation at the spectacle of skilled biologists labouring to find a remedy for pellagra that would be cheaper than food.

I had no interest in Orage's mysticism and am unqualified to define it. I was thankful he had it simply because it kept him in action. He prized the moral indignation of his contributors. I don't know that it helped the clarity of our writing. But, on the other hand, the lack of it in our contemporaries has not always produced better results, nor on the whole a clearer outlook.

Mere abuleia, or the sheer cowardice that causes a man to shun a decision inside his own mind as to the right or wrong, the rightness or wrongness, the sanity or unsoundness of a given idea or congeries of ideas does not of itself lead to lucidity of perception or precision of judgment however much it may help a ninth rate or even a third rate wordster in the avoidance of immediate trouble.

Orage had the concept: rectitudo. On that rock was his

edifice. If the reader knows a better rock let him take it with my benedictions and compliments.

Orage's *rectitudo* demanded justice, justice in the division of the "eredità culturale," the cultural heritage; of the increment of association.

It demanded that the price charged the plain man and consumer should have a just ratio to the real cost of his food and clothing, and that adequate monetary-tickets should exist.

I doubt if Orage had any political talents whatsoever. He was a moralist, and thence an economist. He loathed above all other animal categories the dog in the manger. Only the descendant of this canine species can hold this against him.

Those of us who saw the Major's point in the first weeks of his first declarations* find it rather difficult to unsee it, or to put ourselves in the role of non-perceivers.

For three or four years after that, Orage repeated, now soft, now loud, now irate, now ironic: "consumption is the cost of production. You cannot cure unemployment. Unemployment is not a disease. We could get all the food and goods needed if the banks would get out of our way, if the banks wouldn't sabotage our exchange and consumption." And so forth.

Then he took ten years' vacation. The trams of the Lord move slowly. The screw propellor for ships was invented as soon as the paddlewheel.

Three years ago Orage thought the light might have penetrated Albion's occiput. I suppose our old gang was then in at least three corners of the spherical planet.

From the day Roosevelt entered the White House, Orage

* In Orage's office at the *New Age*, London, c. 1918. Douglas's first article "The Delusion of Super-Production" was published in the *English Review*, December, 1918.

was perhaps his fairest and most open critic. If his hopes and his rages varied as mine have his expression was calmer and he seemed less given to excess in either direction.

As to this question of the public's being able to buy its own produce, Orage's answer (for the 94th time one would think it WAS the answer, an answer, the answer, the ultimate answer) to the persistent question: Why isn't it (Douglas economics) just persistent never-ending inflation?

That answer I quoted in print in 1933. "Would you call it inflation to issue tickets for every seat in a theatre, regardless of the fact that the theatre has until now been always two-thirds empty *simply* because no such number of tickets was printed?"

Even in Jefferson's time people were saying you "have to have more money in circulation when you have a greatly increased quantity of goods," meaning that for a higher standard of living it will be convenient to have both faster and more ample exchange of products, and to be adequate the number of tickets, or the accounting, must keep up with this increase of available or usable goods.

Lack of historic knowledge keeps people from comparing life in an industrialized country with life in Doughty's desert Arabia or with life in very dark ages, say about 700 or 800 A.D. when they tell us European production had dwindled, in fact Europe was producing hardly anything save human beings, and there was an oriental market for eunuchs.

Historic detail sometimes starts a man thinking. Orage wrote *into* a public that had been blindfolded by generations of books produced under the heel of the profit system, fouled by the mentality of decades oppressed by university and educational systems warped by the profit system, by a bureaucracy of education, the bureaucrat being a man who avoids "dangerous" knowledge, who can almost indefinitely refrain

162

from taking, officially, cognizance of anything whatsodamever that is likely to disturb his immediate comfort or expose him to the least inconvenience or ridicule.

There were, and are, arrears of learning for the public to make up, and against this siltage Orage battled until his last heart gripe. It was the sea of stupidities, not a clean sea, it was the bog, the mud storm and quicksand of obfuscation, the ignorance, the non-correlation, the irritation of the jostled, the gross silence of hired concealers and the utter triviality of "men great in the public eye," or notorious authors whose royalties rolled in from the continent, or the U.S.A., or the provinces.

Orage sat in Cursitor Street in the old *New Age* days with a Diogenes lantern of a new pattern, it showed up many curious profiles. Pickthall came in with facts. The young Turks knew somebody was lunching with the high, the HIGH, oh very, and so forth. Whatever one lost in those days in nickle plush and Ritz dinners, one gained in the zest for knowledge.

You could call Orage a damn fool *and* respect him. I don't mean you could do first one and then the other, I mean you could do both at once. Usually you knew that the folly was superficial, that it meant an insistence on something of greater importance than the fancy style or minor merit of a given case up for discussion, that it amounted to no more than his singleness of intention, and his urge to get along toward his goal.

His "pickin' daisies" covered most of the artistic activities of his epoch. He printed my "Seafarer" in the *New Age*, I think he may have printed the first draft of the *Nekuia* (unless it was Granville), he printed my 38th canto, and the 41st went through the press in his last issue of the *New English Weekly*. For twenty-three years I don't think that either of us ever took the other seriously as a critic of letters, and now thinking of it in retrospect, I wonder how far the difference of view was a mere matter of the twelve years between us.

I remember his contended discouragement on one occasion: "Oh well I suppose it just is that I can't make you into a journalist."

To this day I haven't the faintest idea who read that paper. The only man I ever met who had seen my stuff in the *New Age* was an admiral.

To weigh Orage at full value the reader is asked carefully to consider the meaning of the next sentences:

Orage wrote in the British Empire. Even I am old enough to remember a time when the Empire was very efficient. I think it was efficient probably because it could make use of a great number of half-wits (bureaucracy) admirably controlled by a very much smaller number of johnnies who were manifestly ALL THERE.

While the admiral could assure me that his friends were personally honest, i.e. in private dealings, another member of the ruling caste could equally assure me that his cousin so-and-so who was *very* high, had been very much surprised to find so-and-so lunching with so-and-so and addressing him by his front name.

All of which tempts me to a number of less relevant speculations, many possibly pregnant, but all centrifugal, all likely to lead us away from the main theme: Orage's ideal, Orage's concept of justice.

The aim concretely was to equate the nation's purchasing power to available goods.

To that end Orage meant that any and every man's earnings were to be augmented by a share of the "increment of association" (with the nation, and with the accumulated means of production).

164

He meant that the price charged should have just relation to the material cost of the object.

The ultimate distribution to individuals of their daily and weekly supplies is effected mainly by little pieces of paper. The French for fifteen years after 1919 used little brass discs labelled "Chambres de Commerce de France, Bon pour 2 francs," or "1 franc." This fact had no more effect on the thought of English economists than had Mallarmé on Rudyard Kipling. Professor Gubbet went there and never knew what he was using. Dealing with England's Gubbets Orage finally wore himself out.

THE JEFFERSON-ADAMS LETTERS AS A SHRINE AND A MONUMENT ❦ 1937

I

OUR national life might, at least provisorily, be divided into four periods:

1. American civilization, 1760 to 1830.

2. The period of thinning, of mental impoverishment, scission between life of the mind and life of the nation, say 1830 to 1860.

3. The period of despair, civil war as hiatus, 1870 to 1930. The division between the temper, thickness, richness of the mental life of Henry Adams, and Henry James, and that of say U. S. Grant, McKinley, Harding, Coolidge, and Hoover.

4. The possibilities of revival, starting perhaps with a valorization of our cultural heritage, not merely as something lost in dim retrospect, a tombstone, tastily carved, whereon to shed dry tears or upon which to lay a few withered violets, in the manner of, let us say, the late Henry (aforementioned) Adams. The query being: should we lose or go on losing our own revolution (of 1776-1840) by whoring after exotics, Muscovite or European?

"As monument" or I should prefer to say as a still workable dynamo, left us from the real period, nothing surpasses the Jefferson correspondence. Or to reduce it to convenient bulk concentrating on the best of it, and its fullest implications, nothing surpasses the evidence that CIVILIZATION WAS in America, than the series of letters exchanged between Jefferson and John Adams, during the decade of reconciliation after their disagreements.

It is probable that I could pick one crow a week with the American university system "for the rest of my natural," but two immediate crows are quite obvious, one with the modus of teaching history omitting the most significant documents, and second the mode of teaching literature and/or "American literature," omitting the most significant documents, and assuming that the life of a nation's letters is restricted mostly to second-rate fiction.

From 1760 to 1826 two civilized men lived and to a considerable extent reigned in America. They did not feel themselves isolated phenomena. They were not by any means shrunk into a clique or dependent on mutual admiration, or on clique estimation. They both wrote an excellent prose which has not, so far as I know been surpassed in our fatherland, though Henry James had a style of his own (narrative) which was fit for a different purpose.

For the purpose and/or duration of this essay I shall define a civilized man as one who can give a serious answer to a serious question and whose circle of mental reference is not limited to mere acquisition of profit. The degree of his civilization will depend both on the depth of his thought and on the spread of his curiosity. He may have made absolutely no special study of anything outside his profession, but his thoughts on that profession will have been such that his thoughts about anything else will not be completely inane.

In 170 years the United States have at no time contained a more civilized "world" than that comprised by the men to whom Adams and Jefferson wrote and from whom they received private correspondence. A history of American Literature that omits the letters of the founders and memoirs or diaries of J. Q. Adams and Martin Van Buren is merely nonsense. Without competence in matters pertaining to Benjamin Franklin, I should nevertheless hazard the opinion that his public writing will be found slithery and perhaps cheap in comparison. He had not integrity of the word. Or at least there were occasions when it deserted him.

From early "bending of the twig" it is impossible for me to think of certain books save as parts of curricula. Certain books should not be in curricula. Other books belong in curricula. The Adams-Jefferson writings ought to be in curricula.

If we are a nation, we must have a national mind. Frobenius escaped both the fiddling term "culture" and rigid "Kultur" by recourse to greek, he used "Paideuma" with a meaning that is necessary to almost all serious discussion of such subjects as that now under discussion. His "Paideuma" means the mental formation, the inherited habits of thought, the conditionings, aptitudes of a given race or time.

In Italy there is current the adjective "anti-storico" to describe unlikely proposals; ideologies hung in a vacuum or contrary to the natural order of events as conditioned by race, time and geography.

Without Frobenius north of the Alps and the mediterranean sanity south of them our thought would I heartily believe, lack some of its pleasantest pastures.

As Americans we are neither Teutonic nor in any strict sense Mediterranean, though we should be fools to neglect either element of private nutrition.

As far as I remember U.S. school histories, they start with Columbus and/or in another sense with the Pilgrims. None of them starts with the Encyclopedists. Is the term heard even by University Undergraduates?

168

Our national culture can be perhaps better defined from the Jefferson letters than from any other three sources, and mainly to its benefice. I don't think they have been analyzed very clearly in themselves, and I am not sure that anyone has tried very coherently to relate them to anything else.

No one has thought them perfection. Jefferson has been abused as an incredible optimist. I am not going to concede much to these possible accusations.

Henry Adams with a familial and inherited, but very very discrete chip on his somewhat feminine shoulder lacked, on his own implicit, but never explicit confession, the one quality needful for judging action. Adams never guessed right. Take him in London during his father's embassy. He never foresaw.

It was not for nothing that Quincy Adams took up astrology, not anthropology. The discrete descendent wanted a science, almost a mathematic science of history—overlooking, or does he specifically say he didn't overlook, the impossibility of laboratory methods. Take it that he saw the shallowness of historic aimlessness in his time, his first urge is to rectify it by mathematical measurement. And thereby he loses the chance of examining a great many phenomena which were and still are available for any patient man's contemplation.

I am not leaving my subject. You can not "place" the Jefferson correspondence save by postulating some axes of reference, and by some defined method of mensuration.

Frobenius outrages the English because he agrees with Aquinas to the extent of supposing that nothing is without efficient cause.

Before trying to establish type-cycles and accelerated rhythms in history it is advisable to gather at least a few data, and if the urge towards rhythmic analysis obsesses one, it might even be possible to study certain recurrences.

Nevertheless the Flaubertian concept of "l'histoire morale contemporaine" arose not from mathematics but from a perception of paucity. A perception of the paucity registered in historians, the shallowness of their analysis of motivation, their inadequate measurements of causality.

Stendhal, Michelet, Flaubert, the Goncourts differ as individuals, but they were all of them on a trail, they wanted to set down an intelligible record of life in which things happened.

The mere statement that so and so made a war, or that so and so reformed or extended an empire is much too much in the vague.

Frobenius taking things back to supposedly "simpler" conditions does try to sort out tendencies and predispositions. He dissociates modes of living. There are twenty volumes waiting translation. The patient reader must allow me to have them there as possible footnote; permitting me for a moment an anthropologist's dissociation of two systems which have functioned in Europe. Without which dissociation one can not "place" the Encyclopedists or "come to Jefferson," save as isolated phenomenon sprung versatile, voluble, out of chaos. Polumetis, many-minded, distracting, discussable, but minus origins.

A Mediterranean state of mind, state of intelligence, modus of order "arose" out of Sparta perhaps more than from Athens, it developed a system of graduations, an hierarchy of values among which was, perhaps above all other, "order." As a mental and intellectual filing system it certainly did not fall with Romulus Agustulus in A.D. 476.

In fact the earlier parts of it we know almost as palimpsest. We begin to find it in Constantine, after A.D. 300, and we can carry on via Justinian, after 500, Charlemagne, Gratian, in St. Ambrose, and Duns Scotus. This, you see, is by no means confusing a paideuma or mental growth with an empire, such as Propertius debunked under Augustus, slitting out its blah and its rhetoric. Say that this civilization lasted down to Leo the Tenth. And that its clearest formulation (along my present line of measurement) is Dante's "in una parte piu e meno altrove."

Which detached phrase I had best translate by explaining that I take it to mean *a sense of gradations*. Things neither perfect nor utterly wrong, but arranged in a cosmos, an order, stratified, having relations one with another.

This means "the money that built the cathedrals," it means very great care in terminology because the "word" is "holy."

I will take these last terms out of any possible jargon. Translate it, for present emergency, words, an exact terminology, are an effective means of communication, an efficient modus operandi ONLY if they do retain meanings.

This Mediterranean paideuma fell before, or coincident with, the onslaught of brute disorder of taboo. The grossness of incult thought came into Europe simultaneously with manifestations called "renaissance," "restoration" and muddled in our time with a good deal of newspaper yawp about puritans.

Certain things were "forbidden." Specifically, on parchment, they were forbidden to hebrews. The bible emerged and broke the Church Fathers, who had for centuries quoted the bible. All sense of fine assay seemed to decline in Europe.

A whole table of values was lost, but it wasn't just dropped overboard. A confusion which has lasted for several centuries will not be wholly untangled even by this essay. I don't expect to get 500 years onto a shingle.

Lorenzo Valla extended, in one sense, the propaganda for the RIGHT WORD, but at the same time the cult of terminology lost its grip on general life.

Bayle and Voltaire spent their lives battling against "superstition," and something escaped them. The process of impoverishment had set in, analagous in long curve, to the short curve I have given for America 1830 to 60. There are no exact historical parallels. I don't want to be held to strict analogy. For the moment all I can do is to *dissociate* a graduated concept of say good and evil from an incult and gross paideuma. The former created by a series of men following one on another, not neglecting original examination of fact, but not thinking each one in turn that the moon and sea were discovered first by him.

Anybody who has read a labour paper, or reform party propaganda will grasp what I mean by the second crass mode of mentality.

There can be no doubt that the renaissance was born of wide awake curiosity, and that from Italy in the Quattrocento, straight down through Bayle and Voltaire the LIVE men were actuated by a new urge toward veracity.

There can I think, be equally little doubt, that the Church, as bureaucracy and as vested interest was the worst enemy of "faith," of "christianity," of mental order? And yet that doesn't quite cover it either.

Something did *not* hit plumb on the nail. Without saying that anyone was dead wrong, and without committing me to a statement, can we find some sort of split, some scission or lesion in the mental working of Europe? Didn't the mental integrity of the Encyclopedists dwindle into bare intellect by dropping that ETHICAL simplicity which makes the canonists, say any canonist so much more "modern," so much more scientific, than any 18th century "intellectual"?

All I want to do for the moment is to set up two poles of reference. One: a graduated system in which all actions were relative good or evil, according to almost millimetric measurement, but in the absolute. Two, a system in which everything

172

was good or bad without any graduation, but as taboo, though the system itself was continually modified in action by contingencies.

When this second system emerged from low life into high life, when it took over vast stretches of already acquired knowledge, it produced the Encyclopedists. Things were so or not so. You had "Candide," you had writers of maxims, you had "analysis," and you evolved into the Declaration of Les Droits de l'Homme which attained a fineness so near to that of the canonists that no one, so far as I know, has thought much of comparing them.

Out of intellectual revolt. Out of perhaps unwittingly Pico on Human Dignity there proliferated Bobby Burns and to hell with the Duke and the parson . . .

At which point the elder Adams had the puritanical stubbornness to stand up against popular clamour and to question the omniscience of Mr. Jefferson. It cost him four years in the Executive Mansion. But America was a civilized land in those days. Jefferson could imagine no man leaving it for the pleasures of Europe. Both he and Adams had been there and met Europeans.

II

It is only in our time that anyone has, with any shadow of right, questioned the presuppositions on which the U.S. is founded. If we are off that base, why are we off it? Jefferson's America was civilized while and/or because its chief men were social. It is only in our gormy and squalid day that the chief American powers have been, and are, anti-social.

Has any public man in our lifetime dared to say without a sneer or without fear of ridicule that Liberty is the right to do ce que ne nuit pas aux autres? That was, past tense, a definition of civic and social concept. Such liberty was, at least by program guaranteed the American citizen, but no other was offered him.

Jefferson and Adams were responsible. I mean they both were and FELT responsible. *Their* equals felt with them. The oath of allegiance implies this responsibility but it isn't printed in capitals, it passes in an unheeded phrase.

III

Two methods of turning in the evidence of the Adams letters are open. I could quote fragments and thereby be inadequate. The letters are printed. Or I could assert the implications, or at least the chief implications. The MAIN implication is that they stand for a life not split into bits.

Neither of these two men would have thought of literature as something having nothing to do with life, the nation, the organization of government. Of course no first-rate author ever did think of his books in this manner. If he was lyrist, he was crushed under a system; or he was speaking of every man's life in its depth; if he was Trollope or Flaubert he was thinking of history without the defects of generic books by historians which miss the pith and point of the story. The pith and point of Jefferson's story is in a letter to Crawford (1816) ... "and if the national bills issued be bottomed (as is indispensable) on pledges of specific taxes for their redemption within certain and moderate epochs, and be of *proper denominations* for *circulation*, no interest on them would be necessary or just, because they would answer to every one of the purposes of the metallic money withdrawn and replaced by them."

I do not expect one reader in even 600 to believe me when I say these are eight of the most significant lines ever written.

It may take another twenty years' education to give that passage a meaning.* People quite often think me crazy when I make a jump instead of a step, just as if all jumps were unsound and never carried one anywhere.

From that take off I land on the Walter Page correspondence, one hundred or one hundred and one or two years after the Jefferson letter. Page went to Washington and found (verbatim) "men about him (Wilson) nearly all very small fry or worse, narrowest two penny lot I've ever come across . . . never knew quite such a condition in American life."

The colouring there being that Page has a memorial tablet in Westminster Abbey. He cut no ice in European intellectual life. He earned the gratitude of the British. He and Grey passed through those years of racking anxiety, and Page was refined from a perhaps gawky provincial into a character by that anxiety, WITHOUT either of them ever having any idea of what started the war. Page saw things Wilson didn't. He had detailed news of appalling results; but even Wilson saw things that Page didn't. But Europe went blind into that war because mankind had not digested Jefferson's knowledge. They went into that war because the canon law had been buried, because all general knowledge had been split up into useless or incompetent fragments. Because literature no longer bothered about the language "of law and of the state" because the state and plutocracy cared less than a damn about letters. If I say those eight lines of Jefferson should be cut in brass and nailed to the door of Monticello the reader will think me eccentric. Let it pass as a picturesque fantasy.

And literature in the meanwhile? Goes to p-o-t, pot. Steadily it gets duller and duller, steadily it runs into neologism in contravention to T. J.'s moderate precept of style, namely that any man has the right to a new word when it can make

* Give 'em another 20 or 40.—E. P., 1959.

his meaning more clear than an old one. Literature gets duller and duller by limitation of subject. Balzac, Trollope and Henry James extended the subject. EXTENDED the subject, they as Dante before them and as every real writer before them or since, extended the domain of their treatment.

Up till 1820 people read latin. Your Jefferson-Adams correspondence shows acquaintance with latin, note the line of impoverishment. The University of today does not communicate to the student the idea of latin as a window. It instils the idea of "the classics," certain books often of very limited scope, to be read in the acquisition of culture. At some point the whole fact that Berkeley, Hume, whatever serious thought had been printed in English, came in part out of books printed in latin, has just gone by the board. If anyone had told me or any student of my undergraduate time that I would extend my greek vocabulary because I have been infuriated to a curiosity as to the nature of money they would have been greeted by (let us hope at least bland) amazement.

There is nothing more firmly rooted in young America's mind than the belief that certain subjects are dull, there is nothing further from the spirit of American University education than the perception that subjects that have interested the best minds for three, five or twenty-five centuries are not perhaps very dull. There must have been something in them to attract recurrent unstill curiosities.

IV

The historic process is continuous. Or "the historic process is probably continuous." Apparent breaks are probably due to laziness of historians who haven't dug down into causality. When you find two men as different as Marx and M. le

Marquis de la Tour du Pin both blind in the same spot, there is a chance to use curiosity.

In an age beset with cranks we have I suppose heard of Freud. For every man with an anxiety state due to sex, there are nine and ninety with an anxiety state due to lack of purchasing power, or anticipation of same. It is typical of a bewildered society that it should erect a pathology into a system.

The sanity and civilization of Adams-Jefferson stems from the Encyclopedists. You find in their letters a varied culture, and an omniverous (or apparently so) curiosity. And yet the "thinning," the impoverishment of mental life shows in the decades after their death, and not, I think, without cause.

The Aquinian universe, the grades of divine intelligence and/or goodness or goodwill present in graduated degrees throughout this universe gave the thinker, any thinker something to measure by. What was lost or mislaid in the succeeding centuries, or what at least went out of the limelight may have been belief in "God," but it most certainly was the HABIT of thinking of things in general as set in an orderly universe.

The laws of material science presuppose uniformity throughout the cosmos, but they do not offer an hierarchy of anything like the earlier coherence. Call it an hierarchy of evaluation.

The Encyclopedists have a rich culture. What is the Dictionnaire de Bayle? As an arrangement it treats topics ALPHABETICALLY. Voltaire's Dictionnaire is hardly more than a slight addendum. Bayle has Moreri to make fun of, but they all have an ORDER to criticise. They go over the accepted Aquinian universe with a set of measuring tools, reductio ad absurdum etc. The multifarious nature of cognizance remains, but they have only the Alphabet for a filing system.

They are brilliant. Bayle is robust with the heritage of Rabelais and Brantome, Voltaire a bit finer, down almost to silver point. But the idea and/or habit of gradations of value, and the infinitely more vital custom of digging down into principles gradually fade out of the picture. The degrees of light and motion, the whole metaphoric richness begin to perish. From a musical concept of man they dwindle downward to a mathematical concept.

Fontenelle notices it but attributes natural human resistance to abstraction to a hunger for ERROR. I don't think Chesterton ever quite formulated an epigram in reply, but the whole of his life was a protest against this impoverishment.

In fact the whole of Flaubert, the whole of the fight for the novel as "histoire morale contemporaine" was a fight against maxims, against abstractions, a fight back toward a human and/or total conception.

Flaubert, Trollope, and toward the last Henry James got through to money. Marx and La Tour du Pin, not working on total problem, but on a special problem which one would have thought of necessity would have concentrated their attention on money, merely go blind at the crucial point.

In totalitarian writings before Voltaire one does not find this blind spot. The Church Fathers think down to detail, Duns Scotus has no cloudy obsession on this point. There is a great deal of latin on Intrinsic and Extrinsic value of money.

Jefferson is still lucid. Gallatin found banks useful, as T. J. says, because they "gave ubiquity to his money."

Does the historian stop for such details? I mean the pestilent variety of historian who has filled 97% of the shelves in our libraries (historical alcoves)? Venice took over private banking but it took decades to persuade the normal Venetian to keep books, to get down to the office to see whether his butler did the job for him, let alone having the addition correct.

There is a continuity of historic process. The imaginary

178

speech of Q. Xtius Decimus after the battle of Bogoluz or the steaming open of despatches by Metternich is not the whole of the story.

In American history as professed the monetary factor has been left to the LAST. Van Buren's memoirs stays six decades in manuscript. How you expect to have a nation with no national culture, beats me.

"Congress will then be paying six percent on twenty millions, and receiving seven percent on ten millions, being its third of the institution; so that on the ten millions cash which they receive from the States and individuals, they will, in fact, have to pay but 5% interest. This is the bait." (Monticello, Nov. 6, 1813)

The idea, put about I know not why; by I know not whom, that Jefferson was an imprecise rhetorician disappears in a thorough perusal of his letters.

V

There may be a defect in the "decline and fall" method in writing history. There is certainly a defect in it if the analyst persists in assuming that this or that institution (say the Church) "fell" merely because some other paideuma or activity (organized formally, or sporadic and informal) arises, overcrowds, overshadows it, or merely gets greater publicity.

The Church may not have fallen. The steady building up of social and economic criteria, ever with a tendency to control, via Constantine, Justinian, Charlemagne is still there in the records. It is still there as thought and discrimination for anyone who chooses to look at it.

Leibnitz was possibly the last prominent thinker who worried about "reconciliation," about getting all the best European thought "back into" the Church, but one might note that it is not merely theology but philosophy that STOPS with Herr Leibnitz. By that I mean that since his correspondence with Bossuet "philosophy," general ideation has been merely a squib and trailer, correlated to material particular sciences, from which it has had its starts, shoves, incentives. Often splurging in the vaguest analogies.

" 'The same political parties which now agitate the United States, have existed through all time'; precisely. And this is precisely the complaint in the first volume of my defense." (John Adams quoting Priestly to Jefferson, July 9, 1813).

"By comparing the first and the last of these articles" (this follows a table of figures) "we see that if the United States were in possession of the circulating medium, as they ought to be, they cd. redeem what they cd. borrow from that, dollar for dollar, and in ten annual installments; whereas usurpation of that fund by bank paper, obliging them to borrow elsewhere at 7½%, two dollars are required to reimburse one." (T. J. from Poplar Forest, Sept. 11, 1813).

I am not offering proof, because full proof will not go onto ten pages. I am offering indications, which the reader can follow for himself, but which will I think lead to perception:

That Adams and Jefferson exist in a full world. They are NOT a province of England. The letters abound in consciousness of Europe, that is of France, Holland, Spain, Russia, Italy. The truly appalling suburbanism that set in after the civil war, partly from our exhaustion, partly from the oedematous bulging of the British Empire, our relapse into cerebral tutelage, our suburbanism did not afflict Adams and Jefferson. Not only were they level and (with emphasis) CONTEMPORARY with the best minds of Europe but they entered into the making of that mind. Chateaubriand did not come to Philadelphia to lecture, he came to learn.

I do not believe that either public men nor American

writers for the past forty years have dared to face the implications of the Adams-Jefferson volumes. Henry James would have, had he been aware of such works existing.

I doubt if they can be adduced to back up any particular theory, unless you call it a theory to hold that one should look at the totality of the facts or at least at as many as are thrust under your observation and as many more as you can dig out for yourselves.

The first quotation of Jefferson here used, could lead to Gesell. Chemistry and Physics are not mutually contradictory. Faddists and the incult are perpetually trying to refute one set of ideas with other ideas that are sometimes unrelated, sometimes complementary. The just price is a canonist concept. The order of the Roman empire, the possibility of organizing such an empire is indissolubly bound up with reduction of usury rates, with disentanglement of the notion of usury from that of marine insurance (hence the scandal of Cato the censor).

An idea or ideal of order developed with the Roman empire, but it was not the empire. It was an ideal of justice that penetrated down, out, through, into marketing. The idea that you can tax idle money dates back through a number of centuries. These questions have intrigued the best human minds, Hume, Berkeley, a whole line of catholic writers, and a whole congeries of late latin writers. You can not write or understand any history, and you can not write or understand any serious "history of contemporary customs" in the form of Goncourt and Flaubert novels if you persist in staving off all enquiry into the most vital phenomena, e.g. such as search into the nature and source of the "carrier," of the agent and implement of transferrence.

A total culture such as that of Adams and Jefferson does not dodge such investigation. A history of literature which refuses to look at such matters remains merely a shell and a sham.

Adams was anti-clerical (at least I suppose one would call it that), they are both of them heritors of encyclopedism, but they inherit that *forma mentis* in an active state where definition of terms and ideas has not been lost. I mean liberty is still the right to do ANYTHING that harms no one else. For seventy years it has been boomed mainly as effrenis in faenerando licentia, alias to hell with the public.

They both had a wide circle of reference, of knowledge, of ideas, with the acid test for hoakum, and no economic inhibitions. The growth of economic inhibition, I mean specifically in the domain of THOUGHT, is a XIXth century phenomenon to a degree that I believe inhered in no other century. Edward Grey and Page were sincerely unconscious. They "didn't see things that way." There was a vast penumbra about their excitement, and penumbra is the mother of bogies.

Jefferson specifically wanted a civilization in Virginia. Van Buren was at work from very early years. He was servant of the public, and during his public life had, so far as one makes out, time only for good manners. Heaven knows how he spent his time after he was defeated. His memoirs are very well written.

After the death of Van Buren the desire for civilization was limited you might almost say to professional writers, to a very few professional writers and an ineffective minority of the electorate. You have a definite opposition between public life and such men as H. James and H. Adams which you can not ascribe *wholly* to their individual temperaments.

A totalitarian state uses the best of its human components. Shakespeare and Chaucer did not think of emigrating. Landor, Shelley, Keats, Browning, Beddoes did emigrate, and Bobby Burns thought of it. Something had happened in and to

England. An historian, if he were real, would want to pry into it.

And the lesson is, if heaven help us, I am supposed to be teaching anyone anything in this article—the lesson is against raw ideology, which Napoleon, Adams, Jefferson were all up against, and whereto, as Adams remarked, Napoleon had, in those days, given a name.

The lesson is or might be against peripheric acid as distinct from Confucian building of ideogram and search into motivation, or "principle."

If you want certain results, you must as scientist examine a great many phenomena. If you won't admit what you are driving at, even to yourself, you remain in penumbra. Adams did not keep himself in penumbra, he believed in a responsible class. He wanted safeguards and precautions and thereby attained unpopularity.

"You and I ought not to die before we have explained ourselves to each other." (Adams to Jefferson, July 15, 1813). Did Rousseau or Montaigne ever write anything to equal that sentence, given the context (1760 to 1813)?

AMERICA AND THE SECOND WORLD WAR ⇜ 1944

The main events dealt with in this essay are:
1. The suppression of the paper-money issue in Pennsylvania, A.D. 1750.
2. The American Revolution (1776) and its subsequent betrayals.
3. The fall of the United States under the control of the international usurocracy during the Civil War, somewhere about 1863.

These events to be considered in relation to the Second World War.

The Process of History

THE historical process has been understood at various times, but this understanding on the part of a diligent minority fighting for the public good is again and again thrust down beneath the surface. In 1878 my grandfather said the same things that I'm saying now, but the memory of his efforts has been obliterated. The same applies to the revelations of men like Calhoun, Jackson and Van Buren. Forty years ago Brooks Adams assembled some very significant facts, but his books were not widely read. He had no vocation for martyrdom, he confessed with irony.

It took me seven years to get hold of a set of *The Works of John Adams*, published in 1850-56 in ten volumes, edited with a Life of the Author by Charles Francis Adams, grandson

Translated from Italian by John Drummond.

184

of the Father of the Nation. Besides, these works are partly incomprehensible to anyone who is not already provided with some knowledge of economics or, more specifically, monetary matters.

If you can understand the cause, or causes, of one war, you will understand the cause or causes of several—perhaps of all. But the fundamental causes of war have received little publicity. School-books do not disclose the inner workings of banks. The mystery of economics has been more jealously guarded than were ever the mysteries of Eleusis. And the Central Bank of Greece was at Delphi.

This present war is part of the secular war between usurers and peasants, between the usurocracy and whomever does an honest day's work with his own brain or hands.

In the nineteenth century the public more or less believed that political economy had been invented by Adam Smith. Regius professorships were founded to falsify history and teach Whiggery. And even the Tudor monarchs used to talk about "tuning the pulpits."

The cardinal fact of the American Revolution of 1776 was the suppression, in 1750, of the paper money issue in Pennsylvania and other colonies, but history as taught in the U.S.A. speaks of more picturesque matters, such as the Boston Tea Party.

Ethics arise with agriculture. The ethics of the nomad do not go beyond the distinction between my sheep and your sheep. If the study of Aristotle and Demosthenes has not actually been suppressed, it has at least been soft-pedalled for perfectly deliberate and definite reasons. Certain classical authors speak too frankly for the tastes of the Grand Seigneurs of Usury.

The terminology of financial operations has already been studied and set forth with uncommon seriousness by Claudius

Salmasius (*De Modo Usurarum* and *De Foenore Trapezitico,* Lugd. Bat. (Leyden), 1639 and 1640). But even those encyclopaedias that mention his name tend to ignore these two books.

What consitiutes the sound basis of credit was already known and affirmed at the beginning of the seventeenth century by the founders of the Monte dei Paschi of Siena. It was, and is, the abundance or the productive capacity of nature, taken together with the responsibility of the whole people.

I quote these apparently unconnected facts to indicate that certain high crimes are not due to any negligence on the part of a handful of scholars, and cannot be attributed to the ignorance of the whole of humanity, but that they can only happen on account of the ignorance of the great majority.

What the sages understood was recorded, but inscriptions disappear, books decay, while usurocratic publicity floods the public's mind like a muddy tide, and the same greed, the same iniquities and monopolies rise up again subjecting the world to their dominion.

The decrees of the Emperor Frederick II, King of Sicily, used to begin with God the Eternal and the Creation of the World. This medieval style precludes any idea that social factors are without roots.

My ignorance, and yours, and that of the surrounding public is not today a natural phenomenon. Above and beyond natural ignorance, an artificial ignorance is diffused, artificially created.

Among the definitions of the word "banker" collected by Georg Obst we find:

a banker is one who buys money and debts, creating other debts;
a banker is one who borrows money to lend it again at a profit (i.e., at a higher rate of interest).

The advanced stage in the development of cunning marked by the foundation of the (private) Bank of England was clearly registered in Paterson's prospectus: "the bank hath benefit of the interest on all moneys which it creates out of nothing." Paterson, in other words, proposed to lend not money but notes, gambling on the very likely probability that only a small fraction of the "depositors" would ever want to withdraw their money at the same time.

The trick came off, and in a grand way. But the Quakers of Pennsylvania were beginning to enter into competition *pro bono publico Pennsylvanico*. That is to say, they lent their paper money to farmers for purposes of land reclamation up to an amount equal to half the value of the farm in question, requiring payment in ten annual instalments.

The bank in the mother country, through the instrumentality of the British Government, had this beneficial competition, which had brought prosperity to the colonies, suppressed in 1750.

After various other vexations the colonies declared their independence, which they achieved thanks to their geographical position and to the perturbed state of Europe.

During the last thirty years the news-stands and bookshops have displayed and sold a considerable number of more or less "approximative" works detailing the affairs of various monopolies: of petrol, of metals, etc. But the great whodunnit of money never appeared among them.

In a certain sense Brooks Adams had written it, but his *Law of Civilization and Decay* is not in "popular" form.

The modern revelation of the usurocratic mechanism remained at the point reached by Adams until Arthur Kitson gave his evidence before the Macmillan Committee, when he traced the curve showing the relationships between debt and credit after the Napoleonic wars, after the American Civil War, and their bearing on the post-Versailles period.

Every revolution is betrayed.

The victory of the American armies, Lord Cornwallis's surrender, etc., did not end the secular war between producer and usurer which continued, if somewhat subduedly, without the slightest truce.

The idea that a war might ever have abolished interest on debt was regarded with irony by one of the "Fathers of the Republic."

Jefferson, who opposed Hamilton's manoeuvres, pinned his faith on the Secretary of the Treasury, Gallatin, of "Swiss" origin. A certain prejudice was aroused against Gallatin, but Jefferson insisted that he was the "most able man in the administration after the President" (i.e., after himself).

Jefferson professed not to understand agriculture (adding deferentially: but Mr. Madison—he does). He claimed a certain ignorance of economics. He insisted that the bank was useful because it gave "ubiquity" to Gallatin's money. And, in fact, the bank gave it this ubiquity. Giving ubiquity to purchasing power is one of the perfectly legitimate and very useful functions of banks.

Some ten years ago I had occasion to condense the introductory study of American history into a "book" of less than thirty lines. This book shows that Jefferson was less ignorant of finance and money than his modesty would have pretended. Here are my four chapters:

CHAPTER I

"All the perplexities, confusion, and distress in America arise, not from defects in their constitution or confederation, not from want of honour or virtue, so much as from downright ignorance of the nature of coin, credit, and circulation." (John Adams)

CHAPTER II

". . . and if the national bills issued be bottomed (as is indispensable) on pledges of specific taxes for their redemption within certain and moderate epochs, and be of proper denominations for circulation, no interest on them would be necessary or just, because they would answer to every one of the purposes of the metallic money withdrawn and replaced by them." (Thomas Jefferson, letter to Crawford, 1816).

CHAPTER III

". . . and gave to the people of this Republic the greatest blessing they ever had—their own paper to pay their own debts." (Abraham Lincoln)

CHAPTER IV

The Congress shall have Power:

To coin Money, regulate the Value thereof, and of foreign Coin, and fix the Standard of Weights and Measures.

Constitution of the United States, Article I Legislative Department, Section 8, clause 5.

Done in Convention by the Unanimous Consent of the States present the seventeenth Day of September in the Year of our Lord one thousand seven hundred and eighty seven and of the independence of the United States of America the Twelfth. In witness whereof We have hereunto subscribed our Names. (George Washington—President and deputy from Virginia.)

It should be noted that only the last of these statements is to be found in a publication easily accessible to the great majority of the citizens of the great but denatured democracy.

The American Consitiution, from which it is taken, is written in a style that is not very attractive to the average reader. The key phrases come a long way after the beginning and the citizen gets bored before he catches up with them. For years, now, Congress has taken no notice of the powers it has been invested with by this Document. Now and then some crank from Nebraska or Dakota raises an uncouth voice to demand a little of the liberty proclaimed by the Fathers of the Republic, but the roar of the rotary presses soon drowns such rustic vociferations.

One day, thinking of the trouble it had cost me to unearth these four "chapters," I asked the head of the American history department of the Library of Congress if there existed a history of America, whether in one volume or in ten, that contained these four chapters or the substance of them.

After reflecting for a while he replied that so far as he knew I was the first to have brought together and in relation to each other the four great names of the greatest presidents of the Republic.

Lincoln was assassinated after he made the statement given above. The theatrical gesture of the assassin does not explain how it happened that he escaped from Washington, after the alarm had been raised, by the only road that was not guarded; nor its synchronization with the attempted assassination of Seward, the Secretary of State, nor various other details of the affair. The fact remains that Lincoln had assumed a position in clear opposition to the usurocracy.

The usurers, defeated by the operations of Jackson and Van Buren in the decade of 1830-40, directed their beam of obfuscation onto the question of negro slavery, or "chattel slavery," as it was called. The dramatic and sentimental possibilities of this problem were far superior to those immediately visible in the bank struggle.

During the pre-war phase the debates in Congress reveal an extremely penetrating perception on the part of the more intelligent members. But after Lincoln's death discussions lost much of their clarity. The indebtedness of the South to the City of New York took second place. The subject lost its news value.

Usurocracy had discovered that the slave-owning system was less profitable than that of "free" labour. Anyone who possessed a slave had to keep him alive and in fit condition to work. This cost more than "free" labour, in respect of which, under the capitalist system, the employer had no responsibility whatsoever. The defeat of the slave owners was already determined, predetermined.

Perhaps the elements of "conscience" and "idealism" never played so important a part in the preparation of a war as in the present instance. The problem of mass emotion is not a mathematical or a monetary problem, but when the passions of the multitude are aroused certain elements set about to exploit the situation.

The Comte de Vergennes had every reason to say to John Adams that newspapers ruled the world.

John Adams's great-grandson had every reason to write that after Waterloo the power of the usurers met with no serious defeat.

University textbooks, throughout the whole century of usury, known as the nineteenth, were written to maintain the domination of usury, and to keep professors in their chairs. A book like D. R. Dewey's *Financial History of the United States* contains an enormous quantity of incontrovertible facts, but omits those which are really relevant and revealing. These cardinal facts, on which the whole problem turns, are to be found in a few pamphlets that slip through the control, or in fundamental "works" in which their discovery requires great patience on the part of the reader: a hundred pages of reading-matter for three revealing lines.

Conclusion

Wisdom resides less in the means than in affirmation of ends. If there is the will to attain the end, the means will be found. If the end is perfidious, no means can have in itself any inherent virtue capable of preventing the perversion of justice.

Against this, it may be observed that certain systems, and certain mechanisms of means, have been purposely invented and set working in order to mislead the public, and to keep them ignorant of the facts of history and of the best means of creating and maintaining social justice. The ideological and propagandist battle should be directed against this obscurantism.

In recent centuries gold has been used mainly as an instrument for creating scarcity—a scarcity, in the first instance, of gold itself in a certain locality, nation, or nations, strategically determinative.

All the artful dodges used to manipulate the present forms of money would be attempted in the case of any new kind of money.

In this respect the conservatives who cry "No monkeying about with money!" are quite right.

But the fundamental fraud is monopoly. It is necessary to understand this. It is necessary to perceive that Napoleon and several other Heads of State have been struggling against the same snares and pitfalls, the same trickery.

A summary of the League of Nations infamy is contained in Odon Por's *Politica economico-sociale in Italia. Anno XVII-XVIII.*

Stalin's attack on capitalism in his *Foundations of Leninism* merits attention. He thoroughly understands the iniquity of the various Roosevelts, Churchills, Blums, and the rest of them. But Bolshevism stooped to the methods of economic warfare, flooding foreign markets with goods and foodstuffs at cut prices; and with the purchase of Suez Canal shares it has frankly embarked on a financial war. It is allied up to the hilt with liberalism, for the liberals always get around to talking of the export of manpower—of human beings, that is—in exchange for foodstuffs. Stalin disposes of "forty truckloads of human material" for work on a canal. The only difference is one of economic detail: the enormous perversion is common to each tentacle of the monster.

(1) Wars are made to create debts.

(2) War is the highest form of sabotage.

(3) A nation that will not get itself into debt drives the usurers to fury.

Postscriptum

What has been lacking, especially among practical people, among industrialists, large as well as small, among businessmen, and not only small businessmen, is a comprehensive survey of the usurocratic mechanism, an awareness of the relationships between commercial transactions, of the relationship between the management of a factory or business and the international monetary system, not on a short-term basis, at three-monthly or three-yearly intervals, but over periods of centuries or half-centuries: and always with the same object: lucre. And always with the same mechanism too, namely the creation of debts for the extortion of interest, of monopolies so that they can keep prices continually fluctuating, including the prices of the various monetary units, of the various national currencies.

The following are some of the sources at which the student may be able to slake a little of the curiosity that I hope this essay will have stimulated.

George Obst: *Das Bankgeschaft,* C. E. Poeschel Verlag, Stuttgart.

Aristotle: *Politics.*

Claudius Salmasius: *De Modo Usurarum,* Elzevier, Lugd. Bat. (Leyden), 1639.

Claudius Salmasius: *De Foenore Trapezitico,* Joannis Maire, Lugd. Bat., 1640.

Historie Générale de la Chine ou Annales de cet Empire, traduites du Tong-Kien-Kang-Mou, par le feu père Joseph Anne-Marie de Moyriac De Mailla, 13 volumes, Paris, 1777-85.

T. Louis Comparette: "The Reorganization of the Municipal Administration under the Antonines," *American Journal of Philology,* Vol. XXVII, No. 2.

The Works of John Adams, Second President of the United States: with A Life of the Author, notes and illustrations, by his Grandson, Charles Francis Adams. Little, Brown & Co., Boston, 1850-56.

The Writings of Thomas Jefferson, Memorial Edition, XX volumes, Washington, 1903-4.

The Autobiography of Martin Van Buren, written in 1860 or thereabouts, remaining in manuscript until its publication as Vol. II of the "Annual Report of the American Historical Association for the year 1918," Govt. Print. Off., Washington, 1920.

Claude G. Bowers: *Jefferson and Hamilton,* Houghton Mifflin, Boston, 1925.

Willis A. Overholser: *A Short Review and Analysis of the History of Money in the United States,* published by the author, Libertyville, Ill., 1936.

Odon Por: *Politica economico-sociale in Italia. Anno XVII-XVIII.* Florence, 1940. English translation by Ezra Pound: *Italy's Policy of Social Economics 1939-40,* Bergamo, 1941.

And for a wider view of the historical process:

Brooks Adams: *The Law of Civilization and Decay,* first New York ed., Macmillan, 1896. Also Vintage Books, New York, 1955.

Brooks Adams: *The New Empire,* Macmillan, New York, 1902.

Arthur Kitson: *The Bankers' Conspiracy,* Elliot Stock, London, 1933.

NOTE. In all studies of economics and the historical process we need a freshly clarified terminology. Even a writer like Obst who is careful to define his words, has failed to establish a complete terminology, and to make all the distinctions one would have wished. A clearer distinction between a means of savings and a means of exchange might throw some light on the various subjective obscurities of several authors.

Finale Enfatico

I hope the reader has not "understood it all straight off." I should like him to go back to the facts mentioned and think over their significance for himself, drawing his own conclusions. In case I should have been wanting in clarity of expression, I repeat:

After Lincoln's death the real power in the United States passed from the hands of the official government into the hands of an evil combine. The democratic system perished.

From that time it has been useless to speak of the United States as an autonomous entity. From what precise moment it became useless and absurd to speak of the British Empire as an autonomous entity still remains to be determined.

It is so much waste of time to talk of this or that "democracy." The real government was, and is, to be found behind the scenes. The system works as follows. Two or more parties appear before the public. As a matter of form, and to reassure the simpletons, some honest men are allowed to do a little clean work as long as they don't touch the big rackets. The biggest rackets are those of finance and monopolization, including the monopolization of money itself, both within the nation and in combination with the various foreign currencies.

Even before the previous war Anatole France, in *L'Ile des Pingouins*, ironically informed his readers of the workings of "commerical" wars:

"Certainly," replied the interpreter," there are industrial wars. Nations without commerce and industry have no reason to go to war, but commercial nations are forced to adopt a policy of conquest. Our wars must, of necessity, increase in number as our industrial activity increases. When one of our industries fails to find an outlet for its products, we must have a war to open up new markets. This year, in fact, we have had a coal war, a copper war, and a cotton war. In Third Zealand we have massacred two thirds of the natives to force the remainder to buy umbrellas and braces."

This book by France was immensely popular round about 1908, but the world failed to learn its lesson.

196

IMMEDIATE NEED OF
CONFUCIUS ◆§ 1937

In CONSIDERING a value already age-old, and never to end while men are, I prefer not to write "to the modern world." The *Ta Hio* stands, and the commentator were better advised to sweep a few leaves from the temple steps. This is no shrine for the hurried tourist or for the conductor with: "One moment, and now for the alligator tanks so that we can catch the Bombay Express at 8-47."

Dante for a reason wrote *De Vulgari Eloquio*—On the Common Tongue—and in each age there is need to write De Vulgari Eloquio, that is, to insist on seeing the words daily in use and to know the *why* of their usage.

No man has ever known enough about words. The greatest teachers have been content to use a few of them justly.

If my version of the *Ta Hio* is the most valuable work I have done in three decades I can only wait for the reader to see it. And for each reader to discover its "value" to the "modern world" for himself.

Mr. S.V.V. (*The Aryan Path*, December 1936) has indicated the parallels in Indian teaching, but the Western reader will first see the antithesis to the general impression of Indian thought now clouding Occidental attention. This cloud exists, and until some light or lightning disrupts it, many of the better minds in the West will be suspicious of all Eastern teaching.

It is "our" impression that an Indian begins all talk with an allusion to the Infinite and that the Ultimate Unity appears four times on every Indian page.

I am not saying what ought to be. I am not expounding Indian thought, but indicating a misapprehension. It is the opinion of the hard-headed, as distinct from the bone-headed, West that Westerners who are drawn to Indian thought are Westerners in search of an escape mechanism, Westerners who dare face neither the rigours of medieval dialectic nor the concrete and often exhausting detail of the twentieth century material sciences.

Writing, which is communications service, should be held distinct from the production of merchandise for the book trade. And the measure of communication was defined by Leo Frobenius when he said:

"It is not what a man says but the part of it which his auditor considers important that determines the amount of the communication."

In considering the Occident the Oriental should allow for a fact that I have not yet seen printed. Western contact with the Far East was made in an era of Western degradation. American contact with Japan was forced in the very middle of "the century of usury." Western ethics were a consummate filth in the middle of the last century.

You can probably date any Western work of art by reference to the ethical estimate of usury prevalent at the time of that work's composition; the greater the component of tolerance for usury the more blobby and messy the work of art. The kind of thought which distinguishes good from evil, down into details of commerce, rises into the quality of line in paintings and into the clear definition of the word written.

If the editors complain that I am not confining my essay

to Confucius, I reply that I am writing on the "need for Confucius." I am trying to diagnose Western disease. Western disease has raged for over two centuries. Western disease shows in the sixty per cent racket on ink money. This is a *symptom* of moral obtuseness.

The Oriental looking at the West should try more often to look at the total West over a longer period than is usually drawn to his attention.

For over a thousand years the acute intellectual labour of Europe was done *inside* the Catholic Church. The readers of *The Aryan Path* (December 1936) were reminded a few months ago that Scotus Erigena was a layman. A "movement" or institution lives while it searches for truth. It dies with its own curiosity. *Vide* the death of Moslem civilization. *Vide* the very rapid withering of Marxist determinism. Yeats burbles when he talks of "withering into the truth." You wither into non-curiosity.

Catholicism led Europe as long as Erigena, Grosseteste and their fellows struggled for definitions of words.

Today the whole Occident is bathed daily in mental detritus, that is, the "morning paper" in ten millions of copies rouses the Western brain daily. Bunkus is called a philosopher, Puley an economist, and a hundred lesser specimens swarm daily over acres of print.

Ex diffinientium cognitione diffiniti resultat cognitio— "Knowledge of a definite thing comes from a knowledge of things defined," wrote Dante, rubbing it in. You can't know a canzone, which is a structure of strophes, until you know strophes.

"Man triplex, seeks the useful, this is common with vegetables; the delectable, in common with animals; the *honestum*; and here he is alone; vel angelicae naturae sociatur."

This kind of dissociation and tidiness is "medieval."

When the experimental method came into material science giving a *defined* knowledge in realms whereto verbal distinctions had not then penetrated, and where they probably never will penetrate, the Occident lost the habit of verbal definition.

The Church, at least in the eyes of outsiders, seemed to have lost its faith, and considerable confusion prevailed in regard to it.* Curiosity deserted almost all realms save those of physiology, chemistry and kindred material sciences.

A tolerance of the most ungodly indistinctness supervened. The life of Occidental mind fell apart into progressively stupider and still more stupid segregations. The Church of England for example remained a bulwark of usury and/or a concatenation of sinecures, for the holding whereof neither courage, character nor intelligence was required or even wanted.

Hence (leaping over a certain amount of barbed wire, and intermediary gradations), hence the Western need of Confucius, and specifically of the *Ta Hio*, and more specifically of the first chapter of the *Ta Hio*; which you may treat as a *mantram*, or as a *mantram* reinforced, a *mantram* elaborated so that the meditation may gradually be concentrated into contemplation. (Keeping those two grades of life separate as they are defined in the Benjamin Minor of R. St. Victor.)

There is respectable Western thought. There is Western thought that conforms to Confucius just as S.V.V. in December reminded you that there is in Indian Scripture a stress on Confucian "self-examination etc., with emphasis on action."

* Mr. Eliot's "Primer of Heresy" (*After Strange Gods*) was not examined with sufficient care, nor did the present author chew on it sufficiently, especially in regard to the distinction between A Church, an orthodoxy, and a collection of intelligent observations by individual theologians, however brilliant. Eliot's use of Confucius in *The Rock* (section 5), is worth noting.—E. P., 1959.

Yet I fail to understand S.V.V. when he adds "without concern for its fruits." This phrase of his seems to me capable of grave misinterpretation. Does he mean "profits"? Does he mean "material profits"?

In any case the *need* is a matter of emphasis. We in the West *need* to begin with the first chapter of the *Ta Hio*, not merely to grant a casual admission of it in some out-house of our ethics or of our speculations.

There is nothing in this chapter that destroys the best that has been thought in the Occident. The Occident has already done its apparent utmost to destroy the best Western perceptions. Official Christianity is not universally respected by the ethical. Catholicism sank fairly low with, let us say, Antonelli in the eighteen hundred and fifties. It has started a new ascension with the encyclicals, Rerum Novarum and Quadrigesimo Anno. But the whole of Western idealism is a jungle. Christian theology is a jungle. To think through it, to reduce it to some semblance of order, there is no better axe than the *Ta Hio*.

I, personally, want a revision of the trial of Scotus Erigena. If "authority comes from right reason" the shindy between Leibnitz and Bossuet was unnecessary.

Ernest Fenollosa emphasized a difference between the approach of logic and that of science. Confucius left his record in ideogram. I do not wish to confuse the ideogrammic method with the specific and basic teaching of the *Ta Hio*, first chapter.

There are here two related matters. The good scholastic (mediaeval) or good canonist recognized the limits of knowledge transmissible by verbal definitions:—

Scientes quia rationale animal homo est, et quia sensibilis anima et corpus est animal, et *ignorantes* de hac anima quid ea sit, vel de ipso corpore, perfectam hominis cognitionem habere non possumus; quia cognitionis perfectio uniuscuiusque terminatur ad ultima elementa.

(Knowing because man is a rational animal, and because a sensible soul and body is animal, and *ignorant* what this soul is, or what this body is, we cannot have complete (perfect) cognition of man, because the completeness of cognition of anything in particular ends with the ultimate element.)

Fenollosa accented the Western need of ideogramic thinking. Get your "red" down to rose, rust, cherry, if you want to know what you are talking about. We have too much of this talk about vibrations and infinites.

There is here a common element with the Confucian method of getting in to one's own "intentions."

Naturally there is nothing in this which is hostile to Dante's concept of the "directio voluntatis." There exists passage after passage in our serious mediaeval thinkers which contains the terms "virtu," *virtus*, with vivid and dynamic meaning. But it is precisely the *kind* of thought that is now atrophied in the Occident. This is precisely how we do *not* now think.

It is for these values that we have need of *Ta Hio*, and as S.V.V., approaching the work from so different a background, agrees, "here is a very treasury of wisdom."

S.V.V. did not, I take it, awaken to consciousness in McKinley's America, his early boyhood was not adorned with the bustuous noises of Kipling and the first Mr. Roosevelt. Apparently the *Ta Hio* offers us a meeting-place, a field of agreement.

In so far as "at the centre of every movement for order or reconstruction in China you will find a Confucian" (this referring to the procession of centuries) in so far as my knowledge of Kung has come *via* Tokio, there appears to be here a common field not only for men of Bombay and London, but for pilgrims from an even wider circumference. To my mind there is need, very great need of such common *locus* of mutual comprehension.

The late A. R. Orage claimed to have read the *Mahabharata*. Very few Occidentals *can* read it. It is manifestly *not* the possible meeting ground for Eastern and Western man in our era.

Suma Gengi has just been televisioned from London. The news reaches me between one page and another of this essay. There are common denominators. There are points and lines wherein the East can make contact with us Occidentals.

But the "need of Confucius." Let me try to get this as clear as possible. A "need" implies a lack, a sick man has "need." Something he has not. Kung as medicine?

In every cranny of the West there is a mildew of books that start from nowhere. There is a marasmus of books that start "treating of this, that and the other" without defining their terminology, let alone their terms, or circle, of reference. A thousand infernal self-styled economists start off without even defining "money" (which is a *measured* claim, transferable from any one to any one else, and which does not bear interest as does a bond or a share-certificate).

I take that as example. These unhandy writers then go on to muddle their readers with discussion of "systems" of inflation; of cancellation, of credit problems. And naturally their work is useless and merely spreads ignorance. Think, gentle reader, if the greasy fog in so concrete a science as economics is thus dense, what density is it likely to attain in metaphysics. Where is ethical discrimination to end or begin among us?

If only for the sake of understanding and valuating our own European past, we have need of the Master Kung.

And that is by no means our whole need. The fact that we have such a past, is but an encouragement. It is perhaps but a tentative reassurance that we have a chance of understanding part of the Orient.

The "value" of Confucius to the Modern World is not, I think we agree, limited to medicinal value for the Occident. There is visible and raging need of the *Ta Hio* in barbarous countries like Spain and Russia, but above all questions of emergency, of hypodermic injection or strait-jacket for fever patients and lunatics, there is also a question of milder and continuous hygiene.

No one has ever yet exhausted the wisdom of the forty-six ideograms of the first chapter. No one has ever yet attained so complete a wisdom that he can find no further nutriment in this *mantram*. And no one, least of all a twentieth-century American with only a superficial acquaintance with Oriental intuition and language, should aspire to emit the "last word" on this subject. I certainly cannot condense the *Ta Hio*. I have tried to present as much of it as I understand, free from needless clutteration of dead verbiage.

I am ready to wrestle in friendly manner over the words used even by S.V.V., but such contest would at this point obscure my main meaning. I hope some day to see a proper bilingual text, each ideogram with full explanation so that the American reader may have not merely the one side of the meaning which seems to one translator most imperative in a given passage, but one full meaning held in such restraint that a hierarchy of imperatives be not lost.

As in the Dantescan symbol for the universe truth is not lost with velocity, so an age-old intelligence is not lost in an era of speed. We are bedevilled with false diagnoses. We are obfuscated with the noise of those who attribute all troubles to irrelevant symptoms of evil. We are oppressed by powerful persons who lie, who have no curiosity, who smear the world and their high offices with Ersatz sincerity. His grace the

Wubbok of Wok dare not investigate this, that and the other, and so forth . . . Neither does so-and-so nor his colleague (protected by libel laws) *dare* read the *Ta Hio*.

Name, nomen, cognomen etc., dare not be left alone in a lighted room with this document. They cannot face the forty-six characters in the solitude of their library. All this testifies to the strength of the chapter and to their need of it. Men suffer malnutrition by millions because their over-lords dare not read the *Ta Hio*.

II

Gists ✒ Shorter Pieces and
Extracts from
Uncollected Essays

GISTS

BOURGEOIS

What the workingman becomes the moment he has the least opportunity.

SPENDING

The value of a nation's money depends, in the long run, on what the nation (which includes its inhabitants) spends its money FOR.

A SLAVE

A slave is one who waits for someone else to free him.

THIERS

Thiers borrowed from the bank at 3% when they were charging individuals 5 or 6%. He then got money for 1%. When he proposed to follow Andrew Jackson, the whole set of 'em, Orleanists, Bourbons, Bonapartists ganged up against him. Hence the lack of interest in Thiers on the part of professorial historians.

CRITICS

To be judged far more by their selections than by their palaver.

CERTAIN CIRCLES

Any proposal for reduction of government personnel causes a curious uneasiness in certain circles.

BOURGEOIS

A term of abuse applied by young writers to writers seven years older than themselves when the latter can afford seven francs more per day for hotel bills.

NATIONAL WELL BEING

No country can suppress truth and live well.

POISON

It is not arsenic in bottle and labelled that is dangerous, but arsenic in good soup.

LAW

The right aim of law is to prevent coercion, either by force or by fraud.

UTOPIA

Where every man has the right to be born free of debt and to be judged, in case of disagreement, by a jury capable of understanding the nature and implications of the charges against him.

ONE AT A TIME

Every man has the right to have his ideas examined one at a time.

USURY

Usury, a charge for the use of purchasing power, levied without regard to production, sometimes without regard even to the possibilities of production.

210

SOVEREIGNTY

Sovereignty inheres in the power to issue money, or to distribute the power to buy (credit or money) whether you have the right to do so or not.

CIVILIZATION

Civilization depends on local control of purchasing power needed for local purposes.

SHORTER PIECES AND EXTRACTS FROM UNCOLLECTED ESSAYS

Our Contemporaries

The *New Age* has, in a recent and gracious recognition of us, very greatly misrepresented our "tendency," not by a front attack, but by an exaggerated statement of our aloofness. Let it pass. The careful reader will read both us and our critic and make his own due adjustment.

In this melange of bouquets and brick-bats we make but our minimum acknowledge to the *New Age* when we indicate the growing prominence of that paper in England. The cause of this advance during the last four years is not far to seek. For several years prior to Armageddon, Mr. A. R. Orage was the sole editor of any London weekly who encouraged mental activity.

On every other weekly, from the hyper-grand-ducal *Saturday*, still clinging to King Charles the martyr and the divine right of ancestry; the arid *Spectator*, "written in London for the provincial and colonial audience"; the *Nation*, chief envoy of the Dublin lower-class to the English suburban back-parlour; to the *New Statesman*, last refuge of doctrinaire committees; the statistic Webbs, the haven of Shaw's worn out theories,—in every one of these papers a set point of view was demanded. To every possible question, for every possible situation in life, art or politics, there was a carefully prepared, "correct," opinion. The writer for these papers knew to a jot just what was the *proper* view in every possible case.

Suddenly hell broke loose, the normal and comfortable conditions of occidental life were suddenly cast into confusion. There were cases for which no ready made answer was available. On none of these antique staffs, or of these staffs suffering from premature senility (as the *New Statesman's*) was there anyone accustomed to form conclusions from external facts. Neither were their editors acquainted with people of "that sort," i.e., people accustomed to think from facts. They were "flummoxed"; for years they had carefully avoided that type of disturbing mind.

Only in the small company of "unorganized," uneven, unsystematized *New Age* writers was there any spark of this curious kind of activity.

Now in the year of grace 1918 let us hearken to G.B.S., to this amusing, uncultured old satirist, to this old chap who amused us fifteen years ago by his sparkling satiric levity (melange of Ibsen method considerably trivialized, Wilde (of the plays), diluted Nietzsche), to, in brief, G.B.S. who once had in his work no purpose save to amuse, and to incite people to the use of their mental faculties. Truly he has gone under the earth, he has taken up his abode with his forebears, he has entered the inactive, colourless limbo. He now complains that the *New Age* is "a hotch-potch, stimulating thought in general, but not prompting opinion like the *Nation* or the *New Statesman,* nor reflecting it like the *Spectator. . . .* Its freedom is the freedom of the explosive which is not confined to the cannon, spending itself incalculably in all directions."

Poor old Shaw, he was pretty far gone when he had to take

up with the Sidney Webbs, but here he exposes the white hairs of his long beard almost with indecency.

Also he is perhaps a little inaccurate. Mr. Orage's notes which are the back-bone of the *New Age*, are anything but a bolshevik chaos, (as Mr. Shaw admits). Shaw has incorporated himself in committees, and the most illustrative account (personal) of a recent Webbist committee meeting, reported the chairman (female) as follows: "And now we know what to do with the children, *and* with the mentally deficient, but what *shall* we do with the able-bodied men. . . .?"

That is the sum of these fabian crankist unhumanizing kulturbunds. Man is a unit to be dealt with via committees. Christ, with his embarrassing question regarding the value of the individual soul, has died in vain, etc.

And Mr. Shaw is out for "forming," no, for "promoting" opinion. His objection to the *New Age* can be boiled down to the complaint that the *New Age* does not insist on all its contributors having an "English public school point of view" (*Spectator*, and *Saturday Review*—this last, Eton age 13), or a board school vulgarian mechanico-committee-sub-Cambridge-heretics point of view (*New Statesman*, etc.); that the *New Age* has a cosmopolitan staff, that its oriental notes are done by a man who has lived in the Near East, that its continental notes are done by a continental, that its art notes are not done by a man with the same temperament as its writer on guild socialism, that its notes on Balkan literature are not harmonized with its criticisms of English music, etc., a condition of things not to be tolerated on any other British weekly publication.

A decided improvement has been noticeable in the *New Age* since the paper became Mr. Orage's exclusive property, and since he has been wholly free in its management. (*Little Review*, July, 1918)

214

Pastiche: The Regional (II)

Clemence Isaura endowed the local literary society of Toulouse a century after the troubadour vein was exhausted. The funds still insure her celebrity; but the form of endowment is typical of provincialism. It rewards not the best work submitted, but the best local product. The Jeux Floraux are in result as dull as any other high school performance, and have had the same literary value as other high school performance, despite their six centuries of history. The capital, the vortex, is that which draws intelligence into it, not that which builds up a wall for its own "protection"—i.e., isolation or "advantage." (*New Age*, June 26, 1919)

Pastiche: The Regional (VII)

It is the curse of our contemporary "mentality" that its general concepts have so little anchor in particular and known objects; that, for example, in a legislative body (read House of Commons) trying to make laws about coal, there is only one man who knows how coal lies in the rock.

·   ·   ·

A religion is damned, it confesses its own ultimate impotence, the day it burns its first heretic.

·   ·   ·

Spain lost its democracy, the *cortes* their liberties, in the time of Charles V. Liberties as easily acquired have been as easily lost—always for a bribe or a fanaticism. The American people have sold theirs for a mess of soda water and walnut sundaes; each race as it likes, and always in the name of salvation. (*New Age*, August 21, 1919)

Pastiche: The Regional (VIII)

Provincialism of time is as damned as provincialism of place; our evils come in great part from the fact that we are governed by men who take count of too few of the facts, as the poverty of modern art movements lies in the paucity of the mental reference of the artists.

In art and in politics this paucity of reference results in febrile stirs and excursions; legislator and artist alike are over-excited by a phenomenon because they have no means of judging the frequency or infrequency of its occurrence. The rare faculty and the significant datum are lost in the sea of clichés. (*New Age*, August 28, 1919)

Pastiche: The Regional (IX)

The Machiavellian circle occurs; the man of goodwill may find himself first on one side and then on the other of any given dilemma, first for concentration, then for freedom or for decentralisation; but this is not merely the "swing of the pendulum" cliché of opportunism. (*New Age*, September 11, 1919)

Pastiche: The Regional (XV)

At least two factors in the "social question" have been insufficiently recognised, or have at any rate lacked sufficiently sharp verbal definition. Luxury exists as a function; one does not deny that it is abused, but one ascribes the failure of many revolutionary parties to their failure to recognise it, by plain letter and proclamation, as a beneficent part of the social machine. The simple expedient of sacking the West End gets no one any further; any baboon can sack; the function of luxury is to set a model for living; the luxury of one age becomes the convenience of the next.

It is the duty of a sane manufacturing system to overproduce every luxury which tends to increase the comforts and amenities of existence—to overproduce until these things are within every man's reach. No man will get the full force of this until he has read *Arabia Deserta*. The function of an "aristocracy" is largely to criticise, select, castigate luxury, to reduce the baroque to an elegance. For this there is need of only a limited number of functionaries; as there is need of only a limited number of "tasters" in the tea trade, or of smellers in perfume manufactories. A fine model of life, as of architecture, or in the arts, has its value, and any real system of sociology, as opposed to a doctrinaire system, must recognise this value and its nature. (*New Age*, October 30, 1919)

The Revolt of Intelligence

A League of Nations backed up by force is a danger; its chief danger is that every local dispute may produce a world conflict. A League of Nations with the power in the hands of a small committee appointed by Governmental inner cliques in each nation is a peril; on the basis of the *New Age's* demonstration of the recession of power from the people. (*New Age*, January 8, 1920)

Credit and the Fine Arts

One recognises that there is no functioning coordinated civilization in Europe; democracy has signally failed to provide for its best writers; aristocratic patronage exists neither in noun nor in adjective. The function of an aristocracy is selection; illiterate motor-owners are incapable of that function.

. . .

The only thing one can give an artist is leisure in which to work. To give an artist leisure is actually to take part in his creation.* (*New Age*, March 30, 1922)

Definitions

1. A good state is one which impinges least upon the peripheries of its citizens.

2. The function of the state is to facilitate the traffic, i.e., the circulation of goods, air, water, heat, coal (black or white), power, and even thought; and to prevent the citizens from impinging on each other.

3. The aim of state education has been (historically) to prevent people from discovering that the classics are worth reading. In this endeavour it has been almost wholly successful.

Nature of war depends entirely on the state of civilization of the parties contending. Nature of social revolution depends entirely on state of ignorance and barbarism of elements cast to the top.

The only way a nation can render itself safe is by civilizing its neighbours. The duty of an aristocracy is to educate its plebs; failure in this simple precaution means its own bloody destruction. History presents no more imbecile a series of spectacles than the conduct of aristocracies. Without whom civilization is impossible. (*Der Querschnitt*, January, 1925)

* Leisure is time plus money, or at any rate time without monetary worry.—E. P., 1959.

218

The Public Convenience

The republic, the res publica means, or ought to mean "the public convenience." When it does not, it is an evil, to be ameliorated or amended out of, or into decent, existence. Detailed emendment is usually easier, and we await proof that any other course is necessary. But in so far as America is concerned, we should like to know whether there is *any* mental activity outside the so called "revolutionary elements," the communescents, etc.

At present, in that distressed country, it would seem that neither side ever answers the other; such ignoring, leading, in both cases, to ignorance. I should like a small open forum in which the virtues or faults of *either* side might be mentioned without excessive animus.

Both Fascio and the Russian revolution are interesting phenomena; beyond which there is historic perspective. Herrin and Passaic are also phenomena, and indictments.

The capitalist imperialist state must be judged not only in comparison with unrealized utopias, but with past forms of the state; if it will not bear comparison with the feudal order; with the small city states both republican and despotic; either as to its "social justice" *or* to its permanent products, art, science, literature, the onus of proof goes against it.

The contemporary mind will have to digest this concept: the state as convenience.

The antithesis is: the state as an infernal nuisance.

As to our "joining revolutions" etc. It is unlikely. The artist is concerned with producing something that will be enjoyable even after a successful revolution. So far as we know even the most violent bolchevik has never abolished electric light globes merely because they were invented under another regime, and by a man intent rather on his own job than on particular propaganda.

(Parenthesis: a great deal of rubbish is emitted by "economists" who fail to distinguish between transient and permanent goods. Between these there are graduations.

1. Transient: fresh vegetables
                luxuries
                jerry-built houses
                fake art
                pseudo books
                battleships.
2. Durable: well constructed buildings
                roads, public works, canals.
                intelligent afforestation.
3. Permanent: scientific discoveries
                works of art
                classics.

That is to say these latter can be put in a class by themselves, as they are always in use and never consumed; or they are, in jargon, "consumed" but not destroyed by consumption.

Note: the shyster is always trying to pass off class 1 for class 2 or 3. This is, naturally, bad economics. Just as the writings of Keynes, Pigou, and the rest of their tribe are bad economics. end of parenthesis.)

The artist, the maker is always too far ahead of any revolution, or reaction, or counter-revolution or counter-re-action for his vote to have any immediate result; and no party program ever contains enough of his program to give him the least satisfaction. The party that follows him wins; and the speed with which they set about it, is the measure of their practical capacity and intelligence. Blessed are they who pick the right artists and makers. (*The Exile*, No. 1, Spring, 1927)

Summary of the Situation

The American view is expressed in the Harding memorial postage stamp. The American view as expressed by the leading American intelligentsia is that America is *the* most colossal monkey house and prize exhibit that the astonished world has yet seen; and that for this reason one shd. delight in the spectacle; and that as spectacle it is unrivalled and diverting. Not being a descendent of M. le Marquis de Sade, or a follower of the, I believe, Hungarian Massoch, I am unable to appreciate this form of pleasure. The old world view is that one is foolish to disturb one's leisure by taking thought or action, even to enquire into the possibility of saving a few fragments from the disjecta, or of starting a new plantation. Never having met an angel I am unable to define their fear-states or to say where they would rush. (*The Exile*, No. 1, Spring, 1927)

Prolegomena

The drear horror of American life can be traced to two damnable roots, or perhaps it is only one root: 1. The loss of *all* distinction between public and private affairs. 2. The tendency to mess into other peoples' affairs before establishing order in one's own affairs, and in one's thought. To which one might perhaps add the lack in America of any habit of connecting or correlating *any* act or thought to *any* main principle whatsoever; the ineffable rudderlessness of that people. The principle of good is enunciated by Confucius; it consists in establishing order within oneself. This order or harmony spreads by a sort of contagion without specific effort. The principle of evil consists in messing into other peoples' affairs.

Against this principle of evil no adequate precaution is taken by Christianity, Moslemism, Judaism, nor, so far as I know, by *any* monotheistic religion. Many "mystics" do not even aim at the principle of good; they seek merely establishment of a parasitic relationship with the unknown. The original Quakers may have had some adumbration of the good principle. (But no early Quaker texts are available in this village.) (*The Exile*, No. 2, Autumn, 1927)

The Arts

What largely ails the "arts" is unemployment. If painters would paint on walls instead of scraps of paper their work wd. not so easily become prey of speculators, and at fifty an artist wd. not find his most bitter competitors (in the market) the people who had bought his first work. (*The Exile*, No. 3, Spring, 1928)

Desideria

Quite simply: I want a new civilization. We have the basis for a new poetry, and for a new music. The government of our country is hopelessly low-brow, there are certain crass stupidities in administration that it is up to the literate members of the public to eradicate. Voila tout.

I say "new" civilization, I don't know that I *care* about its being so different from the best that has been, but it must be *as good* as the best that has been. It can't possibly be the *same*, so why worry, novelty is enforced (ineluctable as the post-Joycians call it). We have a new building material, we have several new media, whatever they are worth in themselves they have an effect on the consciousness. If you have a thousand architects of great talent working ten hours a day, you can not exhaust the new possibilities of steel structure. If you have a hundred musicians of genius working half the day and all night, you can not exhaust the new impulse in music. Why worry? There is plenty of work to be done.

(Parenthesis: No, dearie, when I say: the basis for a new poetry, I don't mean the vers libre movement as it was in the year 1912.) (*The Exile*, No. 3, Spring, 1928)

Drive Back the Government

The job of America for the next twenty years will be to drive back the government into its proper place, i.e. to force it to occupy itself solely with things which are the proper functions of government. (*The Exile*, No. 4, Autumn, 1928)

Peace

There are certain *known* causes of war, or let us say there are certain perfectly well-known forces that constantly work toward war. "Foundations" etc. supposed to be labouring for peace would do well to stop studying the "effects of war" (e.g. "Early Effects of the European War upon the Finance, Commerce and Industry of Chile." List of Pubctns. Carnegie Endowment for International Peace, Sept. 1, p. 17) and study the causes.

The known causes of war are:

1. Manufacture and high pressure salesmanship of munitions, armaments etc.

2. Overproduction and dumping, leading to trade friction, etc., strife for markets etc.

3. The works of interested cliques, commercial, dynastic and bureaucratic.

The useful research, in fact the only research that is not almost a sabotage of intentions of peace foundations would consist in contemporary (not retrospective) i,e, up to the minute gathering and distribution of information re/ these activities—thru commercial channels or thru any other.

Where retrospection is necessary or commodious, the life of Sir Basil Zaharoff wd. be a fascinating document, any well informed record of the exact procedures followed by Vickers or Krupp, in getting off their products onto "les nations jeunes," of passing the guns into China or other areas of absorbtion wd. not need painful distribution. Needless to say the individual unsubsidized author is in less advantageous position to gather such data than a whole staff of paid researchers with a ten million dollar endowment behind them.

Probably we need a repentent Machiavelli, a private secretary to Messrs Creusot to tell how the wiggle is waggled. Too bad Carnegie is dead, *he* might have seen the point of this argument, as it is we must depend for action on Dr. Nicholas Butler, Dr. Nicholas Murray Butler.* (*The Exile*, No. 4, Autumn, 1928)

Open Letter to Tretyakow

I begin this letter with diffidence. It is generally supposed that the contemporary Russian (whether author or commissar) is too proud to answer questions or to give instruction to anyone who has not already declared an unquestioning and more than religious faith in the allwisdom of whoever happens for the moment to be in command of the Soviet State. I have read Tretyakow's "Report" with interest.

Having landed in Europe with 80 dollars and having, for a number of years thereafter, had considerable difficulty in finding work that wd. pay me a living wage I feel that Mike

* See Appendix, p. 281.

224

Gold's statement that I came to Europe "as the Russian Grand Dukes used to come to Europe before the war" should be somewhat qualified. My gross earnings from 1914 to 1915 were £42/10 (forty two pounds sterling ten shillings). I can not feel that this corresponds to a *pre-war* grand duke's allowance. I think that the difference must in some way have affected my outlook.

I do not think that the more intelligent American and European authors have advocated anti-bolchevik activities in Russia. I think there is a great deal of doubt as to whether anything like the Russian revolution is possible, advisable or necessary for either the U.S.A. or for Western Europe.

I can not see that a course of action suitable or necessary where there "are not enough specialists" can be applied to a community where there is a superfluity of specialists. "We" live in a community where everybody tries to do too much work. If and when we let machines do the work there is more leisure than people will use.

McAlmon and plenty of other American writers have worked on farms before, after and during their writing. There is nothing new for us in a writer's living the life he writes of.

In fact he is likely to be laughed at if he doesn't.

Frost farmed and wrote and was taken over into the educational system.

Tretyakow wrote, became a kolchoznik and was "charged with cultural work."

His article commands attention largely because he is the "author of Roar China" but there is nothing in the article that indicates any other reason for its not having been written by any teacher.

What he does in the kolchos could be done by a teacher who was not an author.

"Our" situation as American European authors is that all

the possible jobs on councils and in "cultural work" have been filled by teachers and that there is nothing whatever left for us to do but to perform extra, voluntary inspections at our own risk and charge.

No serious author outside Russia could be found arguing that there is any subject whatsoever that can possibly be "too vulgar" to need his attention. It is only the dilettantes who fail to take an interest in "class war, socialistic construction etc."

I strongly differ with Tretyakow's remarks about the Russian "classic authors," or any other writers on "l'histoire morale contemporaine" merely "delighting one" etc.

I shd. say that for the non-russian the reading of these pre-revolution authors usually left the reader with a conviction that there was something very wrong in Russia and that it needed alteration. I shd. say that all writing that describes contemporary life accurately is like a physician's diagnosis of disease.

Even Disraeli, a British Prime Minister wrote a novel calling attention to the conditions of British coal mines.

Even if not written with a social purpose, a serious, i.e. accurate realist novel is almost sure to have a social effect.

It is largely because of this "bourgeois" pre-revolution Russian Literature that the rest of the world was in no way surprised at the Russian Revolution and that most of us thought it was due. A mere study of Marxian theories would not have told us very much about mujiks.

The things that became plain to Tretyakow have become plain, I think, to most of us. But we are situated in a different milieu and the subjects for our profound study are possibly different and are certainly difficult.

For example: You can not "introduce" a village tractor in a community where each farmer already has a tractor of his own. Neither can you use machinery intended for wide fields

226

on a plain, for the cultivation of an Italian hill side having a terrace fifteen feet high for every ten feet of cultivated surface. Etc.

Tretyakow's article commands respect.

THE DIFFERENCE

The difference between propagandist literature and "serious literature" is that propagandist literature starts with a ready made solution. It belongs to the era of theology and dogma.

Every piece of serious literature starts with a free examination of the data, if the result happens to confirm the opinion of any party, the work of literature then acquires a propagandist value vastly exceeding any that a work starting with propagandist purpose can have.

Every such work is a new corroboration.

A DIFFERENTIATION

I see no need for a revolution in the mere forms and mechanism of American (U.S.A.) govt. I see many reasons for a social and intellectual revolution. At the present moment the American people are too hog lazy and too unfathomly ignorant to use the mechanism they have inherited to better economic and intellectual advantage. They have practically no "aristocracy," their idle well-to-do have practically no intellectual interests and no will to perform any useful "cultural work." But this state of mind is not confined to the well-to-do. It is to be found among the friends and intimates of Al Capone and the other prominent Americans who wd. find their way to the White House if a political revolution occurred.

There is for the moment, the year, the decade, nothing for the serious American author to do but to learn what he can

227

and to struggle to instruct those who know even less than he does. (*Front*, February, 1931)

Hunger Fighters

This book* begins with a bit of sound Douglasism cited from Jas. Mackenzie. Re cultural heritage: "all great enterprises are based on work that has been done by individuals whose past is lost in obscurity."

De Kruif, as historian, is concerned with leaving a just record of heroisms that have solved vital problems of food production. He demands a cut of glory for his heroes. One is conscious of men in action, but it is correlated action, a handful of underpaid men working at apparently tremendous pressure surrounded by ignorance and stupidity but at least conscious of one another.

One wonders whether these scientists participate in any general intellectual life, or whether the whole idea of a nation's having an intellectual life is alien to the American people; in fact, a nasty latinism, not quite proper, almost indecent.

And if such is the case, one might also wonder which racial stock carried this disposition into the aridity of that continent.

Mark Carleton enriched America by countless millions. His salary was 3,000 dollars a year. He was put out of his mangy little job during the reign of that priceless Administrator and second-come Jesus, Mr. Woodrow Wilson.

Half the American wheat crop now comes from varieties that Carleton introduced. It would be difficult to say to whom this wealth ethically belongs. One might suppose that this was a value based on cultural heritage.

When we come to the pellagra chapters we have definitely

* *Hunger Fighters*, by Paul de Kruif.

228

an economic factor in medicine. This disease comes from poverty alone. During the decades *after* the scientists had determined the cause, there has been a constant scientific fight to find some remedy cheaper than the cheapest food.

Carleton's life is a perfect illustration of the Anglo-Saxon ethics of his era. It seems quite possible that no epoch of history will arouse in future historians quite the nausea of the century stretching from 1834 to 1934.

There is a literary, even a stylistic, cure for evil. I mean that the men who are responsible for reducing printed language to a non-conducting paste of vague phrases are as worthy of hell as those who pay them for this villainy.

The early marquis wheat is the result of the activities of a conglomeration of men; the collaboration is so subtle that no patent law could possibly cover it. It is not even the result of a series of intentional acts, chance enters the compost. You can't catalogue the fountain of value under any personal heading. (*New English Weekly*, February 22, 1934)

Peace Pathology

It may be mere chance that I have never met an honest pacifist. It may be that Nic Butler is not consciously an accomplice of Baron de Wendel. It may be that all things are due to chance.

The place to cure war is in the domestic economy of the nation.

Pacifism is subsidized. I have never heard of any pacifist organization that will face facts. The Carnegie Foundation persistently turns its attention away from facts.

Is pacifism merely a symptom of lust for power, manifested by the weak and peeving?

At any rate it is a dishonest movement. It is a subsidized

movement. Christianity resigned when the Church surrendered economics. The medieval church distinguished between right and wrong in the economic domain. The ecclesiastical bureaucracy withdrew tactfully from any such endeavour. The baked meats were too rich to risk on a mere question of righteousness. (*New Democracy*, April 15, 1934)

To the Historical Society of America

Change in University life is so slow as to be almost undiscoverable. Once the normal graduate has obtained a steady job it seems to require inhuman cruelty to suggest that he use his mind in any way whatsoever. Possibly my own student experience still indicates the condition of method in teaching American history.

Despite the fact that I had a most excellent professor, who in 1901 and '02 was considered "very advanced," it now appears to me that the history of the U.S. has been very greatly obscured. One most flagrant negligence has been leaving the Van Buren autobiography unpublished until 1920. But the ignorance of all the economic history of America is wholly inexcusable. I am writing to ask whether any section of your society, or any group that might be formed among individual members, is willing in any way to collaborate in an effort to connect the teaching of history with reality.

Reality for the purpose of this question can be defined as the accumulated results of the historic process now felt or discernible in the year 1935.

Without going into personalities, a sufficient number of highly placed and highly esteemed persons, from the Pope and the Dean of Canterbury to Lord Tankerville, Basil Blackett and Dr. Soddy, onward and outward, have, whatever their divergence of views as to economic law, concurred in branding the system emitted from chairs of Economics during the past century as a mass of lies, confusions, perversions and general hog wash.

Notwithstanding which, various men are still kept on as professors who have been discredited time and again as to their science and in some cases it might not be excessive to say, as to their motives.

I should welcome correspondence on this subject. (*New Democracy*, February 15, 1935)

Private Worlds

Private Worlds (by Phyllis Bottome), widely known in the U.S.A., insufficiently known in England, a distinctly Adlerian product, is as good a "slide" of the psychotherapeutic world as we are likely to get.

Admittedly, "all the doctors and everyone who goes in for the study" are "abnormal." Take the cases in the novel, as representative or as illustrative of the usual thing:

1. Shell shock cases, result of war, which was a result of monetary system.

2. Female lunatic, neurosis due to loss of male during war; due to finance.

3. Doctor, under financial pressure, need of job.

4. Female doctor, rebuilt after war calamities.

5. Superintendent, plagued by sister, impelled by greed.

6. Doctor, apart from need of feeding family and acute economic pressure in private life, finding the whole of his research dependent on wangling appropriations.

7. Inferiority complex and embarrassments of the children of the rich.

8. (Or 8 to 80), neuroses of secondary and tertiary economic causes; sex suppressions of indirect (or direct) eco-

nomic source, the whole neomalthusian whirligig, fear of this, that and the other.

The effect of reading any vivid work on psychiatry, or at any rate the initial sensation to anyone sane enough to dislike it, is that they themselves are "going bugs," the whole subject is a quagmire, to the extent that while one is seriously considering insanity one must, or at least is very likely to, give disproportionate importance to the subjective, and to lose all, or too much, of one's sense of relative importance of the total external world.

Some few explorers must, doubtless, go down, and explore these submarine areas, but it is a specialist's job. It is especially a specialist's job until the proportion is established between economics and psychiatry.

If a civilized man today cuts his finger, he swobs on a little iodine (when possible) and goes on about his affairs uninterrupted, he doesn't normally set up as amateur bacteriologist to see what he can grow in the fissure. (*New English Weekly*, May 2, 1935)

So-Called "Writers" Congress

The piffling snobism of thirty incompetent writers who set themselves up as better than an equal number of non-writers is unjustified by anything I have found in *Das Kapital*. The idea that Marx expected all human inventiveness to end on the day of his death, is also apochryphal.

Among all these people, not one has conceived a communism developed from the state of America in 1930 as distinct from one growing out of black Russian superstition, mujiks and mouldy Czars.

Nowhere among the American Marxians has there been even a murmur such as: bring your Marxism up to date.

Sure, let's have a congress, and lets have the admission focussed onto

A. writers, meaning people who have written something, or show signs of being likely to do so.

B. Americans who know at least a little American history.

C. If the congress proposes to reform society, let at least the executive committee contain a few members who know something of economic history, outside the dogmas of some one bigoted sect. (*New Democracy*, May 15, 1935)

Cromwell

By great wisdom sodomy and usury were seen coupled together. If there comes ever a rebirth or resurrection of Christian Church, one and Catholic, a recognition of divinity as

La somma sapienza e il primo amore

it will come with a recognition and an abjuration of the great sin *contra natura*, of the prime sin against natural abundance.

Art registers the state of man's soul (or whatever you want to call the compendium of his faculties). The grossening and fattening of European architecture was the contemporary imprint of man's diseased condition with the fall of medieval civilization.

John Buchan, although professing no very clear economic ideas, has been fairly clear on pages 8/9 of his "Cromwell"* as to the decline of English mentality from Bucer and Latimer toward the decadence.

It shows in England's versification. These things move parallel. Spectamur agendo. From all the beauty that was full of light, from all the medieval respect for intelligence, the sanity that could see the theologian as athlete of the spirit, this curve descends in ratio with the rise of old-testament-olatry, with

* Oliver Cromwell, by J. Buchan.

the commodity theory of money, and the elevation of usury to pre-eminence, with the cant about purity, the kowtow to sterility.

Thomas Cromwell, born about 1485, travelled and learnt international banking, settled in London as merchant and money-lender. Zealous for publication of Bible in England, "cared nothing for religion." P. 56, "the difficulty was money." (*New English Weekly*, June 6, 1935)

Towards Orthology

P. Sargent Florence lends triviality to an otherwise almost uniformly serious collection of brochures.* He is a clever playboy with a smartly barbered style. In the course of pirouettes and entrechats he does define "orthodox economics" as a trifling card game, limited by the rules of the gaming room. That being so, it is not worth scientific attention.

Kitson said: "The first two professors who started using my work in class room, were promptly dismissed from their jobs."

The case of Scott Nearing at the University of Pennsylvania might perhaps shed a little more light on America under the yoke of Mark Hanna and company.

The "Psyche" series represents the only serious attempt in England during 14 years, to maintain a serious focus of intellectual life.

I may seem to be blaming Mr. Florence for being a butterfly instead of a draught horse, but the butterfly flutters over a dung heap. His brochure was published in 1927 so that attention now given it can scarcely be ascribed to malevolence. On page 65 he does fairly blow the gaff on the Cambridge economic curriculum.

* Psyche Miniatures, General Series, *Economics of Human Behaviour*, by P. Sargent Florence. *The Standardization of Error*, by V. Staffansson.

234

On page 76, I am impelled to enquire why Orthologists of all people should use the term "philosopher" when they would be better advised to say "writer on abstract topics," or one who discusses general questions, showing no specific and detailed knowledge. Mr. B. Russell ranks along with Hugh Cecil, among English institutions.

So far (up to page 78) I have treated Florence with amiability. His suggestions for terminology are contemptible. Nothing can be worse for honesty than to make what is plain man's sense into nonsense, and to erect a new set of meanings either diametrically opposed to the daily plain sense, or just enough off it to permit the Lloyd Georges, political quacks, camouflagers of vile politics, and usurer's tricksters, to be elevated into Educational bureaucrats.

Were it not buried in this highbrow series, Staffansson's *The Standardization of Error* would be selling like Ed. Wallace on the book-stalls. This is an uproariously delightful volume, the sort of thing one can't read to one's self with anyone in the room, but continually has to communicate. (*New English Weekly*, June 20, 1935)

History and Ignorance

History that omits economics will not eternally be accepted as anything but a farce or a fake. It, as a matter of fact, has not always passed as enlightenment. The real foci of power have never swallowed this sort of tosh. *Vide*, let us say, the Venetian ambassador, Barbon Morosini's report on John Law, to the Venetian Senate, Jaunary 28, 1723.

Somewhere or other, perhaps in Barney Baruch's private files, there is or has been some history. Zaharoff once knew some history. An intelligentzia that accepts anything less is merely an ignoranzia with an Ersatz lion's skin draped over its ass ears.

"Because no one
can sell the moon
to the moon."

As an historian I have a legitimate curiosity as to why so little attention has been give to economics as a factor in incitement to war (direct or indirect) or why so little curiosity has been shown as to economic determinism as a factor in cause of hostilities; or why American education so tamely accepts titular heads whose cause of being is wrapped in so many veils.

Should a National Academy have or not have intellectual curiosity, should it stimulate inquisitive minds? Should the education of the elite be focussed solely or predominantly on the manufacture of robots and tame rabbits?

Should a national academy desire a correlation of active knowledge? Should it take any action to promote it? Has the American Academy ever shown the faintest interest in living thought? And if so, who hides the documents that would prove it?

What percentage of American college presidents owe their advancement to complacency?

In the stratosphere on a pink cloud we observe the era when someone will look into American education and find it vapid; into American "foundations" and find them putrid.

The best of us can not avoid contagion. Major Douglas himself, can resist strictly economic lies, but somewhere comes the moment of fatigue or inattention. I have known it and I know no man who has not. By sheer dint of repetition we have all of us imbibed, absorbed prejudice, if not about the matters we were specifically intent on, certainly on periphery matter.

The teaching of literature was so inefficient in my young

days (and probably still is), that I have had to find out at 49 what I might perfectly well have been told at 17. Dr. Rouse's correspondence during the past months, shows that he has not escaped similar experience.

The intelligentzia do not get ideas, they merely get the spare parts of ideas. Put it another way: cranks and doctrinaires try to propagate specific details of a system often without understanding the system to which these details belong, let alone the relation of that system to any other.

A work of art, any serious work vivifies a man's total perception of relations.

It makes no difference whether the work is a Bach fugue or a drawing by Dürer or the movement of words in the Odyssey.

Naturally the bastards who do not want truth, who do not want a democratization of the perception of relations, howl and weep whenever poetry emerges from the lavender sachet and bric-à-brac category.

There are even in England people so low they want to eliminate the whole major domain of writing—let us say, the major domain of the *Divina Commedia*—from the scope of the poets.

This degradation has been fostered by insularity, by the reading of an anaemic list of purely local mediocrities—Wordsworth, Tennyson, etc., and their local contemporaries. It obviously plays into the hands of people who wish to maintain slavery, and to whom any perception of truth re social or any other kind of relation, is a menace. (*New English Weekly*, July 25, 1935)

The Movement of Literature

The general nit-wittedness of books by contemporaries who do not perceive the economic factor becomes more and more apparent. Not that one expects them to write about econ., but that novel writing being properly the history of contemporary customs, an ignorance of the root of these customs produces a corresponding idiocy in the writing. A man who don't know how life is, and why things happen, does not become a writer of interesting stories. This is entirely separate from the acceptance of any dogma. It is not the refusal of particular ideas about economics, but the absence of curiosity that paralyzes the writing of these left-overs, this debris of earlier literary eddies and ripples.

A single item, such as which big British cake firms are using Chinese liquid eggs, or "Messrs. N. M. Rothschild are ready to issue warrants against deposited fine silver," is of more interest and its collection shows more literary ability, than a rehash of a rehash of a rehash of an imitation of an imitation Maupassant story, or of a hind-side-before pseudo post Joycean sentence void of contents but trying (15 years late) to get in before the death of the fashion.

Literary ability is not something less than or lower than journalistic ability, it is something solider and more durable.

There is plenty of room for another Flaubert. That is one pleasure of literature. By the time one record of *L'Histoire Morale Contemporaine* has been written, there is already a different contemporaneity. Flaubert saw "l'art industriel," he created the real Marxist literature and the Marxist (alleged Marxist) didn't discover it.

The America of Wilson, Harding, Coolidge, Hoover offers plenty of chance for a Flaubert, tho' the subject matter is nearer Dostoievsky's idiot than to human record.

The lack of curiosity, the lack of any desire for knowledge, festers throughout the whole flaccid English and American organism.

I remember Hugo Rennert remarking on some ballyhoo

238

about "the plant," the U. of Penn. "plant" was, according to the ballyhoo, not to lie idle. Rennert observed on the part of himself and faculty: "But damn it *we* are the plant." Naturally the gombeen men weren't ready for any such outbreak of real humanism.

The idea of an American university being a live and active component in the intellectual life of America is taboo.

There will be no restoration of American manhood, until the citizen insists on his rights under the constitution, among which that his representatives in congress govern the currency.

For fifty years the traitors, wormed into our educational system, have kept the significance of this right, from their pore pupils.

(New Democracy, October 15, 1935)

The Individual in His Milieu

Twenty years ago little magazines served to break a monopoly, to release communication, mainly about letters, from an oppressive control, and they now wither on the stalk because they refuse to go on from where the late Henry James was interrupted.

H.J. perceived the *Anagke* of the modern world to be money; he thought he ought to "go down town," and found that he couldn't. He left, for posthumous publication, an unfinished meditation on the money-acquiring faculty. Proust was, by comparison, an insignificant snob, with no deep curiosity as to the working of modern society, apart from his own career in it.

The diseased periphery of letters is now howling that literature and poetry in especial, should keep within bounds. I find this limitation entitled "respect itself," which phrase is perverted to mean that literature should eschew the major field by omitting and leaving untackled a great deal of the subject matter that interested such diverse writers as Propertius, Dante and Lope de Vega.

The *Anagke* of our time is money. Cf. Columbus' rhapsody in Lope de Vega's *Nuevo Mundo*. Curiosity sank very low during the XIXth century. Marx and La Tour du Pin were equally deaf, dumb and blind to money. La Tour du Pin managed to write a whole chapter in denunciation of usury without looking into its substance.

Economics in our time is where medicine was when professors studied the subject in Aristotle and refused to look at dissecting tables. The history of money is yet to be written. Even the scattered fragments are comprehensible only to men who start clean, that is with observation of present day facts, and refuse to lie down until they have studied the relations and causes of actual present phenomena.

Literature that tries to avoid the consideration of causes remains silly bric-à-brac.

The archaeologist and serendipidist can wander back through Claudius Salmasius and find the known beginnings of usury entangled with those of marine insurance, sea lawyers, the law of Rhodes, the disputed text of Antonius Pius on the limits of his jurisdiction. Even then the dealers in metal appeared to be privileged over other merchants, and the insurance risk mainly paid by the takers of greater risk. Vast mines of anecdote lie still unexploited.

Apart from the eminent Claudius Salmasius; we offer the restrospector and serendipidist, the labours by and of Gabriele Biel, doctissimo viro or vir doctissimus, Francisco Curtio, Albert Bruni, Antonii Solae, if not as enlightenments at least to show that human curiosity does not set sail for the first time into these regions.

The revivers of Hebrew mythology lose interest when they

come to Leviticus. The Roman Empire may have risen via the substitution of land usury for sea usury. The "Church" declined and fell on this issue. Historians have left the politics of Luther and of Calvin in the blurr of great ignorance.

Gesell was right in thanking his destiny that he had begun his study of money unclogged by university training. But as focus in 1935? What other possible subject could bring together the Pope of Rome, a Scotch engineer in the orient, the English Church Assembly, a German business man in the Argentine, a physicist, a biologist, a medical journalist, an orthologist and historian of philosophy, and the present practitioner of versification?

Volia l'estat divers d'entre eulx!

The only class excluded being blind journalists, second rate writers, literary hangers-on and their ambience.

The little magazines rose with the need for cleansing our language, in the domain of logic and philosophy, this meant the elimination of false dilemmas and indefinite middles, in the domain of morals it was basic and essential. Until a man can speak of one thing or one category of actions as distinct from another it is useless for him to try to define right and wrong.

The Church slumped into a toleration of usury. Protestantism as factive and organized, may have sprung from nothing but pro-usury politics. And the amazing history of the XIXth century is summed up in: "Marx found nothing to criticize in money." That phrase applied to all the latter half of one XIXth century. It applied down to 1915 when Gesell opened fire. We have yet to improve on Gesell's criteria:

"He would judge money not by its chemical analysis, but by the number of unemployed and by the unsold inventories. These he regarded as the real tests of monetary efficiency.

With regard to the compilation of an index number, he would have the relative importance of each commodity determined according to the number of men employed in its production."*

I attempted in my *ABC* to proceed in more or less Euclidean fashion to list the essential elements of the whole problem, i.e., those few elements without which no economic system can be.

The question for our time is: "What is money?" After reading and writing and before arithmetic, or even before reading and writing the first human instruction, in our time, should lie in this query. We have seen an American administration tricked because it did not observe a transition from pure mathematics, the pure science of arithmetic (numbers) to numeration in terms of money (i.e., to the numeration of something unstable).

The appalling decadence of architecture, stone cutting, art forms after 1500 etc., the loss of moral and terminological clarity, the reduction of philosophy to mere lackeyship toward material sciences all of them run contemporary with each other, and in that barrocco was lost the distinction between usury and partaggio.

Whatever Gesell saw, he did not make clear or emphasize Marx's failure to focus the source of value and he, Gesell, did not proclaim the distinction between usury and the increment of association.

No economic system can neglect these fundamental dissociations, and no monetary system can rise above the status of gadget if it be not in concord with some order of thought, with some system of moral criteria.

If the present writer has been of any use, it may be found (bar competitors unknown to him) that he at least tried to summarize, lay out the essential elements in any economic

* *Stabilized Money*, by Irving Fisher, assisted by H. R. L. Cohrssen.

system, as you would find the elements and primary machines in the opening chapters of a text book on physics, and that the great mass of economic literature is either special pleading, special description beginning haphazard, talking of a state of things, or moving in vaguely chronological order.

Rabid doctrinaires, the extremely non-perceptive red left, attack Douglas because he leaves a bit of our civilization standing. Why philosophic communists haven't flocked to Douglas, and why canting levellers haven't flocked to Gesell is a mystery or would be if one failed to allow for the non-existence of philosophic communists, or for the lack of any real reasoning or intelligence among levellers (dominated by hate and envy and deficient in the greater part of the sensitive and perceptive gamut).

The truth about economics has had no warmer welcome than had a few simple and known facts about the tradition in metric and poetry during a couple of preceding decades. The parallel would be comic were is not freighted with tragedy, death, malnutrition, degradation of the national health in a dozen countries.

Nothing breaks cliché or will break any writer's use of it, save first-hand knowledge of individual phenomena. (And in another dimension: rien ne pousse à la concision comme l'abondance d'idées.)

In another eighty years a few people may begin to see that the present author's insistence on *Ideogrammic* method has not been mere picking daisies. Fenollosa saw the possibilities of a method. The effects of his vision were sabotaged right and left, and the small group of men comprising "the learned world" will some day feel a disgust for Paul Carus in particular.

You can study economics almost entirely as dissociation of ideas. It has not until now been so studied. For ten thousand bigots who quote the Bible on work, there is scarcely one who will, or can, quote it on usury.

You can not make good economics out of bad ethics. (*Criterion*, October, 1935)

The Acid Test

Any act has at least two dimensions, its motivation and its effect. The philosopher is probably less concerned with the external shape given an act by external causes and circumstances.

Shallow thinkers, poor mystics may wallow in a good deal of loose argument trying to judge the two dimensions as if they were one.

No man who has been writing for a quarter of a century can get all his philosophy or all his economics into one article. If a man be serious, almost anything he writes after 40 in a single essay must be judged in relation to its (per force absent) context. I have had one brief *ABC of Economics* published in England. I have always believed that a man should leave his religious or philosophic writing till the end of his life, as either subject demands his total accumulation of knowledge, not merely a few general ideas taught him in school. The "old philosopher," the "young zealot," are type ideas, and justifiable as such.

Confucius repels the lazy because he insists that the results of an action matter. Aristotle and Aquinas annoy sluggish minds by insisting that "nothing is without efficient cause."

Remy de Gourmont was a profane writer and his advice about one dissociation of ideas did not at once penetrate either theological, philosophical or economic thought.

The moment any man is sufficiently developed to assume a position in regard to the total consciousness of the universe (whether he regard it as a coordinated whole, or as merely so

244

many scattered sparks), whether he knows it or not, whether he wants it or will confess it or not, he has a religion.

A religion is incomplete, and an organized religion decays when it excludes from its domain any specific area of thought or action.

The mystic or moralist who excludes economic right and wrong from his scheme of things, is a shirker. (*Biosophical Review*, Winter, 1935)

Without a Distorting Lens

Frobenius in very concrete exposition, as Aristotle in general statements, insists that nothing is without efficient cause. If the art of a given time and race has defects, those defects are caused by something, not necessarily in control of the individual craftsman, however great his energy or fine his perception.

The perception is more likely to defect than the urge toward exteriorization. The cliché covers what nobody sees. Mr. Landseer was the godfather of the S.P.C.A., but had fits of homicidal mania toward the end of his life. He was, in fact, *of* his era.

A physician may like health above everything else in the universe, but must keep awake to disease.

There is, and abundantly, a place for an English literature that will look at England without a distorting lens, and that will try to see the various generations and strata, the temporal and social categories as phenomena objectively there to be studied by particulars and not simply shovelled into the already stated categories of a Marx, or even of an autocthonous Tennyson, though the latter would, or at least could, probably tell the unbiased reader more about England than any German or Russian.

England neglected Trollope for the same root cause that

she refuses Frobenius. A bandage grows into a wound if not changed, and after a time the sensitive child squeals if a tardily arrived doctor tries removing the bandage.

As witness I must say what I have seen; and I put it on record that when I got to England the men ten years older than Gosse were *simpatici*, and had a very much larger humanity than the men of E.G.'s generation. Note that Gosse's generation was *brought up* Victorian.

No need to deny the charm of life in the 1860's in viceregal lodges, where the paideuma was pre-Victorian and the culture tempered with Paris, in order to object to Lord Frederic's hat-trick about the bad taste of the era.* Lord Frederic's "world" went west 1914-19.

The hat-trick that concerns us more crucially is the trick of those reformers who want to impose a Marxian category on a less simple situation. When the white-collar denizen of the pinched London suburb, as distinct from the over-fed occupier of a somewhat clumsy but draught-proof and upholstered villa set in its own grounds, etc., but classed also among suburbanites, gets ready to look at himself and his ambience with something like Trollope's care, you may have a social reformation. At present, reform is blocked along all lines, both economic and social, by the desire to romanticize up or down.

As case of romanticizing down, observe the Cambridge student masquerading as moujik, as one of the proletariat or as communist.

A war, a social war, if you like a class war, exists between the British workingman and something or other. But it also exists between six or eight other English categories and something or other.

Several of these categories have almost ceased to exist, so subtle and penetrative has been the warfare.

* *The Days Before Yesterday*, by Lord Frederic Hamilton.

All these apparently unrelated pieces belong to a picture. Another bit or sliver of the design is my recollection that during twelve years of London almost the only Englishmen who knew anything were those who came back from the edges of Empire. Years later, I thought I had met an exception. It was in Vienna, but when his passport dropped on to the table it was inscribed "born in Pekin." (*New English Weekly,* May, 1936)

Race

Communism is Muscovite, Socialism is German and embodies the worst defect of that race, democracy with representation divided in respect to geographical areas is Anglo-American, and the corporate state is latin.

Resistence to any one of these modes of government by races whereto it is alien, is a sign of health, submission to any one of them by a race whereto it is alien, is a sign of decay.

Emergency measures in any country, or contingencies, are a temporal matter. The spread of civilization from the mediterranean basin is recognised by the most English of English historians. The Roman Senate preceded the Witanagemot.

As to Spain it can not be too frequently reiterated that Europe ends with the Pyrenees. Neither Spain nor Russia has ever contained more than a handful of civilized individuals. A cafe or two in Madrid, a little circle of Parisian or Dresden-ized people in one or two Russian cities.

Socialism as seen in England shows all the worst features of German stupidity. All the lacks which made the average German the butt of the Great Frederick's sarcasm. The mentality of the Webbs is not a sign of the German adjunct to civilization. The overplus of energy in Leibnitz or Bach has nothing to do with the desire to blow other people's noses and to have the collective nose blown by a committee of half wits. And that letch is the indelible mark and stigma of all organized socialism on earth, in hell, or in Hampstead.

The only spark of luminous reason in any socialist organization was lit in Paris, with the insertion of the non-teutonic, utterly non-Webbite, unDaltonian proposal embodied in "et les moyens d'echange." And the medium of exchange. To socialize the medium of exchange, the one factor in economic life which is subject to socialization without having committees of vegetarians, Wellses, carrot-eating Shaws, dogberries and endocrine deficients interfering with individual life, is French. It may be Gaelic. It was not a German idea.

The stupidity of Stalin & co. in not setting up a ticket system is no more crass than 40 or whatever years of dither in the British Socialist party. That party represents German mentality fogged by Baldwin's disease.

Socialism and communism are against the whole fibre and grain of the English and American people.

If Quincy Adams evolved a peculiarly Anglo-Saxon communism it was so pervaded by his personal genius that no Muscovite has ever heard of it, or will ever be capable of grasping Adams' reasons for proposing it in America. Adams' personal limitation and lack of timing are ample explanation as to why the idea did not go into action at the beginning of the last century.

Between a democracy wherein the representation is sectored geographically, and an organization of society, sprung from city organization in guilds, there are means of mutual comprehension. If centuries ago England learned law from Roman prudence, there may be means of understanding corporate entity in our time. To understand corporate entity or even the Corporate States does not imply "going fascist." Danger of tyranny exists wherever men pay taxes without protest and resentment.

248

The essential health of representative government consists in its being de facto representative. There was never any talk of decline of parliamentary government until imitations of it were set up in countries whereto it was racially alien.

To suppose that a difference of policy is due to mere ideology or mere reason, when it has its roots in blood, bone and endocrines, is to take a very superficial view of society, humanity and human coordinations.

There is no more danger of squadrismo, of a love of military drill (other than in an occasional serio-comic parade) in the U.S.A. or in England with an occasional coronation or Lord Mayor's show, than there is of legal requirement for Javanese temple dancing in Essex or Philadalphia for the entire populations thereof.

Typical Roman products have been the legion and the pageantry of the Catholic Church. The typical German expression of racialness was the Children's Crusade and the choral society. If the British square grew out of the legion, so much for a possibility of mutual comprehension.

It is latin to be disgusted with imbecility. It is not English to be disgusted with imbecility and therein is manifest one of the limitations of the English component in civilization.

The United States was founded intellectually with an injection of latin intelligence. This drove in, on a foundation of British law, which was itself compounded on and/or with latin prudence. (September, 1936?)

Sincerity

If a man starts with "God looking upon the heart," etc.; if his will be right; be righteous; he will not get into a tangle.

If he starts with the intention of avoiding anything that is not utter sincerity there will be very few clouds in his mind.

But if he begins by trying to do his partner, he will be able to spin most subtle and enveloping cobwebs.

We share the cost of a ship: we share in the cost of the cargo; and we take returns in proportion—this is good sport and good fellowship: partaggio.

But; we share in the expenses; I take a profit if there be one; but if the ship sinks I take your house.

That is a different arrangement: usura.

You can spin the cobwebs never so fine. The passion for security; the fear of the future; the mistrust of providence, are all human characteristics; they are all known frailties of humanity. Cosa di male?

Che l'intenzione per ragione vale, wrote Cavalcanti. You can carry this up to religion; you can carry it to the summits of poetry. We are not in a "cold thing like economics"; we are in the roots of human existence; in the heights of the spirit.

What did the man *will* when he did this? The Monte dei Paschi arose in the will to remake Siena; to re-establish the good life in Siena.

The Banca di San Giorgio rose in the determination to get money out of the people of Genoa.

There may be a whole PRAXIS of diagnosis; there may be borderline cases; there may be operations of every tint of grey; greyish; pinkish, or bluish grey; but the deep economist will keep his head clear.

Two kinds of mosquitoes. Strongest microscope shows no difference, but they lay different kinds of eggs. And one carries malaria. (*Fig Tree,* September, 1936)

On Theorists

Every dogma or doctrine arises in a particular ambience and is coloured by the vocabulary and ideology of that ambience.

You do not understand the founder's meaning until you study his words in relation to the time and place of their origin.

Studying Lenin one finds that his followers have not studied him very well. Study any great protagonist in history and you find his ideas diluted and then perverted by lesser men who mistake contingencies for ideas.

The idea in many cases remains hidden. Perhaps no idea ever is disengaged and understood until it goes into action. The deed is often "half understood" because armchair critics fail to see that the idea itself was not a "principle" but the comprehension of how a general or vague principle would and could apply in a given case.

Lenin's great idea seems to have escaped most of his professing followers. He told us that every revolutionary situation shd. be studied by itself. Parlour pink and street corner communists have tried for years to set up a Russia, dated 1917, in places where no Russia was or could be.

They insist on creating such a Russia, often out of most unsuitable materials, in order that they can apply the methods which served in 1916,17,18 against Romanoff and Kerensky. (1936?)

On Military Virtue

A nation which does not respect its literature is uncivil and the less it respects its literature the more quickly it rots. Literature at rock bottom is the right use of words.

A nation which is slack in distinguishing the meaning of words, and which tolerates the use of ambiguous phrases, rots.

A confusion between war and the military virtues is a very grave confusion. The military virtues are a possession so precious that it is almost worth a war to preserve them. No soldier makes war. Armies do not make war. Fear makes war;

economic pressure makes war, and men make war when they are in no personal danger. That is why my dislike of professional pacifists scarcely permits me to name them.

In 1927 Count Mensdorf the head of the Austrian section of the Carnegie Foundation for Peace, sent to the Central headquarters of the Foundation a list of the causes of war (the economic causes of war) and a few suggestions as to fruitful lines of legal study. Naturally the Foundation paid no attention to this letter other than to acknowledge receipt of it.*

War is what General Sherman called it. His military virtues were above question. Sangue, merda e fatica, was the definition given me by an officer in the last European war. Blood, dung and fatigue. Had he been English he would have said damnable boredom.

The softness and mental slop and lack of guts among young men who have had no trouble, who have been brought up easy, often drives elderly soldiers and even men like myself to think a bit of war wd. be good for 'em. I am not asserting that it would be, I am registering the state of disgust mature men sometimes feel in the presence of fops.

But hatred is not born in the trenches, hatred comes out of arm chairs, hatred comes out of fear. Soldiers no more make war, than policemen make burglaries. We are flooded with a slush of pacifist sentimentality that does not come from courageous men, it comes from men who either will not or dare not analyze the real causes of war. Some of these causes are at least guessed at by the public. There has been a campaign against gun-makers but even that is half camouflage.

A financial system wherein it is more profitable to sell guns than to sell farm machinery, textiles or food stuff is fundamentally vicious.

* See Appendix, p. 281.

The place to regenerate an Empire is at home. Pacifists who refuse to consider Confucius' formula for world peace are not worthy of respect.

To promote the peace of the world by the good internal government of one's country.

That is the honest man's aim, and no more efficient method of pacifism has been invented during twenty-five hundred years. (1936?)

Our Own Form of Government

Our own form of government was our own. No single man did more to destroy it than, to my mind, Woodrow Wilson. With its defects, if any, with its virtues bred in the race of our founders we can at any rate conserve a clear idea of what it was and what they intended.

The office of president was first given and intended to be in futurity given to a ripe man, to a man of judgment and experience. The initiation of such little national legislation as was wanted was set in the representative body. One House to reflect the will and even the emotions of the people, the other to bring maturity of experience and knowledge of tradition.

The ideological riots could and should have occurred in the Lower House. That is what it was made for. There is not the shadow of a doubt that the "House" was intended as the high debating club for the nation.

There is not the shadow of a doubt that the impulsiveness and instability of the people was there given a chance to enjoy itself in all proper exuberance.

There is not the shadow of a doubt that we were founded by ideological war. No mere essurience brought the Mayflower and the Lyon and the other early ships to New England. No mere sense of business or desire to get into fat land erected our constitutional documents.

253

To confuse the ideological with the racial in one's own mind, or to cause such confusion in other minds is no aid either to clear thinking or intelligent action.

An ideological war in Europe drove some men into the wilderness with constructive intentions. With, if you like, utopian intentions. No New Englander of the old stock ever blushed for his idealism. He did not expect plums to grow unaided from granite. He joked about shooting seed into New Hampshire stone from his shotgun.

Gloom did not reign unquestioned. No other settlers record a new pair of boots utterly consumed in a night celebrating the installation of a new parson. They were the parson's own boots. The dance had we presume been fairly vigorous.

The descendants of the founders have not presented their case to the nation, to the melting pot of germanic, slavic, semitic, scandinavian and 44 other stocks now mixed, diluted, coagulated from California to Minnesota. We have not even asked them to keep or even to consider the contract signed by their fathers on landing or in some cases signed by themselves.

Communism is Muscovite. Socialism is German. Whether the Anglo-Saxon-Scotch-Irish stock in the United States means to look itself in the face and take measure of its own racial heritage I do not know.

Out of centuries of matured law and tradition, Jefferson and the Adamses erected an instrument. John Adams chose the man who could bring it into action, and cheap school books have set up a stuffed image. Washington was respected in Tuscany at least until 1850. He was made president because these ideologues respected his judgment and his balance. They didn't ask him to put on a series of side shows.

The nation controlled its own credit for a few years. It reasserted its right in this field 40 years later.

John Adams saw the defects, at least some of the defects of the system, but did not, so far as I know leave any analysis of basic causes. He saw in his lifetime certain dangers, certain defects which he attributed in the main to Jefferson's disagreement with himself.

The racial intelligence of the New England stock formulated a system of government. Ideological warfare eliminated hereditary privilege and retained most of the racial institutions. In fact it retained all of them save for a list of exceptions. British Common Law was assumed wherever there was not expressed law to the contrary. One chamber for debate, with emotion. That is, to reflect the feeling and immediate will of the people, to initiate, to start legislation. Another chamber of mature men, to keep the keel level. One still more mature magistrate to have the final words in such matters, and to decide in times of emergency on immediate actions *in the frame* of the national principles and legislative decisions.

And one body to decide when these decisions were coherent and concordant with the root principles of the constitution.

The president when elected was supposed to have got over the power lust of adolescence. He was not there to initiate legislation. He was there to use a ripe judgment.

The press has usurped the functions originally intended for the nation's debating club.

The Lower House was, by nature, from the beginning the most imperfect component of the system of balances. Being imperfect is no excuse for sending up all finance bills to the Senate in the state of mere rough draft or sketch, and thereby abrogating one of the chief Lower House functions.

Obviously the House and every other department and bureau in Washington will be overloaded if the central government assume all or 98% of all activity intended by the

Fathers for local treatment and properly governable by local treatment. (1936?)

W. E. Woodward, Historian

With the appearance of *Washington Image and Man* it was apparent to any acutely perceptive reader that here was an historian considerably more serious than he himself thought and more vitally alive than the book trade was likely to believe for some time. Woodward's value showed not so vividly in the main biography as in the vignettes. I mean to say there are a number of good biographies, but there are none known to me wherein the incidental figures are so justly weighed and summarized on a page or two.

In the present work* the author has, I suppose, had little pleasure. He likes to do a full-size portrait and will have felt cramped at having to give the whole history in so small a compass.

We have passed from parliamentary government to news-paper government. At his best, the journalist is the best of the age.

There is also the pejorative sense of the word journalist meaning hired liar, suppressor of fact. I am not here using the term journalist in that sense.

The journalist, in honorific sense, is a man out for the facts, and capable of printing his accounts of them in language that anyone can read, and does read.

A live personal curiosity breathes through this book of Woodward's. We have at last a book for the schools. There is interpretation, but not axe-grinding. Woodward has a sound sense of the sequences of cause and effect. Henry Adams noticed that American democracy was breaking down or that

* *A New American History,* by W. E. Woodward.

the original mechanisms devised to keep it functioning were breaking down. Adams' vague gropings have been followed by Beard, Bowers (*The Tragic Era*), by Lewis Corey. The kind of historic sense that has come into being in these authors and in books on special topics, and in biographies, has at last been concentrated into an American History.

Woodward is not indifferent. No historian with his desire for truth and his respect for justice could be indifferent. His preferences may not be mine. I may, and very probably do, give excessive importance to constructive programs and to individual volitions as causes.

I do not think Woodward has given quite enough weight to Van Buren's life-long fight for economic and social rightness in the U.S. I do not think Jackson could have accomplished his work, and I do not think that Jackson himself thought he was accomplishing his work, without the brains of Martin Van Buren. I do not think that "Van" ever turned aside in his aim from the time he was 14 years of age, until the end of his career.

It is manifestly impossible to get everything into a book of 900 pages. What Woodward does give is an adequate picture of what the monopolists did to defeat Van Buren. The ballyhoo of the Harrison campaign had a reason. The few people who know the story will put "two and two together" and take this as tribute to "Van." But the neophyte will not, and cannot.

On the other hand Woodward is drawing a different lesson from the total mass of his book, and an attempt to more fully light up a single decade might be incompatible with what he may consider a major objective.

His study of the causes of the Civil War would gain by a three-line footnote on Southern debts to New York City (which he might have found in Chris. Hollis's *The Two Nations*).

If Woodward can view the figures of our time without passion, I as reviewer, simply cannot. It is hard enough for me to pardon Burr for not shooting Hamilton sooner.

Nevertheless the effect of such a writer on students comes from something deeper than any statement of detail, or any rightness or wrongness in his estimate of any one character. It comes from the total spirit back of the writing, and in the present case that spirit is one of such fairness that the reading of the book is bound to benefit any adolescent (it is also bound to interest any mature reader or living historian).

Apart from the main drift, which I leave for the reader to divine for himself, I should like to emphasize one strand of the story.

From 1763 onwards there has been an unending war in America. The same forces that rot England in our day have festered in America for 150 years. Alex Hamilton served the devil. The banks put up a series of facades. They made use of two types of men, military figures unfit to govern, and "rag dolls," men with no brains of their own, no strength of character and no ethical value.

Van Buren fought privilege and monopoly all his life. The banks put in Wm. Harrison but providence was kind to the rising nation, Harrison obligingly died and Tyler was honest. This was the greatest joke providence ever played in America, on Biddle and on London's American agents.

Bowers and Woodward have rescued Andrew Johnson. Woodward also brings out the worth of Chester A. Arthur. The silent points, the epochs unmentioned hitherto in school histories all emphasise John Adams' statement that usurers have never failed to obliterate all monuments of the honest men who have opposed them. Time and again the truth is found, and re-buried.

258

A lesson that could be to our profit is to be found on the pages on Greenback and Populist parties. In all these currency reform movements there appears to have been no sense of measure. The "parties" which rose singled out some one issue, often irrelevant or semi-relevant, and if they had an effect it was merely as stimulant to curiosity. Woodward does ample justice to the effect of single books, and/or authors. Owen, Bellamy, the unknown and forgotten author of a book on *The Coming Economic Crisis in the South,* and Sinclair's *Jungle.* His summaries of particular doctrines are notably lucid, as are his perceptions of their limitations.

This note is primarily to urge the use of Woodward's history by American School Boards as a school text book. It is a great boon to anyone who wants to know what has happened, and why, in America. A great deal comes to light that our public enemies would like to keep hidden. A generation brought up on this book will not be fleeced as easily as were their forebears. Perhaps that will delay its adoption by public schools. (*New English Weekly,* February 4 & February 11, 1937)

When Will School Books . . . ?

Thirty years ago in the last and after midnight train from Philadelphia a tough bloke reproved me for hoarding knowledge. I was dead tired, I had with me a pile of books appertaining to graduate study, and suddenly two minutes before my station it emerged that the tough customer envied me to the point of dislike. He thought it just as unlikely that fellows that had "that learning" would unbuckle and hand it out to someone that hadn't, as that J. Wanamaker, whose country place lay alongside the railway, would hand out a slice of money.

Such shocks come once in a lifetime. It was a thick and heavy voice: "Huh! 'n 'yuh fellers! Wot got a lot of learnin' wouldn't *give* any of that!" That call to order has stayed with me thirty years.

When Mr. Hatfield of *The English Journal* tells me that my *ABC of Reading* is too advanced for the students, or when the archaeologist who provided Chicago with stone Assyrian bulls writes that my proposal for a correlation of specialists' results (graded by human interest) is a dream floating above the heads of the people (and specifically of the professoriate) I simply do *not* believe them.

Fancy writers in England and America have been too proud to fight in the text book field. Great men in the Middle Ages were not, Gaston Paris and S. Reinach were not. Dante wrote text books, Aristotle wrote text books, Leibnitz and Berkeley wrote text books.

To despise writing text books is to proclaim the degradation of schools as such. It is a blasphemy against knowledge as such.

A perverted sense of property, "literary property," has got in its dirty work. In the Middle Ages when books weren't printed, a grade A man did not think it beneath his dignity to collaborate with another. He did not think it degrading to write his own work in the margin of another man's book.

With a clean and intelligent economic system it would be possible to attain once more this love of real knowledge, without anyone's suffering from starvation.

In the meantime I want to see particular text books put into use. I want to see W. E. Woodward's *New American History* put into high schools and colleges now. Being human I want to see a million or half million college students actively saving their own time by using my *ABC of Reading* until someone provides 'em with something better. I want to see the work of Larranaga and Butchart put into use.

For twenty-five years, with Fenollosa's posthumous papers on one hand, and Leo Frobenius on the other as stimulants,

I have called for a METHOD, that is for a revival and revision of what was once called dialectic, but which you can call proper articulation of subjects, if you like that term better.

A text book on anything must start with an articulation of the problem. The writer must tell us what he is trying to find out. He must tell us at least something about the width, depth and kind of ignorance, which is plaguing him and for which he seeks a cure.

He must next define his terms. Aristotle failed to define money in an adequate manner. And that has cost mankind millions of dollars in printing bills.

Definition is two-thirds of education. People forgot it when Galileo succeeded in improving the telescope.

A real text book is "the dope," it is "the low down." If a subject or book is presented to the student as something dull, naturally he resists it. Time and again it is not the professor's fault. The text which he is given is *not* the "low down" on the subject, it is a dead book designed to keep the student from learning too much. Naturally it does not stimulate curiosity.

In the study of literature the student is constantly offered stale news. He is offered authors who may have told mankind something that was (past tense) pertinent at the time.

There is a stone tablet in Verona stating that "Here Dante lectured on the proportion of water to land." It would seem a dull enough subject, geographical physics! No poet in 1937 would dare risk his position as a romantic figure by speaking of it in public. What modern education needs is a trace of curiosity, an aroma of more inquisitive nature. (*Delphian Quarterly*, April, 1937)

Reorganize Your Dead Universities

The whole of oriental studies and of the study of musical history is in process of revolution. The fact that you can use a Leica or other small film or even midget film to photograph pages of ideogram or of music manuscript or of any other script in Persian or Bengali means that the student is no longer a victim to enormous and necessary expense when he wants to see his material.

If there is not a great onrush in these studies within the next three years it will mean disease, not of material things but in human curiosity.

Following Aristotle, Hume, Berkeley and Anthony Trollope my first step in any enquiry is now economic. I look to the cost and the profits. Your American periodicals are now full of peace advertisements, one before me says war costs 25,000 dollars per corpse.

I want to know WHO gets the 25,000 dollars. That question seems to me to be elementary criminology. (*Delphian Quarterly*, April, 1938)

A Dull Subject

Economics is a dull subject both because it is complicated and because it is simple. It does not arouse the breathless interest of the common detective story solely because the spectator does not understand the connection between public finance and his own private emotions, love affairs, kitchen, and bath room.

A crime has been committed? Well; that is putting it very mildly, for over two centuries an innumerable and unending series of crimes has been committed by a number of the slickest gangs ever dreamed of. And once a man is on the trail of *that* set of bleeders the mere theft of a diamond necklace is no more exciting than the idea that little Jimmie has pinched a couple of marbles.

To preserve a "democratic" system of government (or perhaps we are too late to do much preserving) say to preserve even the forms of our American government and be decently governed, at least a nucleus of the electors has got to understand the meaning of congressional bills concerning money. And, above that, they have got to elect at least a nucleus of congressmen who can understand a half dozen simple dissociations of ideas. (*Delphian Quarterly*, July, 1938)

Marx

With all due respect to Marx and his intentions, the Russian revolution has betrayed Marx. Marx attacked "Capital," the Russian movement has been perverted into an attack on Property.

Naturally, a man or party which is too apelike to distinguish between Property and Capital can be hoodwinked by this substitution.

Marx attacked the cancer of the long working day and the sweat-shop. He unfortunately lacked sufficient historic perspective to see where he merely repeated St. Ambrose and St. Antonino. He attacked, quite properly, ownership with the usury gadget attached.

Lenin meant well. He saw Mussolini as the one man who could get anything done in the Italian peninsula. The tradition is that he also foresaw Stalin as a danger. I have no reason to mistrust that tradition. He saw Stalin as more capable than Trotsk'. (*Purpose*, July-September, 1938)

Emergency

You will never get the hang of fascism if you persist in the habit of regarding every act as a precedent.

Surgeon amputates leg / NOT as precedent / he don't mean to go on amputating the patient's leg every week or year.

Operations to save life / ONLY in an emergency / What are called CONTINGENT. Things to be done ONCE and not erected into a system. (Letter to Basil Bunting, November 24, 1938)

Text books have been despised and neglected in the anglo-saxon system in our time. There is the well-known American racket in text books. There is the pedagogue's taste in text books, the mentality which reads nothing else and fed on sawdust begets sawdusty dolls.

Knowledge stands on accumulated knowledge of particulars, it can not be buried in them, and after this particular knowledge, above it, beside it, is the accumulation of skills. I say "beside it" for the skill can grow in the child, ignorant of the relations and unconscious possibly or semi-conscious of the informing pattern.

The academic career has in many cases seemed to foster defective sensibility. "The University is not here for the exceptional man." Only an age rotted with mercantilism could have elicited this dogma from the head of a university department. My interpretation of the above symptomatic remark is quite plainly to the effect that the "university" is dead, at least in all branches where such degraded outlook prevails. It is dead in that it has no intention of participating in the intellectual life of its nation or continent, let alone in any larger sphere of vitality. Its pretenses of wanting original research need careful examination.

As a test I offered a few years ago my Cavalcanti *Rime* (not the essays reprinted in *Make It New,* but the paleographic edition) to an American university in lieu of thesis for doctorate: it was rejected. This caused me no surprise, but anyone interested in assessing the value of university degrees is invited to compare that volume with any batch of theses for Ph. D. that he fancies.

The effect of mercantilism, the League of Nations' mentality, is that nearly everyone is caught in the gears of the system. A few rogue elephants, possibly a hero or serpent or two escape. The higher you go the more intense the unemployment, and the lower you go the more multitudinous the unemployed.

Knowledge is nailed down under the costing system. In a craftsman's world errors would be noted and corrected without delay. Publishers of reference books would be interested in having them accurate.

An educational system or cosmos is not a one man job. Under mercantilism the job holder is on the defensive. And the law of bureaucracy is: never irritate the man just above you.

The problem of university education as positive consists in finding out what the student, between say 16 and 24 can learn. To what degree and in what fields can his perception be made more active, what basic data can he acquire, coordinate and keep.

In music the perception is of two things: what note, and how long.

In economics the man who understands the meaning of ten or twelve words is better prepared than the whole congeries of economics professors now operating in England and America.

In literature, the base is the word. And as words function in groups, I probably wasn't far wrong in starting to study groups of ten syllables. At any rate the student who knows a few master works is better off than the man who has a smear of two hundred.

A survey course can be definite, the text book for survey should be a definition of the field. A few masterpieces of this sort exist. They are books that a man can keep all his life, refer to for precisions or restart from when and if he wants to go further into their subjects.

Reinach: Manuel de la philologie classique.

Gaston Paris: Chrestomathie du Moyen Age.

Lavignac: Musique et Musiciens.

The list seems fairly short, I hadn't thought it would be all French. (1938?)

Social Credit

All value comes from labour and nature. Wheat from ploughing, chestnuts from being picked up.

But a lot of work has been done by men (mostly inventors, well-diggers, constructors of factory plant, etc.) now dead, and who therefore can not eat and wear clothes.

In respect of this legacy of mechanical efficiency and scientific advance we have at our disposal a large volume of social credit, which can be distributed to the people as a bonus over and above their wage packet.

Douglas proposed to bring up the total purchasing power of the whole people by a *per capita* issue of tickets proportional to available goods.* (*What Is Money For?* 1939)

The American System
Why Not Revive It?

May I begin patiently with the suggestion that you cannot understand what is going on today either in America or in Europe unless you have some idea of how things got to where they are? If you don't like news from Europe, wouldn't it be advisable to begin with a little real American history? *Delphian Quarterly*, July, 1940)

* The following footnote, signed E. P., appears on p. 136 of *Italy's Policy of Social Economics* by Odon Por (translated by Ezra Pound: Bergamo, 1941): "The family allowances provisions approach steadily nearer and nearer to C. H. Douglas's Social Credit principles. They do not constitute, obviously, a national dividend per capita as Douglas proposes, but they are definitely consumer credit. On Feb. 11, 1941, they were extended far beyond the working class and made to include college graduates, sons and daughters of professional men, who weren't yet earning their own livings."—Ed.

III

Letters to America

LETTERS TO AMERICA

To Senator S. S. Brookhart

Rapallo, March 18, 1931

DEAR SENATOR: Your speech against Meyer (Cong. Rec. Feb. 28, p. 6598) seems to me very important. Parts of it at any rate seem to me the most important historical document of the period I have come upon.

Newspapers do not have to lie to mislead the public, all they need do is to omit significant fact.

At any rate want to express personal appreciation of your clear statement. Can get at Cosimo Medici's letter files (What's left of them) but not at Morgan's, hence easier to study past than present history.

The following points of interrogation arise. I don't know how exactly the Federal Reserve Board is composed or how it is *supposed* to function.

Is there any reason why it should not be elective (by the people)? I see several based neither in divine nor human justice but in human imperfection (to put it mildly).

I take it that suggestion does not belong for the moment to practical politics.

Is there any reason why the board should not sit as a senate committee?

Still simpler. Is there any reason why a tribune of the people should not be present at its meetings to notify the senate and house of reps. of action hostile to the people's interest?

There are two parts of govt., the real (which is economics)

and the eyewash, bureaucracy, passports, laws interfering with personal habits, designed mainly to raise dust and keep populace from thinking about economics.

The Fed. Res. Bd. is not only the most important "financial" office, it is THE most important office: and there is no reason why it being official should not be also responsible to the people.

Purely Bolshevic idea? or merely a democratic one?

Personally I believe control and responsibility here would be simpler than nationalization of any mere railroads or steel works. It would not create a lot of god damn bureaucrats and red tape, and could cause audit and check up both on watering capital and on padded expense lists before extending credit to the unworthy.

Sincerely yours

To W. E. Woodward

Rapallo, February 7, 1934(?)

DEAR WOODWARD: Do it strike you as gauge of the economic illiteracy of the country if you (on the advisory board) don't know what an auxilliary currency is? And that F.D.R. is probably equally vague.

The only defense a people has against "tyranny," i.e. gettin' rushed into war and having its eye teeth cheated out of it in peace time: is a diffusion of econ. knowledge.

France has had an auxilliary currency since 1919. There ought to be some paper in the U.S. to print simple facts of this kind.

The damndest bluff is F.D. talking about Andy Jackson. Who PAID OFF AND ENDED the national debt, while he, F.D., is ballooning into billions.

There is no real overproduction as long as there are people

270

who want the stuff. There is plenty of stuff still wanted, the clog is in the money system.

If Christ and the angels ran the farms, with Aristotle, Spinoza and Hen. Ford supervisin', it wouldn't do any good unless the consumers and would-be consumers had currency to buy the product.

To Henry Morgenthau Jr., Secretary of the Treasury

Rapallo, August 7, 1934

DEAR SECRETARY MORGENTHAU: Re your secretary's last answer. The point of my grandfather's money against lumber is not, for immediate application, that it was private money, but that it was *valid money issued against goods*.

The sane thing to do re cotton and hogs is not to destroy them, but to issue money against them up to the limit of what people want (as distinct from what they can buy under present fool system).

As to my grandfather's money. It functioned. It was never repudiated. Money against stuff people want is just as good as money against a lot of zinc or other metal they don't want and can't use.

If the govt. has enough title to hogs and corn, to destroy 'em it has enough title to issue bills against 'em demanding delivery.

cordially yours

To Upton Sinclair

Rapallo, January 30, 1935

DEAR UPTON: Thanks for How you got Licked.*

* *How I Got Licked and Why*, by Upton Sinclair. Account of Sinclair's candidacy for the governorship of California.

I wd/ have done anything in my power to get you IN. BUT
. . . you got a mind like an old family photograph album.

Any idea you get stays.

You are not a monomaniac; but a polymaniac/ with a number of "fixations."

As bad as Perkins. . . .

God hellup the nation if you didn't find ANYone in Washington who knew enough to contradict you. That is the GLOOMIEST phase of yr/ book.

As for that blather about Frank bein' such a sweet suggary man/ what does it matter his being "kindly" / if he don't know a bung from a barrel. . . .

Work is NOT a commodity, in the sense of goods for traffic. You can't eat it.

To T. C. Wilson

Rapallo, November 28, 1936

DEAR WILSON: Your diagnosis of N.Y. might or ought to teach you why I wanted you to get a lung full of European air before permanent suffocation set in. Poem O.K. but time lag shows in it. No reason it couldn't have been writ 20 years ago.

I can develop society on communist base IF they permit development. Go ON from Chap. X of *Das Kapital*. Stalin too stupid to initiate right ticket system. Communists won't think re communization of Product.

You do not yet understand the difference between a tax and a share. Douglas offers every man, every bloody minded tovarisch, kumrad whatnot, his share in the fruits of the nation. What more does communism offer?

If you are serious you will have ultimately to get down to basic principles.

272

To hell with opiums. But do you think mud, mind or will is the determinant in form?

To *William Langer, Governor of North Dakota*

Rapallo, December, 1936

Sir: Senator Frazier has just written me suggesting that I write to you on the subject of text book reform.

I have for 30 years been hammering on need of reviving education.

Among men of letters with international reputation I am possibly the only American who has worked at the problem of better text books.

I have done an *ABC of Reading* and an *ABC of Economics.* Hatfield of the *English Journal* thinks the former above the intelligence of the High School pupil. I consider this an insult to 85% of Americans over 14.

I am not trying to force my own books on you. I am however demanding your attention for 30 years' work and stating that the results of that work ought to be used now, not after a 60 year time lag, in preparing the new text books for Dakota.

This is a state matter and don't need to wait for Hank Wallace or Sis Perkins.

If you know another introduction to economics with as sane a method as that outlined in my *ABC,* I wish you would inform me of its title. I don't mean the book is good enough, it was the first serious job I wrote on Econ. Tribute from Hickok of *Brooklyn Eagle:* "Hell! this *can't* be Economics. I can understand this."

Most econ. fails to enter the pupil's head because the writer does not start by defining the few simple and necessary terms which he has to use on every third page of his book.

273

One fundamental text book should consist of citations from J. Adams, Jefferson, Van Buren.

No reason for Dakota to wait for what London thinks New York publishers think Dakota ought to be told.

Sincerely

To Senator H. T. Bone

Rapallo, 1936 (?)

My Dear Senator: Re/ Morgan's reply to you, as reported in *Time*. I think this is too good a toe hold to lose.

"Destroy the leisure class you destroy civilization," Right OH and very true, but IRRELEVANT.

For 25 years I have been up against the USURERS' class, whereever USURY, not moderate usury on metal coin, but 60% usury on real money called 6% usury on chequebook and bank money, has dominated, LEISURE has been cut down, the leisure class wiped out/

A piffling set of snobs has RUINED all the real work of the artists as fast as possible.

In place of St. Hilaire of Poitiers, the GREAT architecture, the great ART wherein DESIGN is the main factor, has been bitched and greased into a luxury trade, where EXPENSIVENESS and the look of costliness has ruined the work of the mind and spirit.

That claim of Capitalism I attacked some years ago in *The Criterion* (Murder by Capital, July 1933).

Time reports only Morgan's wise crak, but if he caught you off guard once, do give him both barrels next time. Great art (invention and design) is/are slow process and slow processes/ Must have plenty of time (call it leisure)

BUT that is precisely what the hyper-usury of the financial system welches on/

with their damned endowments etc/they constantly build

274

up a barrier against great art, and put out a marketable Ersatz/ oleomargerine etc.

Nye has, I think, slipped by sticking to PAST history. The hell is in the system. (you'd save time by reading the summary of Jefferson's economic perception, Chapter XXX my *Jefferson and/or Mussolini*.

I have no modesty about recommending that chapter as it is all Jefferson and no E.P.

(but you wd. have had to plow through the 10 double vols. of T.J. to GET it, if I hadn't summarized.

cordially yours (I don't mean you need to reciprocate. I am feeling cordial as result of your remarks as reported.

To Henry Seidel Canby, National Institute of Art & Letters

Rapallo, February 14, 1938 (?)

Dear H/S/C: A job, and I think the first job for a serious Institute is the publication in convenient form of the thought of John Adams, Jefferson, and Van Buren. That kind of thing is particularly the sort of thing an institute could and should do.

Creative genius can not be made obligatory of members.

But intellectual responsibility can, and in fact when it is not, the Inst. is a mere sham.

The disgusting torpidity of American universities is a subject for Institute's attention.

Note again my demand for a bulletin, even if only four pages monthly wherein each member when so inclined shall have right to print 10 lines in parliamentary language.

To Claude Bowers

Rapallo, April 16, 1938

MY DEAR CLAUDE BOWERS: As you have dug up Johnson and made a good job of it, and as I note from what appears to be their ONLY publication, that you are a member of a "body" what about using that BODY / not that the elder members will like it, but still what about using it to stimulate the publication of a few documents, notably Johnnie Adams letters etc/ Jefferson, VanBuren, etc? that the Historic Assn/ does NOT make very accessible.

I refer to the American Insteroot of Awt and Letters. whereinto you preceded me by one year, I suppose out of respect to Henry and Brooks Adams. There seem to have been three writers in the earlier phase of the organization. . . .

cordially yours

To Van Wyck Brooks

Rapallo, April 16, 1938

MY DEAR VAN WYCK BROOKS: AS a reasoning member of the Institute (and Academy) you will I suppose grant that these bodies shd/ either function or cease to exist.

Naturally I know nothing of the functions of the inner body; but the outer body appears to have no means of intercommunication between members/ and therefore can not function as a body.

Canby writes me "funds cd/ be etc." I might point out that IF these bodies aren't the nucleus of national culture, that is such parts of it as are carried on by living men, then they are a sham.

OBVIOUSLY the first disposition of such funds shd be the collection of writings by members / if their writings aren't worth THAT, then the members are improperly elected. . . .

The last MEMBER I met was Henry James. His communications to the BODY as it then was, were suppressed. . . . very truly yours

276

To Dr. Joseph Brewer, Olivet College, Michigan

Rapallo, September 11, 1939

DEAR BREWER: This dirty war gives the U.S. an opportunity such as in 1917. Wyndham Lewis is at King Edward Hotel, Toronto, Canada. Of course he wouldn't come to Olivet for the meagre fee you can pay, but if you modestly put it to him that you don't regard it as pay, but that you can and would like to provide him with basic necessities in a way that would leave him 80% or 90% of his time free to paint and do his writing without preoccupation, you have just a chance of getting the most active of my contemporaries onto your campus.

You could also line up a few sitters. His portrait of me was bought by the Tate Gallery, hung in room next to Whistler's Carlyle.

To Earnest Minor Patterson, President American Academy of Political & Social Science

Rapallo, February 6, 1940

DEAR DR. PATTERSON: Yours of 18th ult. just to hand. I enclose cheque for life membership in the Academy. I shall probably annoy you or the secretary or a few fellow members by excess activity during the first few months, and then sink into the normal inactivity of academicians. HOWEVER.

If the Academy feels any responsibility for the state of the country, or the American mind or the rising or wilting generation, some of its members must feel as I do the appalling lack of handy compendia of the thought and aims of the American founders. Marx, Lenin, Trotsk, Stalin at ten cents and 25 cents in editions of 100 thousand, and running to several editions, WHEREAS it takes a slikked safe breaker to discover the mind of John Adams, or Van Buren, and even Jefferson is in 12 vols, and Taylor of Caroline, I suppose, inaccessible save in libraries, and Henry Adams' "Gallatin" second hand 30 dollars, and Brooks Adams out of print.

If this is off the Academy's line, one cd/at least STIMULATE a demand. . . . cordially yours

To Ernest Minor Patterson

Rapallo, March 12, 1940

DEAR DR. PATTERSON: A definition is not a one man job. To be useful for a science it must be matured, it must be a consensus, it must be both valid and accepted by at least the group using it. Bales of printed paper go to waste for lack of defining the basic words before writing "about" the subject.

I offer my own definitions only in the hope of getting them polished and perfected. I have improved them since the May issue of the Rassegna Monetaria, 1937, and expect to keep on working at them. But they can't do the work until some authoritative body either adopts them or adopts something better.

To Editor of the Annals, American Academy of Social & Political Science

Rapallo, June 3, 1940

Correspondence with the U.S. not very lively, and this will arrive late, but am wondering whether July issue will face two questions or statements.

1. Among the first rights of a man or nation is the right to stay out of debt.

278

2. (Ref. Brooks Adams, an author whom the American universities have for 30 years refused to face.)

Dumping is an hostile act, whether it be dumping of wheat or of gold. Any attempt to force a nation to take a useless or at least unnecessary commodity like gold is a move toward war.

cordially yours

P.S. Are you touching problem of American responsibility for present war?

To D. MacPherson

Rapallo, November 16, 1940

DEAR MAC: England suffered all thru XIX century from being cut off from France and continent during Napoleonic wars. Present cut off of U.S. from Europe is more than serious for you young. May mean decades of lost time, gulf as between Dickens and Flaubert.

All the poisonous foreign ideas are already IN America and established. What no one can get printing expenses for are the AMERICAN ideas, Adams, Lincoln, Jeff, etc.

No one in U.S. has this time even tried to concentrate IN the U.S. the best international stuff, as was done by *Little Review* 1917/19/23.

yours

To the Committee of Progress, National Institute of Art & Letters

Rapallo, 1941 (?)

MR. CHAIRMAN AND MEMBERS: Now that the Academy has purged itself and removed the unutterable Nic. M. Butler from the presidency, may a simple member of the Department of Literature ask why this man is put in our department? What service has he ever done to letters; what has he ever written fit for a human being to read, and why is not his Carnegie Foundation investigated?

cordially yours

To National Institute of Art and Letters

Rapallo, May 15, 1941

The Institute should stand for continual curiosity as to the nature of MAXIMA standards of excellence in all the arts.

To that end, the members including the worst should be placed in prison until they have read at least the main demands of my published criticism, let alone other critical demands of at least equal critical merit.

There has been plenty of encouragement of commercial efficiency. We need a little looking forward, a little courage in facing facts and ideas, and even in contemplating art that is not immediately and speedily remunerative.

The curse of America has been lack of total curiosity. The Institute should also stimulate specific publications needed for American sanity.

Such as (first and notably) publication of American history, including facts that even meritorious professors like D. R. Dewey omit from standard works used in universities.

Sane and impartial recommendation of work by a group of Institute members ought in some way to be mobilized, so as to effect publication and distribution of better books than are now spread by an advertising system necessitated by the economic system.

A list of definitions of words vital to the nation might be undertaken.

APPENDIX

Minoritenplatz 3 Vienna I
June, 18th. 1928

Professor Nicholaus Murry Butler
Chairman of the Executive Committee
Carnegie Endowment for Peace
New York City.

Sir, On page 67 of your Year Book of 1927 the wish is expressed for suggestions and collaboration of thought. This gave me the idea that I might venture to suggest certain points as worth while some study, considering the causes of war, which it might be perhaps more useful to go into carefully than to investigate the effects of war.

Some of these causes are:

1) Intense production and sale of munitions; the whole of the trade in munitions and armaments might be subjugated to contemporary, not retrospective investigation via trade channels.

2) Overproduction and dumping, leading to trade rivalries and irritation.

3) The intrigues of interested cliques.

All these are general and constantly active forces toward war. Further there are particular present subjects which might be clarified by a Carnegie study.

1) The principles of international law as recognised by

* This letter to the Carnegie Endowment for International Peace was drafted jointly by Pound and Count Mensdorff.

the decisions of the permanent international Court of Justice, should be studied and codified and summarised by clear statement.

2) We should be grateful for a clear explanation or study of the meaning of the reservations of the U.S.A. re adhesion to the permanent international Court of Justice.

3) and also for, the interpretation of the Kellog proposals for the outlawry of war and the war prevention policy of the U.S.A.,

4) and for a further study of the attempt of the League of Nations to codify international law, if you are not already dealing fully with this matter.

I remain very truly Yours
(signed) ALBERT MENSDORFF.

Vienna, 20.8.1928

DEAR MR. EZRA POUND, I herewith send you the copy of the reply of the Carnegie Endowment to Count Albert Mensdorff.

Very truly yours
(signed) F. MATSCH.

Carnegie Endowment of International Peace.
405 West 117th Street, New York City.

July 26, 1928

Count Albert von Mensdorff,
Minoritenplatz 3,
Vienna I, Austria.

MY DEAR COUNT VON MENSDORFF: In the absence of President Butler I have the honor to acknowledge receipt of your letter of June 18 which will be brought to his attention as soon as possible. In the meantime I am writing to Dr. Shotwell, Director of the Division of Economics and History ad-

282

vising him of the first three numbered suggestions in your letter. I am also writing to Dr. James Brown Scott, Director of the Division of International Law calling his attention to the last four numbered suggestions. In studying plans for work in the future we shall consider carefully all of your suggestions and I beg to thank you cordially for giving us the benefit of your advice on the various subjects.

Sincerely yours,
(signed) HENRY S. HASKELL M.P.
Assistant to the Director

Select Bibliography

First
Published

1910   *The Spirit of Romance.* New Directions, N.Y., 1952.

1916   *Gaudier-Brzeska: A Memoir.* Lane, London, 1916.

1916   *Classic Noh Theatre of Japan.* New Directions, 1959.

1924   *Antheil: And the Treatise on Harmony.* Covici, Chicago, 1927.

1926   *Personae.* Collected poems, excluding the Cantos. New Directions, 1949.

1931   *Guido Cavalcanti: Rime.* Ed. by Pound, with critical text, notes, manuscript facsim. pl., etc. Marsano, Genoa, 1931 (ref. V. Scheiwiller, Milan).

1932   *Profile.* Anthol. ed. by Pound, with notes. John Scheiwiller, Milan, 1932.

1933   *Active Anthology.* Ed. by Pound, with notes. Faber, London, 1933.

1933   *ABC of Economics.* Peter Russell, Tunbridge Wells, England, 1953.

1934   *ABC of Reading.* New Directions, 1951.

1934   *Make It New.* Yale Univ. Press, New Haven, Conn., 1935.

1935   *Jefferson and/or Mussolini.* Liveright, N.Y., 1936.

1938   *Guide to Kulchur.* New Directions, 1951.

1947   *Confucius: The Great Digest and The Unwobbling Pivot.* Trans. by Pound, with Chinese text. New Directions, 1951. (First published in 1947 without Chinese text.)

284

1948 *The Cantos.* Nos. 1–84, including Pisan Cantos. New Directions, 1948.

1950 *The Letters of Ezra Pound.* Ed. by D. D. Paige. Harcourt, Brace, N.Y., 1950.

1951 *Confucian Analects.* Trans. by Pound. Square Dollar Series, Washington, D.C., 1951.

1953 *Translations of Ezra Pound.* Introduction by Hugh Kenner. New Directions, 1953.

1954 *Confucian Odes.* "Classic Anthology Defined by Confucius," trans. by Pound. New Directions, 1959.

1954 *Literary Essays of Ezra Pound.* Ed. with Introd. by T. S. Eliot. New Directions, 1954.

1955 *Section: Rock-Drill.* Cantos 85–95. New Directions, 1956.

1955 *Moscardino.* By Enrico Pea. Trans. by Pound. In *New Directions 15,* New Directions, 1955.

1956 *Women of Trachis.* Sophocles' Trachiniae, trans. by Pound. New Directions, 1957.

1958 *Pavannes and Divagations.* New Directions, 1958. (Drawn largely from *Pavannes and Divisions,* 1918 and *Instigations,* 1920.)

1959 *Thrones.* Cantos 96–109. New Directions, 1959.

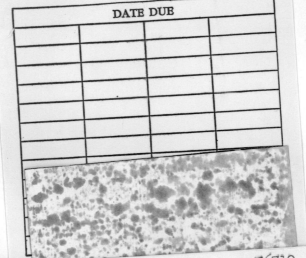